Janna Odabas
The Ghosts Within

Lettre

Janna Odabas, born in 1984, completed the program of the Graduate School of North American Studies at the Freie Universität Berlin. In 2014, she received the Young Scholar Excellence Award of the Society for Multi-Ethnic Studies: Europe and the Americas (MESEA). Her work focuses on questions of identity and migration.

Janna Odabas

The Ghosts Within

Literary Imaginations of Asian America

[transcript]

This dissertation was generously funded by the Excellence Initiative of the German federal and state governments.

Bibliographic information published by the Deutsche Nationalbibliothek
The Deutsche Nationalbibliothek lists this publication in the Deutsche Nationalbibliografie; detailed bibliographic data are available in the Internet at http://dnb.d-nb.de

Cover layout: Maria Arndt, Bielefeld
Printed by Majuskel Medienproduktion GmbH, Wetzlar
Print-ISBN 978-3-8376-4449-4
PDF-ISBN 978-3-8394-4449-8
https://doi.org/10.14361/9783839444498

Table of Contents

Acknowledgements

First of all, I would like to thank my first and second supervisors, Prof. Ulla Haselstein and Prof. Ruth Mayer, for their invaluable help, constructive feedback, patience, and encouragement with my development of the project over the years.

I would also like to thank the Graduate School and its staff for providing a great framework in which to think and write. This dissertation was generously funded by the Excellence Initiative of the German federal and state governments. This scholarship made a focus on the dissertation possible in the first place.

I also thank my friends and colleagues from the Graduate School for their feedback and support: Birte Wege, Mieke Woelky, Melanie Eis, David Bosold, and Gabi Bodmeier. I would also like to thank my third advisor, Prof. Sedlmeier, who gave me great advice in the early stages of the project.

Going way back to the beginnings of this project, I would like to thank my friends and colleagues from Hannover for pushing me into the right direction, for constructive feedback, and for the encouragement to actually live my dream of writing a dissertation: once again, Ruth Mayer, Vanessa Künnemann, Florian Gross, Bettina Soller as well as Christina Lego and Britta Bein.

I also thank the Graduiertenakademie Universität Hannover for providing a "Kurzzeit Exposé scholarship" that allowed me to get this project off the ground.

Finally, I wish to thank my family for supporting me from the first crazy ideas to follow this dream to finally seeing it through.

Introduction

"Chinese-Americans, when you try to understand what things in you are Chinese, how do you separate what is peculiar to childhood, to poverty, insanities, your family, your mother who marked your growing with stories, from what is Chinese? What is Chinese tradition and what is the movies?" (Kingston, *The Woman Warrior* 13)

"My aunt haunts me – her ghost drawn to me because now, after fifty years of neglect, I alone devote pages of paper to her, though not origamied into houses and clothes. I do not think that she always means me well. I am telling on her, and she was a spite suicide, drowning herself in the drinking water. The Chinese are always very frightened of the drowned one, whose weeping ghost, wet hair hanging and skin bloated, waits silently by the water to pull down a substitute." (22)

"They would not tell us children because we had been born among ghosts, were taught by ghosts, and were ourselves half ghosts. They called us a kind of ghost. Ghosts are noisy and full of air; they talk during meals. They talk about anything." (165)

These three passages are taken from Maxine Hong Kingston's *The Woman Warrior* (1977), the most widely known and taught memoir from the Asian American literary tradition. They show how the narrator is haunted by various questions, trying to make sense of her personal and cultural tradition and her position in an American context, of her identity as an Asian American. Where does she belong? How authentic is the channeled imagination that she has of her Chinese heritage? What constitutes an Asian American history? Next to her mother and the movies, who has selected what for her? And for whom will she select, negotiate, remember? And what about the ghost of the aunt that haunts her? This figure is simultaneously a threat, a 'weeping ghost' waiting 'to pull down a substitute,' and an ancestral "forerunner" (Kingston 15) of which the narrator states that "[u]nless I see her life branching into mine, she gives me no ancestral help" (16). What do ghost figures such as these add to a memoir? Are they simply ethnic ornamentation? How are they linked to personal and cultural memory and history? Are ghosts like this one references to an ethnic tradition that informs an Asian American subjectivity? But on the other hand, the narrator is being called a half ghost herself, signaling her distance to Chinese traditions. How is her Asian American identity constituted by haunting presences? What do these ghost figures indicate? How does Kingston's text establish a tradition of ghost figures as central to literary conceptions of Asian America?

With this prominent ghost figure in mind, *The Ghosts Within* addresses all of these questions in focusing on the functions of ghostly presences in contemporary Asian American literature. It shows how these figures shuttle between various traditions, how they simultaneously invite metaphorical/psychoanalytical and folkloristic readings. The specific mixtures that these ghost figures point to are explored in chapter 2 with reference to the postcolonial melodrama that Lois-Ann Yamanaka employs in *Behold the Many* (2006) and in chapter 3 that highlights the Korean German American mixture of Heinz Inzu Fenkl's *Memories of My Ghost Brother* (1996). I argue that ghost figures in contemporary Asian American literature follow a paradoxical logic of providing certain structures – they serve as cultural orientation points, they refer to concrete historical sites, they reference certain ghost beliefs and link this literature back to its beginnings with Maxine Hong Kingston's *The Woman Warrior* –, but they also trouble neat categorizations as they highlight the hauntedness of any conceptualization. *The Ghosts Within* shows how the ghost figures both establish and resist these very structures, highlighting the interlinkages between terms such as colonizer/colonized or Asian/American. The ghosts serve as figures that refer back to literary and cultural traditions and beliefs, but they also reference a present and a future as intertwined with these (hi)stories. As chapter 4 shows, these figures also appear in new territories of contemporary Asian American literature in its move away from the traditional identity politics of the field: the global genre writing of Amitav Ghosh, Amy Tan, and Ed Lin features ghosts. And although these novels re-think the ghosts as less concerned with Asian American identity politics, the specificity of the ghosts' cultural and historical reference remains to be considered. As such, the ghosts continue to be bound to the original reference points of tradition and identity, but they also – at the same time – contour 'Asian America' as heterogeneous and global.

Linking the ghost figures to a larger diasporic context, I argue that they negotiate and challenge the homogenous representation of a unified Asian American 'experience' as it is reflected in the highly constructed pan-Asian label

'Asian American.' A highly effective move by Asian Americans during the 1960s to gain wider political and social influence, the category merged various groups under this one label. However, this unifying category necessitates an ongoing homogenization of a singular Asian American context; and, thus, diversity and differences are subsumed rather than singled out. The label suggests a common background and relationship of all these heterogeneous subgroups with the United States, which is simply not given. But even the split into smaller categories such as Chinese American or Korean American does not do justice to the diversity within each respective group. All of these subgroups share their very own history – of trade, of wars, of immigration – with the United States; and the Asian American diasporas are a direct result of these relationships. Thus, although the label's construction was an empowering move, it is constantly challenged from within. And in my view, the ghosts are references to exactly this kind of negotiation: these figures not only express contradictions and refer to silences, they also point to very specific and concrete stories or events. As such, these figures are important references to the very specificity that the label 'Asian America' stifles. Strikingly, these figures emerge and abound in Asian American literature in a moment in which ethnic pride gains prominence. The ghosts foreground individual diasporic experiences, while they also mark a shared, appropriated Asianness that becomes central to the literary self-conceptualizations of Asian America. This same logic also shapes the current re-positioning of the field in global terms.

Following Avery Gordon, I read these ghosts as "social figures:" they are presences that call for recognition in their reference to social circumstances. While critics tend to emphasize only some aspects of these figures – their reference to a certain ethnic tradition, the struggle with an identity in-between different cultures –, foregrounding a resistance narrative to white mainstream America, *The Ghosts Within* builds on the findings of these scholars, yet, stresses the inherent moral and political ambiguity of these figures. The ghost figures, I argue, negotiate and challenge any homogenous representation of an Asian American identity or history. Most of the novels that *The Ghosts Within* focuses on have been criticized for their (a)political stance. While the ghost's political potential is clearly given, they never allow for easy conceptions or explanations, so that they resist attempts of political usurpation for identity politics or an unchallenged, celebratory resistance narrative. As such, the ghost figures resist the drive of some Asian American critics to 'place' them in a moral or political frame. Foregrounding interconnections and complicity, the ghost figures highlight ambiguity and contradictions as inherent to any conception of history or identity. As *The Ghosts Within* shows, these figures have changed with the field's expansion without, however, deviating from this logic of political ambiguity.

Although the focus of this project is on more recent literature, a beginning with Maxine Hong Kingston's memoir is necessary in order to understand the significance of the figure of the ghost in the Asian American literary tradition. As the first text by an Asian American author to gain wide public recognition, *The Woman Warrior* serves as some kind of a blueprint for what was then, in its aftermath, conceived of and marketed as Asian American literature (Chiang 19). The topics with which its narrator struggles – her identity as an Asian American, her place in America, the authenticity of the Chinese traditions and history – are all tied to the ghost presences in the text. Whether it is her identity as a half ghost, the Americans who are constructed as ghosts in their foreignness, or the ghost of her Chinese aunt, the ghosts embody the central conflicts of this young Asian American girl and they also establish the main topics on which Asian American literature centered. The reception of *The Woman Warrior* in general and its ghost figures in particular nicely highlights the development of the field of Asian American Studies after its inception in the 1970s and 80s. Most secondary literature reads the ghosts according to the current trends of the field, linking them in the early stages to topics of historiography and identity, then moving on to pan-ethnic approaches, before ultimately conceiving of them as global, transnational, and self-reflexive figures.

These readings indicate what I conceive of as the three phases of Asian American Studies in its self-conception.[1] From its initiation, Asian American Studies has been concerned with the struggle of Asian Americans to negotiate their place and position in the United States. It has its roots in the activism of the 1960s (1). As part of the political and social movements of the 1960s, Asian Americans fought for better living conditions (for example, housing, health care, education, unemployment). The field's initiation was also a protest against the absence of Asian American history or literature in the higher education of the

---

1 For my analysis I will be drawing on Bella Adams, *Asian American Literature*, Edinburgh: Edinburgh University Press, 2008; Guiyou Huang, *The Columbia Guide to Asian American Literature Since 1945*, New York: Columbia University Press, 2006; Geok-lin Lim, Shirley, et al., eds. *Transnational Asian American Literature: Sites and Transits*. Philadelphia: Temple University Press, 2006; David Leiwei Li, *Imagining the Nation: Asian American Literature and Cultural Consent*, Stanford, California: Stanford University Press, 1998, especially his conclusion; Sau-ling Cynthia Wong, *Reading Asian American Literature: From Necessity to Extravagance*. Princeton, New Jersey: Princeton University Press, 1993.

United States (Madsen, "Introduction" xvii). The first phase is what I call the initiatory phase, which started in the 1970s and continued into the early 1990s. This phase is basically concerned with the initiation of the field and the creation of an awareness of an Asian American presence in America. It is also a consolidation phase as certain main themes and strands within the field become visible. For example, one can observe a kind of formalization with a prominent focus on feminist projects. This first phase produced readings of ghost figures that ultimately highlight the interconnection of psychoanalytical approaches with identity politics: basically, the ghosts are seen as functioning as ethnic markers that allegorize the narrator's haunted identity as Asian American.

The second phase of diversification dominates the 1990s, which induces a crisis. This phase is not only concerned with a negotiation of the place of Asian American Studies in relation to other Ethnic Studies programs and literature as well as Diaspora Studies, but also highlights the growing diversity of the field. It culminates with the controversy over the fiction award that was presented in 1997 to Lois Ann Yamanaka's *Blu's Hanging* by the Association for Asian American Studies, which basically questioned the representative function of ethnic authors. This reshaping and restructuring of the field also left an impact on the approaches to its ghost figures: although the first phase also linked its readings of ghosts to the specific cultural differences, this aspect becomes more prominent, especially in terms of pan-ethnic conceptions of the ghost figures. The field's diversity demands recognition of the cultural similarities and differences that the ghosts might provide.

The field's crisis produced an awareness of the necessity to recognize the historical and material terms on which Asian America built and builds itself. The reception of the Yamanaka controversy still shapes current projects in the field, which has entered the third phase. This phase is a highly self-reflexive one that also needs to be seen in its dialogic relationship with the larger field of American Studies and transnational approaches. While the ghost figures continue to be read as identity markers and ethnic ornamentation by some critics, a growing tendency to focus on the historical specificity of these figures emerges. Toni Morrison's psychoanalytical conception of an America as haunted by a black presence in *Playing in the Dark* (1992) already foreshadows the approach that dominates the early 21st century: the ghosts are conceived as psychoanalytical yet social forces, linked to specific historical events that haunt certain communities or entire countries. Each phase, of course, overlaps with others and serves only as a general framing to crystallize the most prominent topics of the time. In the secondary literature of these phases that focuses on ghost figures in Asian American literature a development can be observed: from a psychoanalytical identity politics, to a cultural, to a historical material approach. These readings, of course, cannot be evenly separated; all of them include, in a way, psychoanalytical, cultural, historical and material explanations. Not surprisingly, most of the secondary literature attempts to read the ghost figures in terms of the current approaches that shape Asian American Studies, trying to 'place' the ghosts in a marketable, readable narrative. However, a few exceptions have emphasized the ghost's resistance to such political usurpation from the very beginning and it is in these footsteps that I wish to place *The Ghosts Within*.

ASIAN AMERICAN: GHOSTS AS IDENTITY MARKERS AND A (FEMINIST) HISTORIOGRAPHY

The Woman Warrior tells a story of growing up as a Chinese American girl, of finding a voice and an identity, but also of finding a place in America. All of these dimensions emerge as the basic themes and topics around which the early phase of Asian American Studies developed. In this way, Kingston's memoir establishes and writes itself into the dominant discourses of its time. In order to claim a place and a voice, the autobiographical genre seems an obvious choice. Yet, *The Woman Warrior* defies categorizations into fixed genre traditions. Although it is termed a memoir, the ghost figures stretch the limits of autobiographical writing. They are neither clearly marked as metaphoric nor as material presences. Instead, they appear as simply part of the narrator's world and experience. *The Woman Warrior*, thus, presents these figures as forces that demand recognition – like the no name woman –, but the memoir refrains from answering what exactly this recognition should imply: should they be seen as part of Chinese ghost beliefs, as part of a distancing from American norms, as part of an author's creative imagination, as part of an Asian American identity, or as part of the narrator's very personal psychological development? My answer is: probably all of this at once (Odabas, "Do Ghosts Grow Up" 157). The ghosts' 'unplaceability' is the most striking feature of these figures in *The Woman Warrior* and it is this insight that drives *The Ghosts Within*.

Chapter 1 provides an overview of theoretical reflections about ghost figures. It starts with Sigmund Freud's psychoanalytical approach of "The Uncanny" (1919) and connects this to Jacques Derrida's deconstructive conceptions of spectrality. It moves on to Avery Gordon's seminal sociological *Ghostly Matters: Haunting and the Sociological Imagination* (2004), which connects Freud and Derrida to emphasize the social function of ghostly presences. The chapter concludes with a focus on ghost figures in literature and how this always already includes a discussion of these figures' reality status, especially in an Asian American context. *The Ghosts Within* is driven by the argument that only a combination of such psychoanalytical, poststructuralist, social, cultural, and literary approaches can begin to unearth the diverse functions that ghost figures employ. It argues, furthermore, that Asian American literature itself playfully engages with the co-existence of these approaches.

Patricia Lin Blinde already cites the appearance of ghost figures in a memoir as a break with the fact-fiction divide. In her article "The Icicle in the Desert: Perspective and Form in the Works of Two Chinese-American Women Writers" (1979) she states that these ghost figures provide a way to question a Western way of perceiving reality. These ghosts are "not simply metaphorical allusions to the Chinese past" but show that the supernatural "encroaches upon daily existence, and the boundaries of the possible are constantly being extended to include what the American sensibility would deem as superstition" (Blinde 68). And although Blinde's article does not discuss these ghost figures most centrally, it is conceptualizations of ghosts such as hers that have inspired my discussion of these figures. Her article already foreshadows what later engagements with ghost figures in relation to the genre of autobiography outline. What does a ghost as part of autobiographical writing indicate? How does this change the narrative and its perception? If these ghosts are not only metaphorical allusions, what else are they?

Inspired by these aspects, Chapter 3 discusses the appearance of ghost figures in Heinz Insu Fenkl's *Memories of My Ghost Brother* (1996). While his novel is not labeled an autobiography, it certainly has an autobiographical dimension as it narrates the story of the young Heinz Insu Fenkl growing up close to the South Korean camptown world. This neocolonial setting provides the backdrop for the development of ghostly selves. The novel is populated by various highly different ghost figures. There are the narrator's mother's Korean ghosts, his father's ghostly presence that references a ghostly American presence in Korea, there is the narrator's ghost brother of the title, and finally the ghostly self that emerges from the pages of this novel. *Memories of My Ghost Brother* plays with the different traditions to which the narrator is exposed: a Western/ psychoanalytical reading as well as a folkloristic Korean approach of these figures. Thus, the novel depicts the morally outrageous situation – often with the help of ghost figures –, while it refrains from simply blaming specific individuals. *Memories of My Ghost Brother* is mostly told from the perspective of a child narrator, the young Insu. This perspective creates an atmosphere which verifies the reality status of the ghost figures: they appear as both coping strategy and real material presences. The materiality of these figures is pronounced, but it is also repeatedly challenged just as the narrative is interrupted by italicized passages which are being told by an older Insu. In this focus on the intermingling of ghosts and life writing, this chapter is indebted to Blinde's early attentive reading of ghost figures.

The Woman Warrior and even more so Kingston's second book *China Men* (1980), take up the idea of re-writing and re-owning an Asian American history (Odabas, "Do Ghosts Grow Up" 151). In accordance with the field's origins in the civil rights struggles of the 1960s, Asian American Studies is initially most centrally concerned with finding a place for Asian Americans in America and its history. This has been done in the early phase through the creation of various bibliographies[2]. Many historians took up the topic of Asian Americans in a similar vein: in an attempt to create "new social histories," (Leong 65) they not only recovered lost histories but moreover reframed Asian Americans as subjects of this history, instead of mere objects in a history being told by others.[3] One of the most famous of these histories is Ronald Takaki's *Strangers from a Different Shore: A History of Asian Americans*, originally published in 1989. He covers the early immigrant groups of Chinese, Japanese, Korean, and Filipino Americans, who came in between the mid nineteenth century and the early 1900s as workers in the Hawaii sugar plantations or to the continental United States as

2 Not surprisingly, these bibliographies often refer to specific Asian American subgroups, to whom the editors felt the need to draw specific attention and to which they mostly belonged themselves. This is very much in line with the activist roots of the Asian American movement. See, for example, Wei Chi Poon, *A Guide for Establishing Asian American Core Collections*, Berkeley, California: Asian American Studies Library, 1988; Yen Le Espiritu, *Vietnamese in America: An Annotated Bibliography of Materials in Los Angeles and Orange County Libraries*, Los Angeles: UCLA Asian American Studies Center, 1988; Him Mark Lai, *A History Reclaimed: An Annotated Bibliography of Chinese Language Materials on the Chinese of America*, Los Angeles: Asian American Studies Center, 1986; Jane Singh, *South Asians in North America: An Annotated and Selected Bibliography*, Berkeley: Center for South and South East Asia Studies, 1988; Cheung, King-Kok and Stan Yogi, *Asian American Literature: An Annotated Bibliography*, New York: MLA, 1988.

3 See for further examples: Yuji Ichioka, *The Issei: The World of the First-Generation Japanese Immigrants, 1885–1924*, New York: Free Press, 1989; Sucheng Chan, *This Bittersweet Soil: The Chinese in California Agriculture, 1850–1910*, Berkeley: The University of California Press, 1986; Sucheng Chan, *Asian Americans: An Interpretive History*, Boston: Twayne Publishers, 1991.

workers on the railroad tracks. Takaki compares these with the new waves of immigrants that followed after the elimination of the national immigrant quotas in 1965 and the great wave of refugees from Cambodia, Laos and Vietnam. Takaki lists and interprets various exclusionary laws like the Naturalization Act of 1870, which excluded Chinese from becoming naturalized citizens, or the Chinese Exclusion Law of 1882, which basically banned Chinese immigration, or the strict enforcements of these laws on the Angel Island immigration station after 1910, or the internment and relocation of Japanese Americans during World War II.[4] Yet, while Takaki does intend to list these racially based exclusions, he insists on giving the Asian Americans a 'voice' in this history, citing letters, poems, and interviews. This claim of 'owning' their history in America even within this oppressive framework is a striking feature of these kinds of new social histories.

As Takaki's example highlights, the early phase was very much about retelling their own history and, thus, implicitly or explicitly, about battling existing stereotypes. Popular stereotypes of bad and good Asians say more about the American national self-image than actually about Asian immigrants' lives, but Asian American self-representations of course engage with the existing and available images. In the early phase from the mid-nineteenth century to the mid-twentieth century bad images dominated. Asian Americans were depicted as coolie workers and pollutants of America. By the turn of the century, the worst image was that of the 'yellow peril,' that constructs Asian Americans as a threat to the nation, the white race, and the family.[5] Positive images during this time represent Asian Americans and Asians as inferior, helpless heathens in need of civilization by the superior white American people. This image was used in missionary accounts or in the stock image of the servant figure (Kim, *Asian American Literature* 3–22); (Lee, *Orientals* 8–12).

The most striking image, however, is that of the 'model minority,' which derived from the racial logic of the Cold War during the 1940s and continues to be a reference point until today. The 'model minority' depiction of Asian Americans builds on the idea of the American Dream and suggests that this

4 For a detailed chronology of historical and literary events, see Bella Adams, *Asian American Literature*, Edinburgh: Edinburgh University Press, 2008, ix–xxvi.

5 The image of the 'yellow peril' originated in Europe, where it was initially linked to military and cultural threats, before, in the American context, its references were redrawn to focus on migration and urbanization, see, for example, Ute Mehnert, *Deutschland, Amerika und die Gelbe Gefahr: Zur Karriere eines Schlagworts in der großen Politik, 1905–1917*, Stuttgart: Franz Steiner, 1996.

minority group has managed its way up the social and economic ladder and into the American nation due to honest, hard work. It emphasizes Asian American virtues such as patience, loyalty, adherence to Confucian ethics, community spirit, and hard work. Although this myth is attached to all subgroups of Asian America, at least one of its features – the Confucian ethics – is clearly a reference to the special philosophical orientation of the Chinese. Calling to mind the general conception of Asian American, such a conflation of differences into one seemingly homogenous and all-fitting category for all Asian Americans mirrors a larger tendency in Asian American Studies. And very often the representative groups are either the Chinese Americans or the Japanese Americans, from which certain aspects are highlighted and then generalized and applied to Asian Americans at large. The model minority myth is, thus, one example of such a tendency.[6] As early sources of the 1960s demonstrate, this myth was constructed to hold up this particular minority as a model for others, more rebellious ones like the blacks. For example, the article "Success of One Minority Group in U.S." from 1966 praises the Asian American as a law-abiding, patient, industrious citizen, who has faced severe discrimination in the past, yet managed to work his or her way into the American nation due to the classical shared virtues of individualism, self-reliance, and loyalty. This is seen as a case in point that minorities actually can succeed on their own, implying that the demands by blacks for financial support are a result of their mere laziness ("Success of One Minority Group" 158–163).[7]

Although this myth certainly opened new possibilities for Asian Americans, it still remains a stereotypical representation that allows for little variation and causes harm in its own ways. While the myth admits the Asian American into the realm of the American nation, it does so under the condition that this group remains an assimilated and subordinated minority that obediently follows the American way of life (Kim, *Asian American Literature* 3–22). Furthermore, with

6 Another example for this tendency in Asian American Studies is Ronald Takaki's focus on coolie workers, which were typically only Chinese (Americans).

7 The same arguments are put forward in other articles of the time. See, for example, "Success Story: Outwhiting the Whites," *Newsweek*, June 21, 1971; with the shift into the 1980s, the model becomes more and more also one for the white American middle class that could improve its performance, see, as cited in Takaki: "Asian-Americans: A 'Model Minority,'' *Newsweek*, December 6, 1982, 40–51; "America's Super Minority," *Fortune*, November 26, 1986; David A. Bell, "The Triumph of Asian-Americans: America's Greatest Success Story," *New Republic*, July 15 and 22, 1985, 24–31.

this depiction in place, any demand of social welfare by Asian Americans meant a loss of face, implying that they simply did not work, and it resulted in various inter-racial conflicts with other minority groups (Takaki 474–84).[8] Many of the early studies in Asian American Studies directly engage with these stereotypical representations.

The first book-length monograph of Asian American literature was written by Elaine H. Kim, published in 1982 and follows this logic. Kim states in *Asian American Literature: An Introduction to the Writings and Their Social Context* that her purpose is to place these texts in their sociohistorical and cultural contexts to avoid misunderstandings resulting from existing stereotypes. Her proposed solution is a study of Asian American "self-images as they have evolved in response to changing social contexts" (Kim, *Asian American Literature* xviii). As Kim's subsequent chapters show, these self-images have developed from rather idealized depictions of both Asia and America in order to bridge the existing gap between East and West for the first generation writers at the turn of the nineteenth to the twentieth century, to claims to position the Asian American and to claim a home in America in the second generation writers in the mid-twentieth century, to an ever increased awareness of the possibility to build an ethnic American identity since the 1960s. Kim's romanticized vision of the American society as a harmonious multiracial one has been challenged in the years since her publication. Yet, her seminal book still provided the groundwork from which further studies evolved.

Early engagements with ghost figures are, accordingly, very much focused on the idea of a rewriting of history and of finding a voice as an Asian American.[9] These early readings of the ghost figures in the field are concerned

8 For a detailed analysis of the origins of the model minority myth, see, for example, chapter 5, "The Cold War Origins of the Model Minority Myth" in Robert G. Lee, *Orientals: Asian Americans in Popular Culture*, Philadelphia: Temple University Press, 1999, 145–179.

9 This historiographic reading tradition is certainly not limited to the 80s, another important example is, Robert G. Lee, "*The Woman Warrior* as an Intervention in Asian American Historiography," in: Shirley Geok-lin Lim, ed., *Approaches to Teaching Kingston's* The Woman Warrior, New York: The Modern Language Association of America, 1991, 52–63; or the reading of history in the mode of the talk story as referring to equally valid interpretations of history in David Leiwei Li, "*China Men*: Maxine Hong Kingston and the American Canon," *American Literary History* 2.3 (Autumn 1990): 482–502. Still, the dominance of these topics in the early studies demands recognition.

with a psychological approach that makes a silenced history available, especially in its concern with identity politics. Mary Slowick, for example, reads Kingston's books – especially her second novel *China Men* (1980) – as the story that is build around her male ancestors, which needs to combine imagination and history in order to tell this silenced history in her article "When the Ghosts Speak: Oral and Written Narrative Forms in Maxine Hong Kingston's *China Men*" (1994). She argues that in writing the larger history of Chinese Americans, Kingston must "start with the X, the erasing, the silences of her fathers, the apparent extinctions of her history" (Slowik 80) so that her story evolves from such "ghostly footsteps" (86). These silenced family histories also refer to the particular silences that surrounded the so-called 'paper son'-system. After the San Francisco earthquake and fire of 1906 in Chinatown many families claimed to have more sons than they actually had, therewith opening immigration slots for illegal immigrants. With the sponsoring of these paper sons' own families after a couple of years, whole family histories were based on fictions, which needed to be kept secret and resulted in the particular silencing among personal family histories.[10] Ruth Mayer convincingly argues that "the cultural memory of 'paper citizenship' is not only formally shaped by the forces of fabrication and narration – fabrication and narration constitute its very subject matter." In order to come to terms with this kind of fabricated history, to make sense of fake and true stories, and to address this silence, fiction might be an appropriate form, "for it is the one mode of representation that focuses most persistently on spheres of experience beyond the outspoken, the rational, the strategic" (Mayer, "Paper Citizens" 89–90). And in that sense the ghost figure is particularly suitable to embody, represent, and negotiate this silenced and neglected history, as Mary Slowick begins to outline and *The Ghosts Within* continues.

In a similar vein, Gayle K. Fujita Sato reads the narrator's aunt's ghost as a "paper daughter" (Sato 197) in her article "Ghosts as Chinese-American Constructs in Maxine Hong Kingston's *The Woman Warrior*" (1991). She argues that Kingston's memoir narrates "a process of gaining access to a familial, communal memory that is initially ghostlike – elusive and hidden" (196–97). Kingston not only "reclaims but reimagines her aunt's story" (198), as this ghost then 'branches into her life.' Such "authoring of American lives" (199) in both fake immigration identities and the literary engagements with this history almost immediately call to mind the figure of the ghostly. Accordingly, Sato emphasizes

10 For a detailed analysis of this system, see, for example, Erika Lee, *At America's Gates: Chinese Immigration During the Exclusion Era, 1882–1943*, Chapel Hill and London: The University of North Carolina Press, 2003, especially chapter 7.

the function of the ghosts in *The Woman Warrior* as ethnic markers: the ghosts highlight the narrator's struggle with her identity in-between two cultures as well as the elusive, ghostlike history that remains hidden to her (210). Sato's reading of the ghost figures as pointing to the identity as well as the history of Chinese Americans fits the paradigm of identity politics that still links Asian American Studies to its beginnings in activism. The psychological approach to the ghost figures as metaphors of a haunted self that is torn between different ethnic cultures re-appears in readings of Asian American ghosts. But in this early stage, the ghosts' appearance is directly linked to the construction of a politically available and ethnically marked identity. And yet, Sato already indicates the ghosts potential for political ambiguity, when she acknowledges the "vitality of Chinese-American culture" as consisting "in opposed energies, represented in [...] the multiple meanings of *ghost*" (212). It is this conceptualization of ghosts as embodying 'opposed energies' that *The Ghosts Within* emphasizes, even though much of the secondary literature on ghosts in Ethnic Studies in general and in Asian American Studies in particular still rather reiterates the image of ghosts as highlighting an ethnic tradition that encroaches upon the identity of Asian Americans.

One strategy in the initiatory phase to draw attention to a muted Asian American tradition and to build ethnic pride, was to create anthologies of Asian American literature (Leong 64–66).[11] Drawing attention to the literary history

11 Some of the early anthologies are pan-Asian American: the very first one featured, like *Aiiieeeee*, Chinese Americans, Japanese Americans, and Filipino Americans, Kai-yu Hsu and Helen Palubinskas, eds., *Asian-American Authors*, Boston: Houghton Mifflin, 1972; David Hsin-Fu Wand, ed., *Asian-American Heritage: An Anthology of Prose and Poetry*, New York: Washington Square Press, 1974, this anthology is striking for its inclusion also of Korean Americans and Pacific Islanders; others emphasized the female experience while expanding the definition of Asian American writers to include other subgroups such as Vietnamese Americans, see, for example, Shirley Geok-Lin Lim, Mayumi Tsutakawa, Margariat Donnelly, eds., *The Forbidden Stitch: An Asian American Women's Anthology*, Corvallis, OR: Calyx Books, 1989; Diane Yen-mei and Asian Women United, eds., *Making Waves: An Anthology of Writings by and about Asian American Women*, Boston: Beacon Press, 1989; Sylvia Watanabe and Carol Bruchac, eds., *Home to Stay: Asian American Women's Fiction*, Greenfield Center, NY: Greenfield Review Press, 1990; there are also ethnic-specific anthologies, for example, Him Mark Lai, Genny Lim, and Judy Yung, eds., *Island: Poetry and History of Chinese Immigrants on Angel Island, 1910–1940*, Seattle: University of Washington, 1980; Jerrold Asao Hisura, ed., *The Hawk's Well: A*

that dates back to the late nineteenth century with the writings of the Eaton sisters, these collections provide overviews as well as easy access for a larger audience and they help shape a self-image of Asian America. Yet, such a homogenizing labeling also invites critical reflections, especially in terms of which groups should belong to this label and whose writings would be authentic as representative for these groups.

The most prominent anthology of the time was probably the 1974 *Aiiieeeee! An Anthology of Asian-American Writers* edited by Paul Chan, Frank Chin and others and its cultural nationalist project. It included Chinese American, Japanese American, and Filipino American writers as well as a preface by Frank Chin, called "Fifty Years of Our Whole Voice." As is well-known today, the anthology in general and Chin's introduction especially, has sparked serious criticism in terms of its exclusionary definition of 'authentic' Asian Americans: according to the editors, these should be non-Christian, non-feminist, and non-immigrant. According to Chin, the predominance of women writers in the Asian American context even furthered the on-going "emasculation" of Asian American men.[12] In the following controversy, Chin attacked writers such as Jade Snow Wong, Maxine Hong Kingston, and Amy Tan for their 'selling out' to white racist American mainstream. He called them 'fakes' because, to him, they were distorting the original Chinese stories to cater to an American white fantasy. Even in terms of genre, Chin objected to the use of autobiographical writing as it is a Western and Christian genre. He criticized the depiction of Chinese American communities as misogynist and anti-individualistic as

---

Collection of Japanese American Art and Literature, San Jose, CA: Asian American Art Projects, 1986.

12 Although most critics today – including myself – do not agree with Chin's rigorous attacks and contest the link he established between a female presence in Asian America and racist stereotypes by mainstream America, the importance of the "feminized" stereotypical representation of Asian men remains a central point to be discussed. This applies largely to Chinese American men, who not only lived for the first years in America in a bachelor society in Chinatowns, but were being pushed into traditionally female jobs due to language problems or racist exclusions in America. For detailed summaries of these developments, see, for example, Jinqui Ling, "Identity Crisis and Gender Politics: Reappropriating Asian American Masculinity," King-kok Cheung, ed., *An Interethnic Companion to Asian American Literature*, Cambridge: Cambridge University Press, 1997, 312–337; or Viet Than Nguyen, "The Remasculanization of Chinese America: Race, Violence, and the Novel," *American Literary History* 12.1/2 (Spring/Summer 2000): 130–157.

catering to white American stereotypes (Chin and Chan, "Fifty Years of Our Whole" xxi–xlviii), (Chin and Chan, "Preface" vii–xvi). Chin's attacks, especially as he repeated and justified them in the introduction to the expanded 1991 edition of *The Big Aiiieeeee!* (Chin) have to be understood as an attempt – although admittedly over-the-top – to advance the position of Asian Americans.

Even though his main concern was the correction of white America's stereotypes about Asian Americans, his cultural nationalist approach inevitably provoked severe criticism. However, with this aim, his project is not that far removed from Kingston's project because both wish to rewrite and redefine the Chinese American 'experience' in a counter-narrative to racist white American accounts. Nevertheless, the controversy shows the early stages of the development of two traditions within both Asian American literature and Asian American Studies: one side's normative aim is a writing of representative social history through literature, while the other camp emphasizes artistic freedom and the necessity to depict different shades of grey in each kind of literature (Yin 229–53).[13] Although they are not mutually exclusive, these two approaches and the questions they raise about authenticity, representativeness, resistance and accommodation remain as binary distinctions in the field of Asian American Studies until today.

The political subtext of these debates also figures largely in the prominent feminist strand to which Chin's criticism indirectly refers. This feminist basis of Asian American Studies cannot be overstated. Fittingly, *The Woman Warrior* has also been taught and analyzed in various contexts besides Asian American Studies: in Ethnic Studies, world literature, Autobiography Studies, or Feminist Studies. With the publication of Toni Morrison's *Beloved* (1987) as the classical ghost story of ethnic literature, a focus on feminist approaches to ghost figures in ethnic literature was again consolidated.[14] This close connection between ghosts,

13 For extended readings of the controversy see, for example, King-Kok Cheung, "*The Woman Warrior* versus *The Chinaman Pacific*: Must a Chinese American Critic Choose Between Feminism and Heroism?," *Conflicts in Feminism*, eds. Marianne Hirsch and Evelyn Fox Keller, New York: Routledge, 1990, 234–251 ; David Leiwei Li, "Emergence," *Imagining the Nation: Asian American Literature and Cultural Consent*, Stanford, California: Stanford University Press, 1998, 19–62.

14 See, for example, Rigney, Barbara Hill. "'A Story to Pass On': Ghosts and the Significance of History in Toni Morrison's *Beloved*." *Haunting the House of Fiction: Feminist Perspectives on Ghost Stories by American Women*. Eds. Lynette Carpenter, Wendy K Kolmar. Knoxville: University of Tennessee Press, 1991. 229–35; or Lawrence, David. "Fleshly Ghosts and Ghostly Flesh: The Word and the Body in

ethnicity, and history in pan-ethnic readings was to shape the phase of diversification that began in the 1990s. But already in this first phase a connection between feminist readings of ghosts and ethnic aspects becomes obvious.

Drawing on the literature of the second-wave feminism evolving at the time,[15] these critics articulate the special case of Asian American writers. The anthology *This Bridge Called My Back: Writings by Radical Women of Color* (1981) edited by Cherríe Moraga and Gloria Anazaldúa acts as the manifesto of feminist women of color of the time. Containing prose, poetry, and personal essays by African American, Latina, Native American, and Asian American writers, these women perceive their feminist project as an umbrella, intending to "reflect our color loud and clear, not tone it down" (Moraga and Anzaldúa xxiv). The two most prominent monographs in this feminist tradition of the time that focus explicitly on Asian American women are probably Amy Ling's *Between Worlds: Women Writers of Chinese Ancestry* (1990) and King-kok Cheung's *Articulate Silences: Hisaye Yamamoto, Maxine Hong Kingston, and Joy Kogawa* (1993). The first addresses only Chinese American writers, for whom she attempts to provide an overview of their tradition. Following Alice Walker's concept of a 'mother's literary garden,' Ling states that she means "to show off the flowers in my mother's garden" (Ling, *Between Worlds* xi–xv). Ling argues that these women writers intend to right the wrongs by writing them, especially to change their doubly oppressed position as women of Asian descent in America and as women in an often misogynist Chinese cultural tradition. King-kok Cheung's *Articulate Silences* focuses on both Chinese and Japanese American female writers. Cheung argues that the value attached to silence is culturally specific: on this basis, she challenges the Eurocentric assumption that

---

Beloved." *Toni Morrison's Fiction: Contemporary Criticism*. Ed. David L Middleton. New York and London: Garland Publishing, 1997. 231–46.

15 Influential and by now classical texts in the field of feminist criticism were being published at the same time. See, for example, Elaine Showalter, *A Literature of Their Own: British Women Novelists from Bronte to Lessing*, Princeton: Princeton University Press, 1977; Nina Baym, *Woman's Fiction: A Guide to Novels by and about Women in America, 1820–1870*, Ithaca: Cornell University Press, 1978; Sandra M. Gilbert and Susan Gubar, *The Madwoman in the Attic: The Woman Writer and the Nineteenth-Century Literary Imagination*, New Haven: Yale University Press, 1979. Even though Asian American critics build their works on this feminist background, they are simultaneously aware of the pitfalls and problems of taking over the white woman's, Eurocentric ideas for an Asian American context.

silence equals passivity, and instead posits that silence in these works needs to be understood as a rhetorical silence that exposes oppressions, as a provocative silence that enhances creativity, and as an attentive silence that breaks up binaries of voice and voicelessness (Cheung 23).

Such an interweaving of feminist identity politics with an ethnic twist that asserts cultural difference as valuable also shapes feminist readings of Asian American ghost figures. Lynette Carpenter and Wendy K. Kolmar provide a feminist reading of ghostly figures in their edited volume *Haunting the House of Fiction: Feminist Perspectives on Ghost Stories by American Women* (1991). Although the volume includes insightful essays, I disagree with some of the arguments put forward in the introduction by the editors. Surely, ghosts are one of the forms "for exploring dangerous territory" (Carpenter and Kolmar 2), but in my view this conclusion does not automatically limit them to a female trope, as Carpenter and Kolmar seem to suggest. Furthermore, they assume an explicitly female style of writing with women writers' as

> "more likely to portray natural and supernatural experience along a continuum. Boundaries between the two are not absolute, but fluid, so that the supernatural can be accepted, connected with, reclaimed, and can often possess a quality of familiarity." (12)

While I agree with their finding that such a continuum is to be found especially in minority traditions that are not Eurocentric, I hesitate to limit this argument to women's writing. It is, rather, a cultural aspect that should be pronounced much more prominently.

Ruth Y. Jenkins, for example, argues in her essay "Authorizing Female Voice and Experience: Ghosts and Spirits in Kingston's *The Woman Warrior* and Allende's *The House of Spirits*" (1994) that "the supernatural is closely linked to female voice" in that "ghosts and spirits provide authority for articulation and identity" (Jenkins 68). Such feminist interpretations of ghosts emphasize the potential for freedom of expression that these figures allow, highlighting a psychological function of these figures especially for marginalized voices. Moreover, Jenkins provides an approach of the supernatural and ghosts as a representation of alternative experiences and histories that realist writing could not sufficiently portray.[16] With this claim, she emphasizes the specific

16 One of the key terms that comes to mind especially in terms of Ethnic Studies and in relation to Allende explicitly, is magical realism. Although it originated in the 1920s in Germany, this concept has gained wide influence since the mid-twentieth century in reference to Latin American literature and its criticism. The fusion of realist and

ethnic value that these figures offer in their questioning of Western perceptions, therewith foreshadowing the growing insistence on cultural approaches to these figures that shapes the second phase of Asian American Studies. *The Ghosts Within* is inspired by such early conceptualizations of the ghosts' possible potential, yet, it broadens the scope to which these figures refer and foregrounds the inherent political ambiguity of the shape-shifting figure of the ghost. So, instead of following such an overly-positive conclusion, it reads the ghosts rather as pointing to those unfinished, messy aspects that each categorization or conceptualization immediately produces.

Although *The Ghosts Within* is indebted to this rich secondary literature with feminist approaches to Asian American literature in general and ghost figures specifically, it will not directly contribute to this line of thought. Rather, it envisions the ghost figures as not referencing explicitly female aspects, or as voicing a specifically female perspective, but as highlighting different, even paradoxical interconnections. As the readings of the ghost figures in the secondary literature tend to reflect the predominant focus and trends of Asian American criticism at large, I believe that these political foci on the specific rewriting of Asian American history, Asian American identity, and its feminist basis still shape the field but, due to their central position by now, have somehow become more self-referential and complex in their overlaps. And this

magical elements into one literary text, whereby the magical is presented as part of the ordinary, allows for a representation of an alternative 'reality' to that of Western post-enlightenment rationalism. The popularity of the concept can be explained by its destabilization of boundaries and by its assumed subversive tendencies due to the questioning of seemingly given facts of causality, materiality, or motivation. With this subversive approach, the concept has been used increasingly also by writers and critics of postcolonial cultures and in a feminist tradition. On the other hand, magical realist writers have been criticized for a selling out of an exotic background to a Western readership by offering an escapist experience finally supporting a colonial attitude, calling to mind the criticisms charged against Kingston or Tan by Frank Chin. For a critical reading of Salman Rushdie's use of magical realism, see, for example, Timothy Brennan, *Salman Rushdie and the Third World: Myths of the Nation*, Houndsmills, Basingstokes: Macmillan, 1989. For good introductions to the concept of magical realism, see, Maggie Ann Bowers, *Magic(al) Realism*, London and New York: Routledge, 2004; Lois Parkinson Zamora and Wendy B. Faris, "Introduction: Daiquiri Birds and Flaubertian Parrot(ie)s," *Magical Realism: Theory, History, Community*, Eds. Lois Parkinson Zamora and Wendy B. Faris, Durham and London: Duke University Press, 1995, 1–11.

shift has been brought about also because of the second phase of Asian American Studies – that of diversification – which dominated the 1990s.

GHOSTS AS PAN-ETHNIC CONSTRUCTIONS IN DIVERSIFIED ASIAN AMERICA

While Elaine H. Kim's first monograph of Asian American Studies highlights the initiation and establishment of the field, Sau-ling Cynthia Wong's *Reading Asian American Literature: From Necessity to Extravagance* (1993) embodies the transition into the second phase: the diversification of the field.[17] The great strength of Kim's *Asian American Literature* is its grounding of the texts in their sociohistorical and cultural contexts. However, this is also its weakness, as Sau-ling Cynthia Wong points out about a decade later. Wong criticizes Kim's assumption that a certain text can be read in its specific context in order to prevent misunderstandings. Influenced by new historicist and poststructuralist theories, Wong complicates this by introducing multiple subject positions for Asian Americans (Wong, *Reading Asian American Literature* 10–12). Wong introduces the helpful notion of intertexuality, arguing that Asian American texts create a sense of an autonomous Asian American literary tradition in that they all "build upon, allude to, refine, controvert, and resonate with each other" (10–12). With this thinking, Wong builds on the ideas of hybridity and syncretism[18]:

17 After its initiation, Asian American Studies had the already outlined concerns: claiming a voice and a history in America. These concerns and the increasing diversity of topics and subgroups are reflected in anthologies of critical essays in the field. The first collection that attempted a rewriting of the American canon from a multicultural perspective was, A. LaVonne Brown Ruoff and Jerry Ward W., Jr., eds, *Redefining American Literary History*, New York: Modern Language Association, 1990; a collection that attests to the prominence of Kingston's *The Woman Warrior* in educational contexts in various academic fields, Shirley Geok-Lin Lim, ed., *Approaches to Teaching Kingston's* The Woman Warrior, New York: Modern Language Association, 1991; a collection that already broadens the scope of Asian American writers significantly by including various subgroups, Shirley Geok-Lin Lim and Amy Ling, eds., *Reading the Literatures of Asian America*, Philadelphia: Temple University Press, 1992.

18 For definitions of and critical conceptions of the terms hybridity and syncretism, see, for example: James Clifford, *The Predicament of Culture: Twentieth-Century Ethnography, Literature, and Art*, Cambridge: Cambridge University Press, 1988;

Asian American literature is an emergent tradition. Combining various elements, a new and different, specifically Asian American literary tradition emerges. As Wong further demonstrates, the label Asian American is a pan-Asian politically oriented construct: the various subgroups chose to combine their forces in order to gain a new visibility (6). For the academic discourse this constructedness implies an uncertainty about the subject matter, as the Chin-Kingston controversy highlights. As a result, Asian American critics "have to establish their professional domain; through doing so, and through disseminating the products of their efforts, they play a role in building *their* community" (9, my emphasis). Wong assumes that the Asian American critics have an important role to play not only in the perception but also in the formation of the Asian American community. As the italicized 'their' in this passage suggests, Wong expects all of the critics to be Asian Americans themselves. With this, Wong shows herself to be very much influenced by the activist roots of the Asian American project.[19]

Wong's emphasis of an Asian American literary intertextuality speaks to the growing awareness and self-assurance of this specific tradition. It also reveals the focus on cultural aspects that becomes so important in this period of diversification. While her intertextual focus has been highly influential and helpful in recognizing the field's specificity, I argue that her conception of the Asian American literary tradition as an autonomous one can even be expanded. Although she lists multiple discourses as constitutive of the Asian American literary tradition and I agree with her conception of this tradition as a hybrid, newly emergent one, her main aim is a conception of a distinctive Asian American intertextuality that feeds into the growing awareness of the specific

---

Christopher Balme, "Inventive Syncretism: The Concept of the Syncretic in Intercultural Discourse," *Fusion of Cultures*, Eds. Peter O. Stummer and Christopher Balme, Amsterdam, Atlanta: Rodopi, 1996, 9–18; Homi K. Bhabha, *The Location of Culture*, London, New York: Routledge, 1994; for the Asian American context, see, for example, Lisa Lowe, "Heterogeneity, Hybridity, Multiplicity: Marking Asian American Differences" *Diaspora: A Journal of Transnational Studies* 1.1 (Summer 1991): 24–44.

19 According to Judy Chu the very first courses that were taught at the universities in California were predominantly concerned with a redefinition of Asian American women's roles, with the intersections of race, class, sex in oppressive attitudes towards women, and, most importantly, encouraged the students to activism within the Asian American community as part of their university projects, Judy Chu, "Asian American Women's Studies Courses: A Look Back at Our Beginnings," *Frontiers: A Journal of Women Studies*, 8.3 (1986): 96–101.

appeal to market this literature as Asian American after Kingston's influential memoir. *The Ghosts Within* builds on such recognitions – highlighting the influence of Kingston's ghost figures as reference points for both Asian American fiction writers and its critics. Yet, while this intertextuality of Asian American literature needs to be emphasized, I argue that one should read Asian American literature more consistently as simultaneously also an intertext with both the Western/mainstream American, the Asian traditions, and most signifycantly the American ethnic traditions as I do, for example, in chapter 2 that alludes to the connections between Lois Ann Yamanaka's *Behold the Many* and Toni Morrison's *Beloved* and foregrounds the specific mixture that emerges in the ghost figures of Christianized Asians.

The growing awareness of the field's own diversity induced – especially in its relationship with the growing field of Diaspora Studies – a wish to establish a strong connection to other Ethnic Studies in order to support its ongoing legitimization. While the origins of African American Studies and Asian American Studies are already tightly intertwined, the overlapping aspects – at least in terms of the predominant readings of ghost figures – are now again being pronounced once each field has successfully claimed a voice of its own.

Bonnie Winsbro's *Supernatural Forces: Belief, Difference, and Power in Contemporary Works by Ethnic Women* (1993) marks this shift towards cultural interconnections that appears in the 1990s in readings of ghost figures. Her aim is to show that a particular use of supernatural figures is a "cross-cultural" trend (Winsbro 10). Arguing that ethnic writers are confronted with a "multiplicity of realities," often mutually exclusive ones, Winsbro sees the supernatural as one area that engages with and stages this conflict. Looking at female authors such as Louise Erdrich, Toni Morrison, and Maxine Hong Kingston, Winsbro claims that they have to find their own conceptions of 'reality' in relation to such concepts as the supernatural in order to arrive at individuation and self-definition (5–6). Even though I find Winsbro's general complication of a universal 'reality' in terms of different ethnic backgrounds convincing, she ultimately reads the supernatural as positive and enriching forces pushing towards a self-definition – especially for women – and, thus, evens out the striking differences between these ethnic groups and their respective ghostly figures. Instead of centering on the internal contradictions and bumps to which these figures point, Winsbro attempts to arrive at a smooth reading of these figures as basically references to non-Western conceptions of 'reality.' While her reading of ghost figures remains in line with earlier feminist conceptualizations, her study moves into new territory in attempting a 'cross-cultural' reading of ghosts as linked to ethnicity.

This emphasis on a cultural approach of ghost figures also drives Kathleen Brogan's seminal *Cultural Haunting: Ghosts and Ethnicity in Recent American Literature* (1998). She establishes the genre of 'stories of cultural haunting' as a pan-ethnic tradition. Her engagement with these figures highlights their function as "agents of both cultural memory *and* cultural renewal" (Brogan 12) in the narrative process of ethnic redefinition. Because of its central status as a reading of ghosts that reflects their cultural function, a more detailed discussion of Brogan's findings appears in chapter 1, where I place her approach of these figures within the larger theoretical frameworks that have shaped our receptions of ghost figures. Such emphasis on ethnic memory and tradition in the reading of ghost figures appears as a reaction to the ongoing redefinitions of the larger field of Asian American Studies in its relation to border fields such as Diaspora Studies. Asian American academic discourse increasingly engages with the re-articulation of Asian America as part of transnational and diasporic influences, constraints, and liberations.[20] This move to a diasporic approach constitutes the replacement of the earlier minority or immigration discourse in the field (Clifford 255); and the pan-ethnic approaches to the ghost figures reflect this move.

These influences of Diaspora Studies mark the growing diversification conceptually during the second phase and show an important re-shaping of the field that prefigures its current engagement with the concept of transnationalism. The classical reference point for a definition of the term 'diaspora' is William Safran's "Diasporas in Modern Societies: Myths of Homeland and Return" (1991). He defines diasporas as communities with a history of dispersal, with mythical memories of an original homeland, with the feeling of not being accepted by the host country, with the idea of a final return to the original homeland, an ongoing engagement with the rebuilding of the original homeland, and whose group identity is centrally shaped by an ongoing relationship with this homeland (Safran 83–84). While Safran's definition proves a good starting point, it has also been criticized.[21] James Clifford argues in his influential chapter "Diaspora" that these features need to be expanded by others. He takes issue especially with the centrality of a return to the original homeland as well as the demand for a specific origin. In his view, diasporic communities are also

20 Another influential text in this line of thought that rethinks citizenship in an ever-increasing transnational set up of migratory life is Aihwa Ong, *Flexible Citizenship: The Cultural Logics of Transnationality*, Durham: Duke University Press, 1999.

21 For a thorough typology of diasporas, see, Robin Cohen, *Global Diasporas: An Introduction*, Abingdon, Oxon: Routledge , 1997.

significantly formed by "[d]ecentered, lateral connections" and "a shared, ongoing history of displacement, suffering, adaptation, or resistance" (Clifford 250). Diasporas, to him, are both about roots and routes: they articulate the tensions of accommodation and resistance, and in this engagement, they signify transnationality and movement, but at the same time a struggle on the local level in which the community tries to situate itself (252). In this way, Clifford demands that the concept needs to be historicized and historically situated in order to be applied fruitfully.[22]

Diasporic approaches challenge the notion of a single national identity that overrides all other identifications. Instead, as David Leiwei Li argues, they emphasize shared histories of multiple transformations and origins (Li 196).[23] And yet, even though these definitions break with simplified relations to nation-states, they are still very much shaped by group identities that are often constituted nationally or ethnically. Ruth Mayer's study *Diaspora: Eine kritische Begriffsbestimmung* (2005) emphasizes the narrative aspect of this identity formation while she challenges oversimplified definitions of the concept. Linking her argument to Assmann's concept of cultural memory and Benedict Anderson's imagined communities, Mayer argues that diasporic groups are constituted by a (mythical) narrative of origin or a communal future (Mayer, *Diaspora* 13). Thus, she questions the synonymous use of the terms 'diaspora' and 'transnationalism.' While diasporas certainly are cosmopolitan and flexible forms of (post)modern living, they do not inherently challenge the idea of nation-states (14). Rather, diasporic communities also produce what Benedict

22 One of the principle sources that Clifford cites is Paul Gilroy's *Black Atlantic: Modernity and Double Consciousness*, London: Verso, 1993. This seminal study is a strategic move out of the race paradigm and the constraints given in thinking solely in terms of nation-states. Gilroy perceives of this 'black atlantic' as a countertradition to modernity. This move allows the creation of a new framework, in which narratives of crossing, exploration, and forced and voluntary travel precede, in order to highlight formerly hidden cultural productions. For a critical reading of Gilroy's 'black atlantic,' see Ruth Mayer, *Diaspora: Eine kritische Begriffsbestimmung*, Bielefeld: Transcript, 2005. Mayer sees the influence of this concept related to the general questioning of concepts such as authenticity, tradition, and nationality at the time. These categories were more and more seen as highly constructed and imagined (compare, especially pages 80–87).

23 For another example of this reading of diaspora at the time see, for example, Rey Chow's *Writing Diaspora: Tactics of Intervention in Contemporary Cultural Studies*, Bloomington: Indiana University Press, 1993.

Anderson calls 'long-distance nationalism.' In his article with the same title, Anderson shows how these figures enter into politics in their original homelands from the save distance of the given host-country. This example highlights the close connections that still exist between nation-states and diasporic communities. Although the limits of a diasporic approach are clear – how far is the term stretchable, how far does it tend towards romanticization –, I still see this as a productive concept for critically reflecting upon the situation of Asian Americans.[24] As long as one follows Clifford's and Mayer's warnings to historize its use and to stick to the tensions that the term highlights, this category remains as a convincing complement to the current use of the term transnationalism.

Although *The Ghosts Within* does not prominently work with the concept of diaspora for the specific close readings in its chapters, an awareness of the development from Immigrant Studies via Diaspora Studies to Transnational Studies and the consequences for the field of Asian American Studies is highly relevant. The engagement with diaspora emphasizes the necessity to include and discuss the historical situatedness of Asian America and its literary productions. This awareness also shapes the re-definitions that appear with reference to the label 'Asian America' at the time. The anthology *Charlie Chan is Dead* is a case in point for the broadening of the concept in the second phase. It includes Asian American authors with ethnic backgrounds as diverse as India, East Asia, Southeast Asia, and Malaysia.[25]

---

24 The 1990s also produce a number of Asian American scholarly texts that critically evaluate the diasporic readings. Rachel C. Lee, for example, laments that gender is almost completely being dropped in this new focus on diaspora in her influential *The Americas of Asian American Literature: Gendered Fictions of Nation and Transnation* (1999). In her opinion, the feminist emphasis on aspects of gender vanished largely because it was initially linked to a protest against the cultural nationalist projects of the initiatory phase of the field. With the loss of credibility of these cultural nationalist claims, the ground for the gendered focus also seemed to disappear. Lee's project fills this gap by asserting a relationship between the gendered cultural representations of Asian America and the (neo)colonial politics of nation-states that are increasingly perceived as global and borderless (Lee, *The Americas of Asian American* 10–11).

25 Next to anthologies like this one, that significantly broaden the definition of Asian America, many new ethnic-specific anthologies emerge that focus on formerly neglected groups. See, for example, Barbara Tran, Monique T.D. Truong, and Luu Truong Khoi, eds., *Watermark: Vietnamese American Poetry and Prose*, New York:

And with this, Asian American Studies enters a crisis of representation. While its self-definition broadens significantly, the category of Asian American becomes increasingly contested. Lisa Lowe's article "Heterogeneity, Hybridity, Multiplicity: Asian American Differences" (originally published in 1991) reflects this shift. Drawing on Stuart Hall and Antonio Gramsci, Lowe argues that Asian American Studies has reached a point where it should move beyond the nationalist/feminist divide or the formalized generational discussions and instead focus on "'Asian American cultural practices' that produce identity" (Lowe, *Immigrant Acts* 64). This also includes recognition of the historical and material differences that constitute any social formation. Even though Lowe acknowledges the political advantages of articulating a unified Asian American identity, she also problematizes the fixation of Asian American identity within this logic and the intricate interrelatedness to the dominant discourse to which it remains bound. Instead, recognizing the constructedness of the category and acknowledging the hybridity and heterogeneity within, allows one to conceive of it as a social *positioning*, to use one of Hall's terms. This highly influential article demands to rethink processes that are, on the one hand, "being appropriated and commodified by commercial culture and, on the other, [...] being rearticulated for the creation of oppositional 'resistance cultures'" (82). Lowe's argument is linked to the concept of multiculturalism that shaped discourses in the 1990s and the critical re-evaluation of difference in culture at large.[26] Her rethinking of the field's central terms has influenced the field at large and *The Ghosts Within* in particular. It is studies like Lowe's or Mayer's

Asian American Writers' Workshop, 1998; or Mai Neng Moua, ed., *Bamboo Among the Oaks: Contemporary Writing by Hmong Americans*, St. Paul, MN: Borealis Books, 2002.

26 A related shift in the field, which is connected to both the self-conscious redefinition of what the category Asian American actually includes and to its self-positioning with regards to Diaspora Studies, for example, is an emphasis on border regions. Arif Dirlik, for example, calls for a reconsideration of the term Asian American, challenging the notion of national categorization that underpins it. Instead, he opts for "Asia-Pacific," in order to highlight that a regional, not a national, focus should be central to this field of study. Dirlik argues that this region is highly constructed to embody the historically produced and contradictory economic, social, political, militia, and cultural relationships within this sphere (Dirlik 3–4). For a critical reading of this concept, see, for example, David Leiwei Li, *Imaging the Nation: Asian American Literature and Cultural Consent*, Stanford, California: Stanford University Press, 1997, especially pages 196–203.

that have inspired my critical rethinking of the ghost figure as a central concept of Asian American literature: as both a reference to the cultural and historical specificity as well as their general questioning of any attempted neat conceptualization.

The pan-ethnic cultural readings of ghost figures that shape this period can be seen as reactions to the call for historical situatedness and the larger inter-ethnic connections in diasporic redefintions. A broadening of the conceptualization of Asian America results in both a stretching of these figures as cross-cultural, ethnic ones and simultaneously a narrowing down and emphasis of the concrete historical reference of these figures. This dual tendency also shapes the third phase of Asian American Studies, which foregrounds cultural psychoanalytical approaches to the ghosts: from ghosts as haunting an American identity and history to those that begin to see a self-critical function of these figures for Asian America.

GLOBAL/TRANSNATIONAL ASIAN AMERICA: GHOSTS AS SELF-REFLEXIVE FIGURES

Beginning in the 1990s and stretching into the third phase of Asian American Studies, there is a body of literature that recognizes America as haunted. Toni Morrison's *Playing in the Dark* (1992) is an early – and probably the most famous – example of this reading. It constructs the American literary scene as haunted by an African American presence. A similar argument is put forward by Renée Bergland in *The National Uncanny: Indian Ghosts and American Subjects* (2000), which focuses on the ghostly presence of Native Americans as constituting the American national self-image. Working with both a psychoanalytical and a poststructuralist approach, Bergland argues that Americans, especially in their literary imaginations, have constructed Native Americans as ghostly figures as a technique of removal. In Bergland's words, "Native American ghosts function as representations of national guilt and as triumphant agents of Americanization" (Bergland, *The National Uncanny* 4). Following from a process of "repression of subjection," the American imagination is structured around these figures: Americans build their own national conception on the repression of the ongoing oppression of Native Americans. By pushing them from the territorial landscape into the imaginary landscape, however, Americans have turned them into powerful ghostly figures that return to haunt this national conception of America. Bergland concludes that these ghosts haunt American literature "because the American nation is compelled to return again and again to an encounter that makes it both sorry and happy, a defiled grave upon which it must continually rebuild the American subject" (22).[27] Crystal Parikh follows a similar logic in her article "Blue Hawaii: Asian Hawaiian Cultural Production and Racial Melancholia" (2002), in which she argues that America's democratic self-image is haunted by Hawaii's troubled history. She argues that novels such as Lois-Ann Yamanaka's *Blu's Hanging* (1997) counter the "exotic/erotic fantasy of Hawaii as Edenic space of escape by figuring the history of traumatic loss that such a fantasy disguises" (Parikh 201) and, as such, appear as haunting images that trouble the American self-conception. Although these readings begin to address the uncomfortable aspects to which ghost figures and haunting point, they ultimately follow a conception of ethnic ghosts as figures of resistance in reading them as challenges to American hegemonic constructions.

Contemporary Asian American criticism begins to move beyond such resistance narratives and instead highlights the *internal* haunting of Asian American communities. In *Haunting the Korean Diaspora: Shame, Secrecy, and the Forgotten War* (2008) Grace M. Cho sees the Korean diaspora as not only haunted but constituted by transgenerational haunting. Drawing on Ramsay Liem's oral history project[28] and Abraham and Torok's psychoanalytical approach to transgenerational haunting, Cho looks at the troubling legacy of encounters between American soldiers and Korean women in Korea for the Korean diaspora. In her words, the figure of the *yanggongju* "emerges as the ghostly figure of all that has been erased" (Cho 4). *Yanggongju* is the term for Korean women, who sleep with US soldiers, and it refers back to the Korean comfort women for the Japanese and forward to the military brides that migrated to the US. In order to represent US involvement in Korea as benevolent, the war brides were used as figures mirroring this possibility for Korean women to enter the US as role models of interracial happy relations. Yet, their integration into

27 Ulla Haselstein's article on Native American literary haunting and highlighting the double processes of deconstructive and reconstructive tendencies of spectrality has also inspired my own readings of ghostly figures (Haselstein 179–198).

28 Ramsay Liem interviews Korean Americans in order to study the influences of intergenerational transmissions of social trauma and argues that silence is often the carrier of such unspeakable pasts. Thus, the "Korean War has been a skeleton in the closet associated with unspeakable pain" (126) which has been transmitted to the younger generations of Korean Americans who have not actually experienced the war. See, Ramsay Liem, "History, Trauma, and Identity: The Legacy of the Korean War for Korean Americans," *Amerasia Journal* 29.3 (2003–2004): 111–129.

the US required a burial of any story that would run counter this myth. As participants of their own erasures, these families became entangled in personal transgenerational hauntings (12–15). With this, Cho re-frames psychoanalytical conceptions of ghosts such as Bergland's to question Asian American self-conceptions. Cho's insightful study exemplifies the potential of reading ghost figures as not only pointing to larger structures of inequality but also to the complex interconnections and internal haunting of an Asian American community itself.

Belinda Kong also emphasizes such internal haunting in her article "The Asian American Hyphen Goes Gothic: Ghosts and Doubles in Maxine Hong Kingston and lê thi diem thúy" (2008). Comparing the function of ghosts in Kingston's *The Woman Warrior* (1977) with that in lê's *The Gangster We Are All Looking For* (2003), Kong arrives at the conclusion "that contemporary Asian-American literature demonstrates an intensified appropriation of the Gothic as it continually expands the representational boundaries of Asian-American identity" (Kong 124). According to Kong, whereas Kingston's ghosts basically follow "cultural singularity" and polarize Asia against America, "lê brings the ghostly into the Asian-American hyphen itself, the very realm that her predecessor had tried to exorcise" (132). And with that, the more recent novel "gives us a narrative of Asian-America's internal alterity" (133). Although I find Kong's reading of Kingston's ghost figures too limited,[29] her general observation of the growing awareness of a haunted Asian America supports not only the claim that the current phase of Asian American Studies has become self-reflexive but also the tendency to read its ghost figures as self-critical references.

These critical insights have significantly influenced my reading of ghost figures. Instead of following a simple resistance paradigm, they offer possible references to uncomfortable interlinkages between larger hegemonic power systems and the marginalized groups themselves. Chapter 2 argues that the ghosts that populate Lois-Ann Yamanaka's *Behold the Many* (2006) expose the paradoxical interconnections that shape the Hawaiian society: they embody the dis-ease that underlines the image of Hawaii as an interethnic paradise and reveal instead the interethnic tensions that shape Hawaii and its Asian American community. Instead of a clear-cut resistance narrative, Yamanaka's postcolonial

29 For a critical reading of Kong's claim that *The Woman Warrior* uses ghosts only as references to one single cultural background and never both at once, see my article "Do Ghosts Grow Up? Ghostliness in Maxine Hong Kingston's *The Woman Warrior* and *China Men*," *The Legacy of Maxine Hong Kingston: The Mulhouse Book*, Eds. Sämi Ludwig and Nicoleta Alexoae-Zagni, Wien, Berlin: LIT, 2014.

melodrama at the same time addresses and disguises these conflicts. Without offering solutions to the problems it raises, the novel uses the ghost figures' affective potential to throw its readers into a roller coaster of emotions, forcing them to re-think or rather re-feel categorizations via emotions and intuition. This reading, then, follows the critical insights of Kong and Cho in that the ghosts challenge the label Asian America from within.

Such critical rethinking of categorizations in terms of Asian American or colonizer/colonized shapes all chapters of *The Ghosts Within*. Chapter 3 engages in a reading of Heinz Insu Fenkl's *Memories of My Ghost Brother* (1996) that highlights the paradoxical subject position that emerges from the neocolonial camptown world in which terms such as victim and persecutor become increasingly entangled. *The Ghosts Within* reads his novel, thus, as an engagement with the origins of what Grace M. Cho calls the transgenerational haunted Korean diaspora as the novel follows the narrator's complicated family life that is build around the haunting presence of the 'ghost brother.' And even though chapter 4 implies a move away from the close entanglements of ethnicity/identity/ghosts in its focus on global novels, my reading of Amitav Ghosh's *The Calcutta Chromosome* (1995) also highlights the uneasy subject positions that his science fiction novel envisions for its postcolonial posthuman agents, addresses the problems and privileges of conceptions of ethnic tour guides for a global readership with reference to Ed Lin's *Ghost Month* (2014) and Amy Tan's ghost narrator in *Saving Fish From Drowning* (2006).

These conceptualizations of ghost figures as self-reflexive and self-critical aspects reflect the ongoing re-negotiation of Asian American Studies as a field. The current, third phase of Asian American Studies is dominated by the question how to engage with the varied experiences, the ever-expanding reach of the term Asian America, and the growing available methodologies in the field. The award controversy around Lois-Ann Yamanaka's novel *Blu's Hanging* marks the shift into such self-reflexivity.[30] The novel is about the death of a mother of three children and how these cope with their loss and the emotional withdrawal of their grief-stricken father. One of the minor characters is Uncle Paulo, a Filipino American, who is a rapist. The controversy centered on this character. After the Association for Asian American Studies committee chose to give the fiction

30 Of course, other aspects such as gender remain visible categories, but I want to show here the new focus on a critical self-evaluation within the field. An example for the ongoing significance of this category is: Patricia P. Chu, *Assimilating Asians: Gendered Strategies of Authorship in Asian America*, Durham and London: Duke University Press, 2000.

award of 1997 to *Blu's Hanging*, it sparked a controversy that resulted in the rescinding of the award. Critics charged Yamanaka with a racist depiction of Filipino Americans, arguing that this stereotypical representation was causing harmful social reactions. Supporters of Yamanaka claimed the right of freedom of artistic expression. Thus, the controversy moved way beyond this single depiction of one Filipino American rapist in one fictional text. It became a fight over the function of literature and the role of the author in general and even more so in the special case of an ethnic author. Do these authors have social responsebilities towards their ethnic groups or other Asian American groups? Is it correct to assume automatically that the voice of the narrator is equal to the voice of the author? Or, are (ethnic) authors free to write whatever they feel like?

This controversy echoes some of the fundamental questions that already concerned the first big controversy within the field, namely, the Kingston-Chin debate of the 1970s. They reflect the renewed tensions between theory and practice twenty years later. The reception of this controversy in academic texts shows two tendencies in which Asian American Studies has moved. According to Mark Chiang in *The Cultural Capital of Asian American Studies: Autonomy and Representation in the University* (2009) these two positions are exemplified by Viet Nguyen's *Race and Resistance: Literature and Politics in Asian America* (2002) and Kandice Chuh's *Imagine Otherwise: On Asian Americanist Critique* (2003). Both texts cite the controversy but draw different conclusions. Chiang reads Nguyen as a call for greater accountability and Chuh as breaking with representation as such (Chiang 1–5).[31] While Chiang's reading is simplified, I agree with the general perception that these texts propose different solutions to address the current crisis.

Both scholars read the controversy of Yamanaka's fiction award as a result of the changing set-up and relationship of Asian Americans and especially the consequences of these for the academic discourse within the field. Nguyen ascribes the controversy to the threat of internal ideological diversity and the resulting inability of Asian America to represent itself as unified (Nguyen 8). Although Asian American authors have always employed flexible strategies in their negotiations, the ideological discourse of scholars has been highly rigid. Building on Jinqui Ling's argument in *Narrating Nationalisms* (1998), Nguyen expands Ling's critique of the rigidity of a poststructuralist criticism (Ling, *Narrating Nationalisms* 4), arguing that scholars tend to see literature as either

31 Chiang explains this gap as a result of the institutionalization of Asian American Studies, which was paradoxical because it created the field as a part of the university while the field considered itself as outside of it (Chiang 1–5).

resisting or accommodating the dominant American context, favoring the first of the two strategies (Nguyen 4–5). He argues that the intersection of racialized capitalism and a pluralist democracy in America have opened the possibility to value 'race' as a commodity and that Asian American academic discourse neglects this option, instead focusing on resistance as a critique of racist capitalism (10). Yet, exactly this unifying theme of resistance to the American nation-state becomes highly problematic in today's globalized world (20–22). For Nguyen, Yamanaka's fiction is a case-in-point for the fracturing of the Asian American community and the development of Asian American subjects that do not fit the favored resistance paradigm (157–66).

Kandice Chuh, on the other hand, argues that today's criticism is not going far enough in terms of poststructuralist approaches (Chuh 5). Like Nguyen, Chuh also views the Yamanaka controversy as a result of the rearticulation of the field (3). Asian American Studies needs to re-situate itself as a formation of multiculturalism in the current development of other, inter-related fields such as transnational studies or postcolonial studies (6). Chuh criticizes the current liberal multicultural basis of reading racialized minority literature as simple mimetic representations (142). She, thus, calls for a reconceptualization of culture as neither given by nature nor through refinement, but as "a site in which the affiliation of meaning to individuals, ideologies, and social structures occurs in negotiation with the material conditions of existence shaped by politics and economics" (19). While the broadening of the term has included more diverse Asian American subgroups, Chuh criticizes the general approach as it always already implies a normative subject (21). In order to move beyond this, she proposes a deconstructive attitude that results in an anti-essentialist 'subjectless discourse' (9). Foregrounding the discursive constructedness of subjectivity, such an approach would allow critics to address the diversity and difference within the field. Thus, she proposes to read the term 'Asian American' as "a representational *sign*" that is "arbitrary but inscribed; it comes to have meaning through and within and as an effect of specific structures of social/power relations that are themselves ideologically valenced constructs" (27). As such, the term becomes a "*metaphor* for resistance and racism" (27). According to Chuh, this general approach allows Asian Americanist critique to engage in a twofold criticism: that of US nationalism and that of Asian Americanist paradigms supporting US nationalism (113).

What I find particularly productive about both Nguyen's and Chuh's approaches, is their focus on discursive practices. Yet, criticizing Chuh with Nguyen shows that she is stuck in the resistance paradigm. The strength of Nguyen's argument is the resulting openness of a critic's approach to literature: it allows the reading of literature as much more diverse than the simple division into accommodation and resistance against a dominant American hegemony. It produces 'fresh' readings in which the result of the reading is not pre-given. And it acknowledges that literature is often ahead of its literary criticism.[32] Although Chuh's 'subjectless discourse' immediately calls to mind the figure of the ghost, I rather agree with Nguyen. Instead of simply searching for a resistance narrative that drives the ghost figures, *The Ghosts Within* is indebted to such open readings that are not grounded in pre-given moral or political considerations.[33] However, I also do not think that the two approaches are that far removed from one another as they both highlight the various connections and interpenetrations of cultural production and social and economic structures. Such an approach also shapes my readings of the ghostly figures in contemporary Asian American literature.

One way to avoid a morally preconceived reading is a focus on form and genre. An emphasis of the alignment with and rewriting of existing genre structures can offer 'fresh' readings that diverge from a resistance/assimilation paradigm in favor of analyses of rules and traditions, conventions and revisions. Offering similar arguments, some publications in recent years have called for a renewed emphasis of formal features in Asian American Studies. Zhou Xiaojing

32 Heiner Bus also claims that Asian American literature is often ahead of its surrounding discourse, Heiner Bus, "Asiatisch-amerikanische Literatur," Hubert Zapf, ed., *Amerikanische Literaturgeschichte*, Stuttgart, Weimar: Verlag JB Metzler, 2004, 473–485. Ruth Mayer made a similar point for postcolonial literatures and the surrounding discourses in her talk at the conference "American Studies Today: Recent Developments and New Perspectives," at the JFKI, November 3rd, 2011.

33 My reading here is influenced by Winfried Fluck's critical readings of what he calls 'cultural radicalism.' He argues that the revisionist projects of the New American Studies shifted the possible location of resistance to culture, following the logic that all other realms were interpellating apparatuses of an all-encompassing domination through the hegemonic system. With this shift, the margins of American society became possible locations of resistance. Fluck also perceives of the transnational turn in American Studies as a similar move to the margins in order to find new areas of possible resistance. Instead of this movement to the margins, Fluck calls for a movement into America and a new way of asking questions about this culture (see, for example, Winfried Fluck, "Theories of American Culture (and the Transnational Turn in American Studies)," Laura Bieger, Johannes Voelz, eds., *Romance with America?: Essays on Culture, Literature, and American Studies*, Heidelberg: Universitätsverlag Winter, 2009, 69–86).

believes that the field needs to overcome the binary structures that have shaped its beginnings. Drawing on Jinqui Ling, David Leiwei Li, Viet Nguyen, and David Palumbo-Liu, she argues in *Form and Transformation* (2005) that Asian American literary productions need to be seen in a "mutually constitutive, reciprocally transformative relationship" with mainstream America (Xiaojing 13). Xiaojing states that

> "[t]his critical perspective breaks away from the expressive and binary models of constructing a literary tradition in terms of a discrete cultural origin or a singular, oppositional subject position. It is crucial for Asian American studies to investigate the various historical, cultural, and discursive elements that determine individual writers' poetics and enable certain modes of signification." (17)

These critics emphasize the necessity and enriching perspective of a focus on form as it reflects neglected interconnections. Sue-Im Lee proposes the category of the aesthetic for such a recognition of formal elements in her introduction to the volume *Literary Gestures* (2006). She argues that Asian American Studies should recognize the constructedness, not only of categories and institutions, but also of literary works as "constituted by and through deliberate choices in form, genres, traditions, and conventions" (Lee, "Introduction" 2). Florian Sedlmeier, for example, reads contemporary ethnic literature as 'postethnic' in the sense that these texts self-reflectively position themselves "from within and against the marked and marketed versions" of their respective ethnic traditions (Sedlmeier 215). Sedlmeier emphasizes the formal strategies that these texts employ – in their paratexts' playful engagement and rewriting of traditions – for such a repositioning within and against an expected representative status (216).

Betsy Huang focuses on the specific appeal of genre as a critical lens for reading Asian American literature in *Contesting Genres in Contemporary Asian America* (2010). According to her, the narrow scope of Asian American literary scholarship – with its primary emphasis on autobiographical and immigrant stories – needs to be expanded in order to disrupt such 'generic' narratives about Asian America (Huang 3). Huang focuses on three types of genre fiction: immigrant fiction, crime fiction, and science fiction. Drawing on Wai Chee Dimock's term of 'regenreing' and her conception of genre fiction as a 'reproductive process,' Huang argues that it is precisely

> "[w]orking within the established boundaries of popular fiction genres and the known quantities of audience tastes and expectations, [that] Asian American writers [...] can

confirm, contest, and, most importantly, rewrite the genericized narratives about Asian American history, culture, and identity." (7)

These formal positions have significantly influenced the approach that shapes *The Ghosts Within*. Each chapter highlights the significant interlinkages of its novels' respective genre traditions: Lois-Ann Yamanaka's *Behold the Many* (2006) is positioned both as an intertext with Gothic/melodramatic modes and Heinz Insu Fenkl's autobiographical *Memories of My Ghost Brother* (1996) is understood in its reference to and reworking of ethnic and postcolonial life writings. My project, thus, hopes to fruitfully engage in a discussion not only of the 'what' of these novels but also of the 'how:' how does the novel present, rewrite, and continue existing genre traditions. The last chapter of *The Ghosts Within* is most directly influenced by Betsy Huang's insightful study as it reads Amitav Ghosh's *The Calcutta Chromosome* (1995), Amy Tan's *Saving Fish From Drowning* (2006), and Ed Lin's *Ghost Month* (2014) as global novels that engage in genre writing in the forms of science fiction, social comedy, and crime fiction.

The Ghosts Within argues that such a focus on form also helps to read the ghost figures themselves: instead of simple ethnic ornamentation, these figures appear as both intertextual citations and as part of cultural/religious traditions. In their various, even paradoxical references, these figures defy a quick categorization that tries to force them into a narrow political or moral framework. Foregrounding genre in its specific use of these figures helps to understand their multiple locations. Just like the ghosts themselves, genre provides preconceived structures and particular traditions, but allows a re-working from within.

Andrew Hock Soon Ng's edited volume *Asian Gothic: Essays on Literature, Film and Anime* (2008) marks an attempt to develop a specific Gothic tradition in relation to Asia. *Asian Gothic* addresses various topics, ranging from exemplary readings of the flexibility of postcolonial Gothic texts to Asian American authors and their use of a Gothic theoretical framework to a Gothic tradition in the national literatures of Asia. Significantly, *Asian Gothic* also focuses largely on Chinese American authors in the section that is entitled 'Asian American Gothic Literature.' The scope of this volume is extensive, and in the wide range of references, contemporary Asian American authors are subsumed rather than singled out. An earlier study of Ng's, *Interrogating Interstices* (2007), focuses exclusively on the aesthetics of the Gothic in Postcolonial Asian and Asian American literature. Here, Ng argues that the diasporic Asian literature shares many similarities with the Gothic: a questioning of binary oppositions, a troubling of selective history-telling, an aesthetic of loss and transgression. Throughout, he stresses the ambiguity, flexibility, and contradictory aspects of Gothic aesthetics. Ng argues that the transgressive aspect of the Gothic is "not in the sense of 'challenging,' or 'resisting' the establishment, but that of stretching the boundaries of the establishment to its limits, and there, fissuring it with its own limitations" (Ng, *Interrogating Interstices* 19). Ng establishes Gothic literature as self-reflexive (21). The flexibility that Ng ascribes to a Gothic aesthetic in an Asian American context also inspires *The Ghosts Within* in its reading of Lois-Ann Yamanaka's *Behold the Many* as a new kind of postcolonial, affective melodrama.

According to Ng, in Gothic "socially proscribed images are given profound visibility; they are transcribed into embodiments which would otherwise remain imaginary and unconscious" (24). Although I agree with the first part of this quote, I object to Ng's use of the 'imaginary.' In my view, these socially proscribed images emerge exactly *through* the imaginary realm of literature, in Wolfgang Iser's sense of the term.[34] In the imaginary, these issues can not only be expressed but furthermore negotiated. Later on, Ng himself calls for equal "attention to the *material* experiences of subjects and the *discursive* rendering of these experiences" (37). Thus, Ng's approach to Gothic elements is similar to mine, especially in his conception of the transgressive elements of ghostly figures. So, Ng's findings are highly important to me, yet *The Ghosts Within* zooms in where his study takes a panoramic view. Focusing on the figure of the ghost in Asian American literature in their various references to genre traditions rather than pursuing a broad diagnosis of emerging Gothicism like Ng, I come to markedly different conclusions with respect to the social and cultural implications of these phenomena.

Ng notes in the introduction to the volume *Asian Gothic* (2008) that the ghost is a particular motif in Asian American literature. He suggests that the ghost story "at least for Asian American writers, does more than merely function as critique of patriarchy and exploration of female entrapment within domestic ideologies" (Ng, "Introduction" 8). Instead, for Asian American writers,

> "ghosts are not just figurative devices, but literalizes [sic] as helpmeets and guardians which assist the liminal subject in her transition across the difficult hyphen. Haunting is

34 For a more detailed discussion of Wolfgang Iser and Winfried Fluck's approaches to literature and the imaginary as it relates to ghost presences in contemporary Asian American literature see the first chapter of *The Ghosts Within*.

not something to be dreaded but, placed in an Asian perspective, represents filial piety, familial attachment, continuity and reparation." (8)

Although I agree with Ng's observation that the abundance of ghosts in Asian American literature serves more functions than a simple critique of patriarchy, I question his conclusion that they should be only read as guardian figures grounding an otherwise lost subject in a filial tradition. This reading is certainly correct up to a point and it pinpoints the specific Asian ghost traditions. It also emphasizes the importance of recognizing culturally specific functions of these figures: the positive associations of ghosts in Asian traditions are certainly a helpful corrective of Gothic horror stories that a Western perspective might expect. Yet, I suggest that the ghost figures trouble any attempts at such a closed reading in terms of cultural references. Rather, they point to the inherent troubles and contradictions of such a positioning of Asian Americans.

However, Ng's studies reflect the importance of recognizing Asian traditions as a background to Asian American literature. Asian conceptions of ghosts as ancestors deviate from metaphorical Western conceptions. Although *The Ghosts Within* does not attempt an anthropological study of ghost figures in Asian or Western traditions, but rather focuses on the specific functions of ghost figures in certain literary representations, the question of the ghosts' status in Asian traditions remains central to an understanding of the ghosts varied references.[35] Where Ng's reading of the ghost figures pronounces the specific Asian cultural background, which also informs my readings in general and of Yamanaka's *Behold the Many* as a postcolonial melodrama in chapter 2 and Fenkl's *Memories of My Ghost Brother* in its reference to Korean folklore in chapter 3 in particular, chapter 4 complements this view by highlighting the paradoxical function of the ghost figures in Amitav Ghosh's *The Calcutta Chromosome*, Amy Tan's *Saving Fish From Drowning,* and Ed Lin's *Ghost Month.* It argues that these figures renegotiate the traditional context of family, ethnicity, and

35 One specific difference that a focus on Asian traditions foregrounds is the reality status of the ghost figures in Asian American literature. Western conceptions tend to read these as merely metaphorical, whereas Asian approaches allow for a material reality of such figures. The question of the reality status is addressed in the first chapter of *The Ghosts Within* in theoretical terms, and it addresses the playful engagement with these differing views in chapter 3 that reads Heinz Insu Fenkl's child narrator as a way to avoid a clear answer of this question and in chapter 4 in Ed Lin's *Ghost Month*, in which the narrator's Western perspective is continuously challenged by his friends.

tradition in the self-positioning of Asian Americans and merge with other global discourses instead; such a reading conceives of these texts as related to the border field of Transnational Studies.

Thinking back to Kandice Chuh's and Viet Nguyen's observations of current Asian American Studies, they both refer to the global status of Asian American literature and the necessity to position itself in relation to fields such as Transnational Studies. One of the changes in the field has been the so-called 'transnational turn' in American Studies in general. In her highly influential presidential address in 2004, "Crossroads of Cultures: The Transnational Turn in American Studies – Presidential Address to the American Studies Association," Shelley Fisher Fishkin argues that America has always been a transnational 'crossroads,' and that it should focus more on the "historical roots of multidirectional flows of people, ideas, and goods and the social, political, linguistic, cultural, and economic crossroads generated in the process" (Fishkin 22) instead of its national configuration.[36] After its first century, current engagements with the concept highlight both the potential and the pitfalls thereof. The openness of the approach provides space for new and expanded foci, viewing America as ever-more embedded in larger contexts, but it simultaneously is marked by a "glaring terminological vagueness" and is criticized for "its implied association with the global spread of neoliberalism" (Benesch 615).

As the collection *Transnational Asian American Literature: Sites and Transits* (2006) exemplifies, transnational aspects are inherently part of the Asian American diaspora. Referring to the diasporic, migratory situation of Asian Americans, the editors argue that the notions of nation-state and those that move beyond this concept have always been a part of this field. In contrast to Chuh's subjectless discourse, the editors argue for a reading of Asian American as a 'multiplier signifier' that includes the various experiences and the interconnections. They argue for the need to acknowledge both the groundedness in specific sites and the decentering of transits in the field (Geok-lin Lim et al.

36 For a good introduction to the field of Transnational Studies in general (and not in its specific relation to American Studies, which is my concern here) and its five intellectual foundations of empirical, methodological, theoretical, philosophical, and public transnationalism, see: Sanjeev Khagram and Peggy Levitt, "Introduction: Constructing Transnational Studies," Sanjeev Khagram and Peggy Levitt, eds., *The Transnational Studies Reader: Intersections and Innovations*, New York and London: Routledge, 2008, 1–18.

22).[37] This call for a recognition and balance of both locality and transnationality has shaped the field from its beginnings.

Linked to this sensibility of transnational interconnections is the marketing of a new genre: the new global novel. Asian American writers have been seen as the blueprint for this development. Writers such as Amitav Ghosh appear as both Asian American but also global writers. According to Tim Parks' definition, the global novel is specifically written and marketed with an international readership in mind. It avoids topics that might cause misunderstandings and its language is kept simple in order to reach many readers all over the world. These novels support a liberal political orientation, promoting world peace. Parks criticizes these works for their dullness and argues that the overstated fantasy devices of Rushdie simply feed into such political sensibility (Parks np). While his observations of the genre are convincing, I disagree with this last point. In my view, the fantasy devices – like the ghosts – support such liberal international political sensibilities, but they also function as references to the specificity and concrete historical situatedness of a certain work. And it is this paradoxical double function that drives the logic of the ghost figures.

Therefore, critical voices such as Sladja Blazan's are highly relevant. Blazan criticizes Kathleen Brogan's focus on ethnicity in her insightful article "Haunting History: The Ghostliness of History in Susan Sontag's *In America* and

37 Even before Fishkin's influential address, Rocío G. Davis' and Sämi Ludwig's edited volume *Asian American Literature in the International Context: Readings on Fiction, Poetry, and Performance* (2002) proposes a reading of Asian American literature in an international context. With this study, they intend a dialogue among scholars from all over the world in order to break with the US-centered research. Furthermore, they do not impose a defining theoretical paradigm, opting instead for an openness of approaches (Davis and Ludwig 9). A similar move to ever-increasing interdisciplinary and global approaches to Asian American Studies is also proposed by Guiyou Huang's edited volume *Asian American Literary Studies* (2005), stressing the heterogeneity within the field. Other texts that emphasize the demand to rethink Asian America as transnational and diasporic, but that tend to use these terms as interchangeable, thus reducing the specificity of each one are: Caroline Rody's *The Interethnic Imagination: Roots and Passages in Contemporary Asian American Fiction*, New York: Oxford University Press, 2009; Feng, Pin-chia. *Diasporic Representations: Reading Chinese American Women's Fiction*. Münster, Berlin: LIT, 2010; and Simal, Begoña, and Elisabetta Marino, eds. *Transnational, National, and Personal Voices: New Perspectives on Asian American and Asian Diasporic Women*. Münster: LIT, 2004.

Louise Erdrich's *Tracks*" (2008). Next to the focus on identity politics, and the psychological and cultural readings, Blazan stands for a fourth reading of ghosts, one that emphasizes the historicity of these figures. While she does acknowledge the ghosts' reference to cultural and communal memory that drives a more culturally focused approach, she laments a singling out of ethnicity as the main feature of these figures. For her, ghosts should rather be studied in their connection to memory as such (Blazan 138). Such a broadened focus on memory instead of ethnicity is a welcome correction to works that over-emphasize the ghosts' inherent ethnic value and cultural function. Still, in cases such as Asian American ghostly figures, the entanglement of ethnicity into memory and into reconfigurations of the past into useable narratives for the present and future demands a critical engagement, albeit one that should be balanced. Blazan's attention to matters other than ethnicity signals a current trend to move beyond such a singular focus, participating in the current discussions about 'post-ethnicity,' which is shortly outlined in the conclusion of *The Ghosts Within*. Blazan's call for a historical corrective of the cultural approaches of these figures fits the general conception of Asian America as historically situated. Instead of an automatic connection of ghost and cultural beliefs, her approach offers another way to produce 'fresh' readings of these figures. Inspired by such rethinking, chapter 4 also emphasizes the current move away from issues of ethnicity and identity politics in Asian American literature.

The chapter rather conceives of the current placelessness that shapes contemporary writings. It focuses on Amitav Ghosh's *The Calcutta Chromosome* and foregrounds the postcolonial global posthuman subject positions the novel envisions via its haunted characters. The possibility of transmigration – the move from one body into another – appears neither as bound to specific national conceptions nor to a positive re-positioning of these characters within the novel. The novel rather features the non-human agency that drives the process. Amy Tan's *Saving Fish From Drowning* also diverges from questions of ethnicity. Its narrator is a ghost: an Asian American woman who lingers after her death to solve the puzzle around her death. Yet, most importantly she has no family and instead watches over a group of her friends during their tourist adventure through China and Burma. Tan's ghost represents the shift into the new genre of the global novel: it revolves around the question of how an Asian American ghost author can function as a tour guide through the rough terrain of Asia for its global audience. A well-established Asian American author such as Tan, thus, uses the traditional trope of the ghost to move into new directions. Whether this shift is a successful one remains for each reader to decide, but the fact that Tan attempts such a shift speaks volumes about the changes within the field of Asian

American Studies since its beginnings. Ed Lin's *Ghost Month* also discusses this aspect of a tour guide: it features a Taiwanese narrator, who tries to solve the murder of his ex-fiancé. In order to do so, he invites his global readership along to a tour through Taiwan: and this is especially shown in the novel's various explanations of Taiwanese ghost beliefs and Taiwanese traditional food. Both Lin and Tan, thus, reengage with the idea of what Sau-Ling Cynthia Wong famously calls "the literary equivalent of a guided Chinatown tour" who argues that "even those works that do not share it will most likely be read as anthropological guidebooks" (Wong, "Autobiography as Guided Chinatown Tour" 262). Originally, this tradition is seen as catering to white curiosity and supporting the positive image of their respective ethnic community. Such an anthropological take implies a representative function of Asian American life writing and it refers back to the controversy between Frank Chin and Maxine Hong Kingston. These later engagements by Tan and Lin provide playful variations of such an approach.

That Amy Tan's and Ed Lin's novels once again feature most centrally ghost figures, grounds their work in an Asian American literary tradition. Ever since Maxine Hong Kingston's highly successful employment of this motif in *The Woman Warrior*, the ghost figure has appeared as a haunting presence in literary representations of Asian America. And while it has changed its outfit – marking the recent trend of transnational, global writings –, the Asian American ghost always inherently references this tradition. The ghosts are always already both: figures that call for a crossing of boundaries and categories, but that also re-employ such cultural specificity. As such, the ghosts remain to a certain extent unplaceable.

The Ghosts Within is indebted to the rich secondary literature on ghost figures that has shaped Asia American Studies. It emphasizes the simultaneous existence of allegorical and spiritual explanations of these figures as an aspect that shapes imaginations of Asian America, especially in highlighting the novels' own play with these approaches. In its close readings, this study employs all of the approaches: psychoanalytical, cultural, and historical ones. It is, however, the push and pull of cultural and historical conceptions that helps to re-emphasize these figures as open and flexible. Each chapter focuses on the specific genre tradition(s) in which its novels engage, which helps to establish the ghost as an intertextual reference to its Asian, its American, other ethnic, and especially its Asian American traditions.

The Ghosts Within, thus, participates in this invention of a tradition that authors and critics of Asian American Studies engage in. As this overview of the development of Asian American Studies shows, the field is largely driven by questions of identity formation and a positioning in an American and later global context. The motif of the ghost is directly linked to this (self-)representation and is therefore always already part of the field's political questions. The literary imaginations of 'Asian America' have been linked – from its very beginning – to a strong identification with the field's intention to directly and indirectly support the standing of Asian Americans in America. The impulse to read the ghost figures as subversive of an American mainstream is connected to this political (self-)positioning. And yet, *The Ghosts Within* argues that the ghosts have more diverse functions than this one. They shatter – in their almost not-presentness – what we tend to take for granted. As cultural and literary images of what belongs to Asian America, they highlight the impossibility to arrive at a conclusive answer. And yet, even though the ghost is in a way unplaceable and defies readings that try to push it into a certain political or moral framework, it still remains bound to questions of culture, identity, ethnicity, and history in an Asian American context. And this double function makes the ghost such a productive figure. It is these diverse, sometimes paradoxical, references that drive my project's engagement with these shadowy, yet ever-present figures.

1 “risk the violence of reading the ghost” – Theoretical Reflections on Ghost Figures

In her insightful article “The Ghostly Rhetoric of Autobiography: Maxine Hong Kingston’s *The Woman Warrior* as American Gothic Narrative” (2008), Carol Mejia-LaPerle focuses on the connections between ghosts and the writing of autobiographical texts and argues that “[g]hosts emphasize what is constructed – therefore fleeting, undependable, ephemeral – yet this constructedness is proof of, and perhaps the only tenable foundation for, one’s identity” (Mejia-LaPerle 119). In Mejia-LaPerle’s view, Kingston

> “chooses to expose, rather than repress, these ghostly manifestations; utilizing them to confer significance to the most troubled parts of her self-construction. Ultimately, American gothic discourse’s obsession with a disturbed and unknowable past is linked to the retrospection inherent in an autobiographer’s narrative of self. Both seek to find a cohesive, articulated identity but reveal, instead, ghosts that compromise, and comprise, the search.” (119–20)

Although Mejia-LaPerle writes about a very particular aspect – the ghostly rhetoric of Kingston’s autobiographic novel –, she addresses many of the concerns of more general approaches to ghost figures: their relation to psychology and identity formation, their literary or fictional appeal, their cultural reference points, and the ways in which the ghosts inherently trouble the neat conceptions that we wish to put them into. This chapter provides an overview of the theoretical approaches that have shaped our perceptions of these figures. It ultimately calls for the theoretical flexibility that these figures demand.

PSYCHOANALYTIC AND POSTSTRUCTURALIST GHOSTS

As early as 1919, Sigmund Freud published "The Uncanny," an engagement with ghostly aspects from a psychoanalytical perspective. His influential conception already addresses key aspects that still shape reflections about ghost figures today. Freud defines the uncanny as something that is frightening. He links it to his concept of repression. In establishing a tripartide model of the structure of the mind – *id*, *ego*, and *super-ego* –, Freud begins to outline the existence of a conscious and an unconscious in *The Interpretation of Dreams* (1900). With this model, Freud argues that subjects are not fully in control of themselves because in any product of thought there is an unconscious dimension. Repression appears as part of this model: it is a defense mechanism by which unwelcome desires or feelings are pushed into the unconscious. In his definition of the uncanny, Freud refers to the concept of repression, arguing that it "is something which is secretly familiar [...], which has undergone repression and then returned from it, and that everything that is uncanny fulfils this condition" (Freud 245). As such, the uncanny is "in reality nothing new or alien, but something which is familiar and old-established in the mind and which has become alienated from it only through the process of repression" (241). The uncanny is accordingly "something repressed which *recurs*" (241). With this conception, Freud establishes the uncanny as a psychoanalytical aspect. Repression is part of every subject formation, but the recurring of repressed aspects becomes a frightening experience that emphasizes the ways in which human beings lack control. It is something that should have been kept hidden, concealed, withheld from others and oneself, but came to light nonetheless (224–25). With this approach, Freud diverges from Ernst Jentsch's earlier theory of the uncanny as something foreign (Jentsch 196) and significantly establishes it as something that belongs to oneself: it belongs uneasily in its changed appearance after repression, but it belongs nevertheless.

In the essay, Freud lists a number of things that appear as frightening and uncanny: the double, repetition, or an omnipotence of thought. Via these examples, Freud establishes the uncanny not only in spatial relations but also begins to refer to its temporality (Lehmann 21), an aspect that Jacques Derrida later emphasizes most prominently. Freud links these fears to animistic beliefs and childhood fears, which educated adults have seemingly overcome, but still register deep within the unconscious of each person (Freud 240–241). Freud's reference to such animistic beliefs of what he calls 'primitive men' are certainly out of place today. Still, such distinctions already hint at different observations of ghosts in other cultures and will appear repeatedly in the theoretical literature that tries to explain these figures – albeit no longer in Freud's outdated terms. Furthermore, a close reading of Freud's essay already shows that he himself is not sure about his own conception. It is very productive to stay with Freud's uncertainty in this case, which once again mirrors his theory of a decentered subject. His tone and choice of words reflect his struggle. For example, Freud argues that "[a]ll supposedly educated people have ceased to believe officially that the dead can become visible as spirits" (242). Qualifying words like 'supposedly' and 'officially' express his own hesitation. Furthermore, he does not give a definitive definition of the 'uncanny;' instead, he seems to collect random reflections.

Interestingly, he is drawn to the realm of literature throughout the essay. Arguing that we need to distinguish between the uncanny "that we actually experience and the uncanny we merely picture or read about" (247), Freud emphasizes the freedom of a writer to construct a setting in which uncanny experiences do not create an uncanny effect, such as in fairy tales. Whenever the setting is close to common 'reality,' it would have to obey the common regulations and would thus create uncanny effects as well (247–51). Yet, as already stated above, Freud himself seems unsure of his own definition. I question not only his neat distinction between the realm of literature and the realm of experience, but also his own conviction of this conclusion. Earlier on in the essay, Freud argues that "an uncanny effect is often and easily produced when the distinction between imagination and reality is effaced" (244) and I believe that this is true for both the realm of experience and the realm of fiction.[1]

Starting with Freud makes sense not only because he is *the* classical reference point when one thinks of psychoanalytical approaches to ghost figures but also because he already addresses the aspects that continue to occupy the secondary literature today. Most fundamentally, his psychoanalytical explanation of ghosts as repressed aspects belongs today, in the West, to the area of common knowledge and appears in almost all discussions of the topic. His approach grounds these figures in the psychological realm: they are not really there, they are simply constructions of the mind, references to earlier fears, expressions of psychic processes and registers.

In *Specters of Marx* (1994) Jacques Derrida evades the question of the ghosts' reality in emphasizing their status as figures that demand recognition. He concludes *Specters of Marx* with a call for such recognition:

1 The complicated status of the ghosts in relation to reality is addressed in detail in the part of this chapter that focuses on the specificity of ghosts in literature.

> "If he loves justice at least, the 'scholar' of the future, the 'intellectual' of tomorrow should learn it and from the ghost. He should learn to live by learning not how to make conversation with the ghost but how to talk with him, with her, how to let them speak or how to give them back speech, even if it is in oneself, in the other, in the other in oneself: they are always there, specters, even if they do not exist, even if they are no longer, even if they are not yet." (Derrida, *Specters of Marx* 176)

Instead of developing a psychoanalytical approach to ghosts, Derrida simply presupposes their presence: he does not question their existence, does not assume cultural (archaic or primitive) traditional beliefs or a child's fears, but simply accepts their presence as 'always there' 'even if they do not exist.' To him, the question of the ghosts' reality is irrelevant, what matters to him is the function they serve for the one who encounters them. The ghosts' function is to show that things are amiss: they represent a return of forgotten histories, unfulfilled debts, unresolved crimes, failed promises, and unsatisfied demands for justice. In order to grasp Derrida's approach of these figures, one needs to understand his relation to deconstruction.

In a nutshell, Derridean deconstruction is part of the poststructuralist developments during the late twentieth century. With its criticism of structuralist and logocentric approaches, deconstruction has both a critical destructive element and an affirmative reconstructive element. It is influenced by various thoughts and developments of the late nineteenth and early twentieth century – Heidegger's destruction of the history of ontology, and Freud's dissociation of the subject, just to name two highly influential ones. These reference points already highlight the deep insults that humanity had to face at this time: along with a biological disillusion following Charles Darwin, Freud offered a psychological offence of the subject's illusion of control. In a first step, Derrida complicates the structuralist equation of a sign as signifier and signified, arguing that the signified is always already a chain of signifiers so that meaning is constantly deferred and reiterated. Moreover, the meaning that language seemingly has is a result of a constant distinction between two opposed terms. The goal of a deconstructionist approach is, thus, the breaking up of binary oppositions and their inherent hierarchies. With this deconstructive background in place, Derrida moves into a second phase, which renews his interests in ethical questions of responsibility. His seminal *Specters of Marx* marks this shift.[2]

---

2 Compare, for example, Jacques Derrida, *Of Grammatology*, 1967, trans. Gayatri Chakravorty Spivak, Baltimore: Johns Hopkins University Press, 1997; Jacques

In this book, Derrida argues that one needs to offer ghosts a welcome "out of a concern for *justice*" (175) and that it

> "is necessary to speak *of the* ghost, indeed *to the* ghost and *with* it, from the moment that no ethics, no politics, whether revolutionary or not, seems possible and thinkable and *just* that does not recognize in its principle the respect for those others who are no longer or for those who are not yet *there*, presently living, whether they are already dead or not yet born." (xix)

In this conception of justice, Derrida refers to a "*politics* of memory, of inheritance, and of generations" (xix). And there "is no inheritance without a call to responsibility" for it "is always the reaffirmation of a debt, but a critical, selective, and filtering reaffirmation" (91–92). Derrida, thus, clearly highlights the political[3] and ethical demands that specters pose to the living, and he links this to the past, the present, and the future.

Derrida, "Structure, Sign and Play in the Discourse of the Human Sciences," *Writing and Difference*, 1967, trans. Alan Bass, London: Routledge, 2001, 351–370. For a great overview of Jacques Derrida's works, see, Jack Reynolds, "Jacques Derrida (1930–2004)," *Internet Encyclopedia of Philosophy*, originally published November 17, 2002, revised January 12, 2010 at: http://www.iep.utm.edu/derrida/; Hagner, Michael, Dieter Thomä, and Cornelia Vismann, *Jacques Derrida zur Einführung*. Hamburg: Junius, 2011. For a classical and detailed overview of deconstruction, see, Jonathan Culler, *On Deconstruction: Theory and Criticism after Structuralism*, London, Melbourne and Henley: Routledge & Kegan Paul, 1983; or Christopher Norris, *Deconstruction: Theory and Practice*, London: Methuen, 1985; critical anthologies about the approach are, for example, Martin MacQuillan, ed., *Deconstruction: A Reader*, Edinburgh: Edinburgh University Press, 2000; or Jonathan Culler, ed., *Deconstruction: Critical Concepts in Literary and Cultural Studies*, London and New York: Routledge, 2003.

3 Deconstruction in general and *Specters of Marx* have been criticized for an anti-political orientation. Aijaz Ahmad, for example, disagrees with Derrida's reading of deconstruction as a radicalization of Marxism, pointing to the neglect of Marxism in deconstructive thinkers such as Paul de Man. Ahmad rather sees deconstruction as primarily a textual hermeneutics than a political force (Ahmad 107–108). Ahmad's critical response to *Specters of Marx* exemplifies a general tendency: while Marxist scholars were highly disappointed by Derrida's claims, critics from other fields, especially Literary and Cultural Studies, have enthusiastically taken up his ideas. For a detailed reading of the interlinkages between politics and deconstruction, see, for

He emphasizes the ghost's status as *revenant* – as a figure that cannot be controlled in its comings and goings, a figure that ultimately "*begins by coming back*" (11). He, thus, highlights the ghost's temporality. The specter troubles a chronological historical development, jumping from the past to the present and back, referring to the past as well as the future and a possible re-appearance (39). Derrida coins the term hauntology. In his own words, to "haunt does not mean to be present, and it is necessary to introduce haunting into the very construction of a concept. Of every concept, beginning with the concepts of being and time. That is what we would be calling here a hauntology" (161). Linking his thoughts to deconstructionist philosophy, Derrida calls for a radical critique of existing concepts (88–90). He criticizes Freud, for example, for trying to press the uncanny into pre-conceived psychoanalytical categories because the ghost as such permanently destabilizes such conceptual distinctions (174). According to this logic, every concept is haunted by what it excludes and includes, by its own borders and its own uncertainty.

Instead of assuming that a specter simply appears out of the blue, Derrida demands to "realize that the ghost is [already] there, be it in the opening of the promise or the expectation, *before its first apparition*: the latter had announced itself, from the first it will have come second. *Two times at the same time*, originary iterability" (163). This iterability entails both repetition and alterity, but most importantly, it negates an origin. For a ghost as ghost can only exist because it returns as a distorted figure that refers to an absent presence. In other words, the specter embodies its own paradoxical relation to being and time: the ghost itself does not have a place or a time, but constantly refers to its own deferral; and yet, the ghost always references a certain place or time. Derrida argues that the "non-presence of the specter demands that one take its times and its history into consideration, the singularity of its temporality or of its historicity" (101). The ghost, however fleeting its presence, calls for a responsible inheritance of its reference point.

Just like Freud in "The Uncanny," Derrida works with a literary text throughout *Specters of Marx*. The quote that runs through his analysis – "the time is out of joint" – is taken from one of the most famous ghost fictions of all times, Shakespeare's *Hamlet*. Hamlet utters these words after he has met his father's spirit, which has told him about his murder by the hand of his uncle, who is now the ruling king. Being called by this ghost to revenge his father's betrayal, Hamlet calms the ghost down – "Rest, rest, perturbed spirit" – and

example, Catherine Zuckert, "The Politics of Derridean Deconstruction," *Polity* 23.3 (Spring 1991): 335–356.

continues: "The time is out of joint: O cursed spite, That ever I was born to set it right" (Shakespeare 54–55). Following from this example, Derrida develops his ethical approach of specters as bringing a debt to an inheritor's attention but also the temporality of specters as *revenants*. In an interview, Derrida once said about the role of literature that while it

> "shares a certain power and a certain destiny with 'jurisdiction,' with the juridico-political production of institutional foundations, the constitutions of States, fundamental legislation, and even the theological-juridical performatives which occur at the origin of the law, at a certain point it can also exceed them, interrogate them, 'fictionalize' them: with nothing, or almost nothing, in view, of course, and by producing events whose 'reality' or duration is never assured, but which by that very fact are more thought-provoking, if that still means something." (Derrida, "'This Strange Institution Called Literature'" 32)

In a way, literature is a text like any other text, but it can 'exceed' these other texts because of its status as fiction, its peculiar relation to reality. There is a certain productive relation between the singularity and the generality of literary texts for Derrida. As Derek Attridge has it, Derrida sees literature as an "institution" which "sheds light on institutionality, as a site of resistance to the philosophical tradition of conceptual thought, as a series of singular (but repeatable) acts that demand singular (but responsible) responses, as a staging of a number of strategic issues" (Attridge 25). Literary texts are, in this aspect, similar to the ghosts themselves: they can stage what might otherwise remain hidden or forgotten. *The Ghosts Within* is indebted to such an approach of both literature and its ghost figures.

The reception of Derrida's text has shifted from its early – often critical – readings in a political framework to Cultural Studies (Lehmann 25–26). *Specters of Marx*, by now, is the key text of what Roger Luckhurst in 2002 terms the "Spectral Turn" (Luckhurst 527–46). The term spectrality implies questions of memory, history, home/familiar and foreign, materiality and immateriality, media and technology, and always also responsibility, debt, and ethics (Lehmann 26). These references make the term so productive and influential, but they also already highlight the broadness of what Derrida calls specters. Therefore, the Derridean approach to ghosts significantly shapes *The Ghosts Within*, especially in its conception of the literariness of these figures, but in order to apply such a reading to its concrete examples of Asian American literature this needs to be balanced out by more specific cultural and historical approaches of these figures.

Still, Freud's psychoanalytical and Derrida's deconstructive readings of ghosts have inspired various re-readings and continue to be the two reference points for all theoretical engagements with these figures. As Anneleen Masschelein argues in *The Unconcept: The Freudian Uncanny in Late-Twentieth-Century Theory* (2011) the uncanny has always been both psychoanalytical and something beyond. It calls for both psychoanalytical and deconstructive approaches. This also reflects the genealogy of the concept, which has become highly influential in the last three decades of the twentieth century. Masschelein argues that the concept was influenced by and adapted to fit (post)structuralist discourses[4] and that this resulted in its status today as a highly flexible theoretical concept (Masschelein 2–4).[5]

Masschelein is in line with Peter Buse and Andrew Stott, who argue in *Ghosts: Deconstruction, Psychoanalysis, History* (1999) that only a combination of these approaches allows for a productive reading of ghosts. Drawing on Freud's concept of repression, Buse and Stott claim that Derrida's theory is highly influenced by the idea of haunting, even in those cases where he does not openly theorize it (Buse and Stott 8). Again in connection to Freudian ideas of having overcome certain fears or beliefs, they emphasize the influence of the Enlightenment on the development of supernatural or uncanny experience. The Enlightenment's focus on reason and rationality and its turn away from magic as

---

4 Prominent examples of rereadings of the Freudian uncanny are, to Masschelein, influenced by poststructuralist approaches such as, Helene Cixious, "Fiction and its Phantoms: A Reading of Freud's Das Unheimliche," *New Literary History* 7 (1976): 525–548, but then split into two axes. One is a 'postromantic/aesthetic' tradition, emphasizing the aspect of the supernatural, for which she cites authors such as Harold Bloom, or engagements with the concept of the fantastic, such as Tzvetan Todorov, *The Fantastic: A Structural Approach to a Literary Genre* (1975), Ithaca: Cornell University Press, 1980; Rosemary Jackson, *Fantasy: The Literature of Subversion*, London, New York: Methuen, 1981; and the other tradition is an 'existentialist/post-Marxist' one focusing more on the aspect of unfamiliarity, with texts such as, Jacques Derrida, *Specters of Marx: The State of the Debt, the Work of Mourning and the New International,* New York: Routledge, 1994; Julia Kristeva, *Strangers to Ourselves*, New York: Columbia University Press, 1994.

5 The concept's broad application and theoretical indefinition have resulted in an almost inflationary use, which has been critically viewed (see, for example, Lehmann 24). My own reading of this unclear definition of the term as not a flaw but rather part of the character of the ghostly itself can be found here, (Odabas "Gespenstisches Amerika," 228).

well as religion only created the uncanny as such. However, they depart from Freud's seemingly rational explanation of uncanny experiences and move towards Derrida's conception of spectrality: in their own words, this reorient-tation towards rationality could not succeed "entirely in exorcising its own ghosts."[6] They argue that "[i]nstead of saying that there is an outside of reason which has been neglected, perhaps we need to inspect the inside of reason and see how it too is haunted by what it excludes" (5). And in order to view our society's hauntings from within, Buse and Stott refer to Derrida's conception of the *revenant*, "the thing that returns, comes to represent a mobilization of familiar Derridean concepts such as trace, iteration and the deferral of presence" (11).

One re-working of Freud's ideas – and in direct relation to Derrida,[7] who even wrote the foreword "Fors" to one of their volumes, *Kyptonymie: Das Verbarium des Wolfsmanns* (1979) –, is Nicolas Abraham and Maria Torok's conception of the phantom. In their conception of the phantom, they diverge from Freudian theories of dynamic repression, where a censored and repressed emotion can force its way back. Instead, they opt for a *preservative* repression, which "seals off access to part of one's own life in order to shelter from view the traumatic monument of an obliterated event" (Rand, "Introduction" 18). Abraham and Torok "explore the mental landscapes of submerged family secrets and traumatic tombs in which, for example, actual events are treated as if they

6 As reference for this claim, Buse and Stott cite the phenomenon of spiritualism during the nineteenth century with its focus on talking to the dead (Buse and Stott 3–5). They cite especially two studies about spiritualism for the British context: Janet Oppenheim, *The Other World: Spiritualism and Psychical Research in England, 1850–1914*, Cambridge: Cambridge University Press, 1985; and Alex Owen, *The Darkened Room: Women, Power and Spiritualism in Late Victorian England*, London: Virago, 1989. However, this phenomenon was also central in the American context, as these studies exemplify: Bret E. Carroll, *Spiritualism in Antebellum America*, Bloomington: Indiana University Press, 1997; Robert S. Cox, *Body and Soul: A Sympathetic History of American Spiritualism*, Charlottesville: University of Virginia Press, 2003.

7 As Zoltán Drogan notes, curiously, Derrida does not mention Abraham and Torok in his later *Specters of Marx*, although this text clearly re-works their findings. Drogan therefore reads Abraham as the phantom that haunts Derrida's hauntology, see Zoltán Drogan, "Derrida's Specter, Abraham's Phantom: Psychoanalysis as the Uncanny Kernel of Deconstruction," *The AnaChronisT* 11 (2005): 253–269, see esp. 265–269.

had never occurred" in order to uphold "the preservation of a shut-up or excluded reality" (18).

Defining the phantom, Abraham states

> "[t]o be sure, all the departed may return, but some are destined to haunt: the dead who were shamed during their lifetime or those who took unspeakable secrets to the grave. [...] It is a fact that the 'phantom,' whatever its form, is nothing but an invention of the living. Yes, an invention in the sense that the phantom is meant to objectify, even if under the guise of individual or collective hallucinations, the gap produced in us by the concealment of some part of a love object's life. The phantom is therefore also a metapsychological fact: what haunts are not the dead, but the gaps left within us by the secrets of others." (Abraham, "Notes on the Phantom" 171)

Although exposed as only 'inventions' – not incarnations of ancestors or something like this – phantoms still appear as defining forces. According to Abraham's definition, the haunting happens because a dead loved one has hidden an important secret from a descendant – and this is how transgenerational haunting begins.

Abraham and Torok are, thus, refashioning Freud's question 'what kind of repression is returning in the guise of the symptom?' as "what is the nature of the phantom returning to haunt? How can the phantom be weakened so as to make it restore the unhappy subject's own speech – whether or not it ultimately refers to repression – that had been victimized by the haunting?" (Torok 180). For Abraham and Torok, the crypt and its phantom, is therefore most significantly a linguistic feature; they are not concerned with the process of repression or the question of the ghost's reality status. What is important for them is that the phantom follows from the gaps in the language which one generation inhabited from the previous one. In Abraham's words, the phantom "is sustained by secreted words, invisible gnomes whose aim is to wreak havoc, from within the unconscious, in the coherence of logical progression" (Abraham, "Notes on the Phantom" 175). As such, the ghost is a lying creature, it tries to veil such shameful secrets, hoping to uphold the familial gap as gap (Abraham, "The Phantom of Hamlet" 188).

Abraham and Torok's psychological research is far less influential today than Freud's or Derrida's. The idea of being haunted by someone else's ghosts seems counterintuitive at first. However, their findings have been fruitfully applied to the transgenerational haunting that shapes families who survived the Holocaust: the children of these families who had never experienced the horrors of the Holocaust themselves were exposed to such transgenerational haunting.

Gabriele Schwab, for example, explores in *Haunting Legacies: Violent Histories and Transgenerational Haunting* (2010) how second generation narratives about the Holocaust offer stories that fit Abraham's and Torok's transgenerational haunting. Grace M. Cho applies their theory to the Korean diaspora, arguing in *Haunting the Korean Diaspora: Shame, Secrecy, and the Forgotten War* (2008) that "it is not enough to say that the diaspora is transgenerationally haunted by the unspoken traumas of war; it is constituted by that haunting" (Cho 12).

Grace M. Cho's text also indirectly references Homi K. Bhabha's work as another re-writing of Freud's uncanny. Bhabha made the concept productive in Postcolonial Studies to analyze the uncanny subjects that appear in postcolonial relations (Lehmann 26–27). Although Bhabha draws on Freud's conception, he rather employs the term 'unhomely,' which highlights Bhabha's insistence on the topological dimension of Freud's uncanny. As Lehmann elaborates, this relates to a 'home' that implies a place as one's own, a certain safety and belonging. The unhomely then appears as the blind spot of this conception of the home: it undermines the narrative of homeliness and exposes it as always already unstable and insecure by and in itself, not just in relation to something foreign (27).

According to Bhabha in *The Location of Culture* (1994), "the 'unhomely' is a paradigmatic colonial and post-colonial condition" for "[i]n that displacement, the borders between home and world become confused; and, uncannily, the private and the public become part of each other, forcing upon us a vision that is as divided as it is disorienting" (Bhabha 13). For Bhabha, then, the interconnection of home and world, their uncanny interpenetration, appears as a feature of the postcolonial society and its uncanny subjects. He thus broadens Freud's psychological, individualized conception to highlight a political dimension. In his own words, the "unhomely moment relates the traumatic ambivalences of a personal, psychic history to the wider disjunctions of political existence" (15). For Bhabha the in-between status of postcolonial subjects shapes the whole society:

> "Private and public, past and present, the psyche and the social develop an interstitial intimacy. It is an intimacy that questions binary divisions through which such spheres of social experience are often spatially opposed. […] [The postcolonial subject] represents a hybridity, a difference 'within,' a subject that inhabits the rim of an 'in-between' reality. And the inscription of this borderline existence inhabits a stillness of time and a strangeness of framing that creates the discursive 'image' at the crossroads of history and literature, bridging the home and the world." (19)

In the larger framework of his understanding of postcolonial society as constituted by hybridity, Bhabha emphasizes the intended hierarchical and political basis of these conceptualizations. With his concepts of 'mimicry' or 'hybridity' he shows how this (post)colonial discourse is in itself instable. Bhabha defines the colonial discourse and constellation as a reciprocal relationship of dependence between the colonizers and the colonized. Both need and crave the other's recognition, they are driven by a simultaneous fear and desire of the other. This creates the ambivalence of the colonial discourse and the inherent instability of colonial authority. He contends that cultural statements and systems are constructed in a 'third space' – which is a contradictory and ambivalent space in-between cultures, in which cultural symbols can be reinterpreted and gain new kinds of meanings. Cultural identity, then, is also constructed in this space that makes hierarchical purity of cultures untenable.[8] This rather creates an empowering, hybrid space in which cultural difference can operate. Hybridity is disruptive because it challenges hierarchies of self and other. In Bhabha's own words, "[h]ybridity is the sign of the productivity of colonial power, its shifting forces and fixities" (159). The concept is particularly helpful because it allows a questioning of binary oppositions without simply turning them around. With this in mind, the unhomely appears in Bhabha's theory as that which haunts the home, which shows that the home has never been as stable as one originally believed. And for him, it appears when the world and the home become entangled.

These applications of haunting in its strong interplay of the public and the private already foreshadow what Avery Gordon outlines in her seminal *Ghostly Matters: Haunting and the Sociological Imagination* (2004): the social dimension of ghosts. Her book is one of the most influential studies in the field in recent years and her ideas are highly important for *The Ghosts Within*. Gordon also draws on Freud's psychoanalytical readings of 'the uncanny' and Derrida's poststructuralist *Specters of Marx*. Her sociological approach to ghostly matter is highly convincing as her engagement with the ghostly figures results from her increasing awareness that common modes of inquiry in sociology have failed her due to their demand to strictly separate fact and fiction. Focusing on haunting, Gordon writes, if it

"describes how that which appears to be not there is often a seething presence, acting on and often meddling with taken-for-granted realities, the ghost is just the sign, or the empirical evidence if you like, that tells you a haunting is taking place. The ghost is not

8 Compare, esp. Bhabha 121–31.

simply a dead or missing person, but a social figure, and investigating it can lead to that dense site where history and subjectivity make social life." (Gordon, *Ghostly Matters* 2004, 8)

In this often-quoted passage, Gordon emphasizes the social aspect of the ghost and the actual consequences that these figures have for a society. Her approach connects history and subjectivity as the two reference poles for how a society constructs and sees itself. For her, ghosts are the ideal figures to remind us of the meeting points of these two poles.

Gordon approaches ghosts from a similar viewpoint like Derrida. Instead of trying to observe their reality status, she simply accepts their presence and focuses on their function. For her, the ghosts' reality cannot be measured in a verified existence or a negation thereof, but in the ways in which these figures demand recognition. Highlighting the power relations that construct a version of reality that attempts to exclude these ghostly presences, Gordon argues that these figures are nevertheless "real, that is to say, that they produce material effects" (17). In her view, writing and reading ghost stories means not only to amend representational faults but also to unveil the circumstances under which a certain memory was produced and created a ghost so that a countermemory can be constructed for the future (22). Referring to Freud's claims, she stresses the importance of haunting in today's societies, which have only seemingly overcome such animistic beliefs. Challenging this assumption, Gordon argues that "*it's not that the ghosts don't exist.* The postmodern, late-capitalist, postcolonial world represses and projects its ghosts or phantoms in similar intensities, if not entirely in the same forms, as the older world did" (12). But these repressed figures remain as "a seething presence" (17) for it would be wrong to assume that invisibility equals nonexistence.[9] The sentence, in its use

9 Gordon's argument is very close to Toni Morrison's theoretical reflections. And although Gordon is referencing Morrison's article "Unspeakable Things Unspoken: The African-American Presence in American Literature," (*Michigan Quarterly Review* 28.1 (1989): 1–34), she largely ignores her influential prior work on an unacknowledged ghostly black presence in the white literary imagination in her argument (Toni Morrison, *Playing in the Dark: Whiteness and the Literary Imagination*, Cambridge: Harvard University Press, 1992). Instead, she focuses on Morrison as a novelist, whom she reads as a social theorist. While I find this latter reading interesting and convincing in her argument as a whole, Gordon could have made more productive use of this already existing tradition of reading ghostly matter by an African American Studies scholar.

of the word 'repression,' shows her indebtedness to psychoanalytical readings of ghost figures.

Even though Gordon draws on psychoanalytical approaches, she also moves beyond the usual reading of ghosts as an individual's reaction to repressed anxieties. Referring to Freud's conceptions of the uncanny, Gordon claims that his essay basically reveals his own uncertainty. In her view, in the end, "Freud will disappoint" and with him the psychoanalytic readings of ghostly matters (42). Yet, psychoanalysis in general and Freud in particular at least problematize haunting. Freud begins by establishing the unconscious as the relation between one's own and another's consciousness. In Gordon's words,

> "in this small moment where Freud is vexed by the possibility of conceiving the unconscious as the life of others and other things within us, the specter of the social raises its head. The Freudian unconscious is not a social unconscious. But his early conceptualizations of the unconscious remains haunted by its origins in the fundamental encounter between self and world, between me and you." (48)

In the end, Freud does not focus on the social implications, as Gordon points out. Instead, he is trying to explain uncanny experiences by "hoping to convince us that everything that seems to be coming at us from the outside is really coming from this now shrunken inside, tormented by its own immortality" (49). Gordon continues, "[t]he uncanny is the return, in psychoanalytic terms, of what the concept of the unconscious represses: the reality of being haunted by worldly contacts" (54–55). In her "Introduction to the New Edition" (2008), she argues that "[w]hat's distinctive about haunting is that it is an animated state in which a repressed or unresolved social violence is making itself known, sometimes very directly, sometimes more obliquely" (Gordon, *Ghostly Matters* xvi). Gordon's focus on a process of collective social repression and haunting helps to think about haunting matters in relation to larger groups such as the Asian American community. It invites considering ghosts as figures of collective concerns – even if they haunt an individual – and this insight has deeply informed my own approach of these figures.

Ultimately a call for political attention to repressed, invisible aspects of a society, Gordon's book emphasizes the "something to be done" that a ghost's appearance signals (Gordon, *Ghostly Matters* 2004, 183–84). Although she is drawing less extensively on Derrida's *Specters of Marx*, her political and ethical approach to the subject clearly aligns her with his prominent call for justice and responsibility. In a way, Derrida also already suggests the ghost's social dimension in his own text, but his conception is less clearly interlinked with the sociological dimension of these figures and more a general, broader diagnosis of spectrality. Both – Gordon and Derrida –, however, offer relevant re-readings of these figures and they are similar in the urgency with which they call for a recognition of these ghosts and their reference points in order to allow for a livable future. And just like Derrida's spectrality, Gordon's *Ghostly Matters* is not so much about the ghosts themselves, but rather points to their signaling of haunted power structures in modern life. While this point is an important one to be made – especially in emphasizing the ghosts' political potential – *The Ghosts Within* complements this broad conception with the very specificity of certain ghost figures that haunt literary representations of Asian America.

Significantly, Gordon argues, these figures have a certain way of bringing their claims to our attention: "[b]eing haunted draws us affectively, sometimes against our will and always a bit magically, into the structure of feeling of a reality we come to experience, not as cold knowledge, but as transformative recognition" (8). They draw us 'affectively' and often 'magically' to question what we have so far perceived as factual, even if we are not yet ready to admit this fully. In *The Uncanny* (2003) Nicholas Royle argues that Freud's essay already teaches its readers to detect foreignness within themselves, to focus on the extraordinary way the text says what it says, to see the text's own uncanny-ness (Royle 6–8), and that to address the uncanny means to "lose one's bearings, to find oneself immersed in the maddening logic of the supplement" (8). This idea of 'losing one's bearings,' of completely giving oneself over to the uncanny and ghostly figures and their demands constructs the readers themselves as haunted. Just like Gordon's ghosts, Royle's create certain – maybe resented – affects, and they directly engage with us/the readers, to use Gordon's and Royle's terminology. *The Ghosts Within* argues that exactly because of this affective potential ghosts appear as such productive figures in Asian American literature.

Taken together, these approaches establish the ghost as a figure of uncertainty. The ghost is unruly. It challenges norms and categories. It expresses an in-between status. And although this seems to invite a subversive reading of these figures, actually, if one follows the radical logic of this argument, the ghosts rather function as figures of uncertainty: their questioning of terms, categories or constructions always already defies any appropriation. They remain, up to a point, unreadable.

LITERARY GHOSTS

While Avery Gordon's *Ghostly Matters* provides us with great insights into the workings of ghostly matter in the set-up of a society, her focus is of course very much on sociology. So, for me, the basic question is: what do these ghosts mean in the context of literature? As Gordon herself is mostly working with literature as her primary sources, namely Luisa Valenzuela and Toni Morrison's fiction, she addresses this aspect from her sociological point of view and distinguishes Literary and Cultural Studies from her field of research:

> "Literature has its own problems or, rather, it has its own business. It has a history and a market that implicates it in the production of a highly ideological enterprise called Culture; part of its economy of literacy situates it within an academic discipline, literary criticism or now cultural studies, where particular struggles over value and access take precedence. My concern is unequivocally with social life, not with Literature as such (even if literature itself is, of course, riddled with the complications of the social life – my object of inquiry – it represents and sometimes influences)." (Gordon, *Ghostly Matters* 2004, 27)

I disagree with the definition of literature as Gordon gives it at the end of the quote. Arguing with Wolfgang Iser, literature is not about a simple representation of social life that it sometimes influences. Rather, literature provides the space to reflect, to negotiate, to imagine what life is and could be like. Looking at Janice Radway's preface to the new edition of *Ghostly Matters* (2008), I see a similar claim, when she states that Gordon "actively *articulates* exactly what these novels [Valenzuela's and Morrison's] unconsciously know." Radway states that Gordon reads theses novelists "*as* social theorists, which is to say as intellectuals who use imaginative fiction both to diagnose the political *dis-ease* of our historical moment and to envision just what it will take to put things right" (Radway xi). Thus, in order to fill the gap that Gordon's text leaves, I complement her study with a special focus on literature. Combining these two approaches produces new readings of these complex figures.

My definition of literature follows Wolfgang Iser's and Winfried Fluck's conception. Following Iser's triadic relationship of the imaginary, the real, and the fictive, Fluck establishes the concept of the cultural imaginary. Iser argues in *The Fictive and the Imaginary: Charting Literary Anthropology* (1993) that the fictionalizing act creates two processes:

"[r]eproduced reality is made to point to a 'reality' beyond itself, while the imaginary is lured into form. [...] Consequently, extratextual reality merges into the imaginary, and the imaginary merges into reality. The text, then, functions to bring into view the interplay among the fictive, the real, and the imaginary." (Iser 3).

The fictionalizing act, thus, links the real and the imaginary in various ways, constructing the text as a combination of signs that disrupt and double the world to which they refer (2–4).

Fluck draws on this conception of literature as language that refers to a 'reality' yet transcends it in this fictionalizing act in *Das kulturelle Imaginäre: Eine Funktionsgeschichte des amerikanischen Romans 1790-1900* (1997). Referencing Iser, Fluck argues that fiction combines these signs in new ways, and that its potential is given precisely not in a mimetic function, but in a communicatory act that allows to transgress existing norms and to playfully act out possible alternatives (Fluck 12–13). As such, fiction turns into a motor of cultural innovation and de-hierarchization (20). Fluck calls this an articulation effect through which so far unspeakable and diffuse things can become articulated (18). Linking his thoughts to literature and early American novels, Fluck argues that the novel allows a renegotiation and redefinition of the 'reality' it intends to structure and make sense of.[10] This imaginary in literature is a cultural imaginary that allows to articulate otherwise not acceptable aspects within a society. This results in an imaginary self-articulation of a culture in literature, which, in turn, influences the 'reality' from which the fiction draws its inspiration (19–21).

Taken together, Iser/Fluck and Gordon allow for a productive reading of ghost figures in literature as both social figures and as part of the cultural imaginary. Fluck's concept of the cultural imaginary provides the link to actual ghost figures in literature. These figures require a reading in their own terms as constructed parts of something unarticulated. As part of the cultural imaginary as well as social figures, ghosts become active agents that not only refer to

10 Although Fluck is drawing on the ongoing revisions within American Studies for his own project, he views the general tendency to simply turn hierarchies on their head as highly problematic. And I agree with this point especially with reference to Ethnic Studies projects, which have the tendency, as we have seen above, to read literature only in terms of its political potential to either accommodate or resist. If freed from this restricted reading, the history of the American novel becomes the struggle over alternative social, cultural, and aesthetic possibilities that fiction lays bare in its triad play (see, Fluck 9–11).

repressed (hi)stories but also open up spaces for alternative possibilities. While I certainly see the importance of psychoanalytical readings of these figures, I agree with the demand to complement and complicate these with a deconstructive approach.

Colin Davis' *Haunted Subjects: Deconstruction, Psychoanalysis and the Return of the Dead* (2007) reads Derrida's specter as a deconstructive figure *par excellence* that upsets binary oppositions on all levels. To him, Derrida's specter embodies the possibility of productive openness of meanings instead of a closed contend that needs to be unburied (Davis, *Haunted Subjects* 11). As Davis states, the secrets of Derrida's specters are unspeakable[11], in that

> "the ghost's secret is not a puzzle to be solved; it is the structural openness or address directed towards the living by the voices of the past or the not-yet formulated possibilities of the future. The secret is not unspeakable because it is taboo, but because it cannot (yet) be articulated in the languages available to us. The ghost pushes at the boundaries of language and thought." (13)

In this reading of Derrida, Davis highlights the connection of ghosts to language. Read in this way, ghostly figures are not only those things that one has repressed or surpassed beliefs that recur to haunt the living as a sole psychoanalytical reading would have it. Rather, such a poststructuralist/deconstructive approach in its close connection to language reads ghosts as highly constructed figures that point to unarticulated aspects. Especially in terms of ghosts that appear in literature, such a reading opens new possibilities of interpreting them as not only destructive, recurring, repressed forces but also as constructed and productive.[12]

---

11 Davis compares Derrida's specters to the phantoms of Nicolas Abraham and Maria Torok, arguing that both approaches constitute the concept of hauntology. The phantom is unspeakable in a very different sense in that it is a subject of shame and prohibition. The phantoms are lying creatures that try to veil such shameful secrets through transgenerational haunting. The main difference between Abraham and Torok and Derrida is the formers' belief that the secrets can and must be revealed so that, in the end, a reconciliation and order can be restored (Davis *Haunted Subjects* 8; 13).

12 Marjorie Garber also works with Derrida's concept of the revenant in *Shakespeare's Ghost Writers: Literature as Uncanny Causality* (1987), claiming that ghosts only "carry the authority of their own belatedness" (Garber 172) in this coming back. She thus establishes the ghost as a self-referential figure. For Garber, a ghost's effect "is related simultaneously to its manifestation as a sign of potential proliferation or plurality and to its acknowledgement of the loss of the original – indeed, to the loss of

Gabriele Schwab assumes a similar process and function of haunting in literature in *Haunting Legacies: Violent Histories and Transgenerational Trauma* (2010). She conceives of literature as a space to re-write traumatic experience. Drawing on Abraham and Torok's conception of the crypt, she argues that "[c]ryptographic writing functions as a transformational object by breaking through the walls of silence or the sealed boundaries of a crypt" (Schwab 7) in order to "force the ghosts of violent histories into the open and work toward social recognition and reparation" (55). The transformational function of literature is directly linked to trauma in Schwab's reading, but in connection with Iser/Fluck this function is part of every literary text. Still, Schwab's connection to haunting indicates a special function that ghosts might serve in literary texts. As figures of uncertainty the literary ghosts mark spaces of the imaginary.

Both Fluck and Gordon address the complicated relation of representation and 'reality.' For the ghostly figures appearing in literature, Tzvetan Todorov's conception of 'the fantastic' has been influential. His *The Fantastic: A Structural Approach to a Literary Genre* (1973) attempts to outline a structuralist analysis of the fantastic as a genre (Todorov 3–23). In order to do this, Todorov distinguishes three categories: the uncanny, the fantastic, and the marvelous. The uncanny and the marvelous are neighboring genres of the uncanny and mark its boundaries. Inherently connected to questions of imagination and 'reality,' the uncanny explains the occurrence of an event as a result of natural causes, while the marvelous relates them to supernatural causes. The fantastic, though, is the genre in between these two and is marked by its unresolved tension between the two poles of illusion and truth, of 'reality' and dream, of supernatural and natural. Once the literary text resolves this hesitation, it leaves the fantastic (25). In order for the fantastic to work, Todorov argues that this hesitation may be experienced by a character in the story, and that the reader must reject an allegorical or poetic reading of the text to accept this ambiguity (24–40). Although my project is not a genre study as Todorov's, his structural analysis is

---

the certainty of the concept of origin" (15). Referring to Shakespeare's plays, Garber argues that these "plays not only thematize," "but also theorize" issues of authorship and origin, asking questions such as: "who wrote this? did someone else have a hand in it? is the apparent author the real author? is the official version to be trusted? or are there suppressed stories, hidden messages, other signatures?" (26). These questions have an uncanny resemblance to the questions that appear in terms of the Asian American literary texts. Who wrote this? For whom?

still important in order to emphasize different approaches to these figures as part of reality or allegorical reference.[13]

Todorov has been criticized for his structuralist approach that remains very much within the literary realm. Rosemary Jackson's *Fantasy: The Literature of Subversion* (1981) expands Todorov's reading with a psychoanalytical reading and focuses rather on the political and social dimension of this literature, providing, in her words, a "cultural study of the fantastic" (Jackson 7). Jackson views the fantastic as a mode of writing that does not only stage a hesitation between 'reality' and imagination but rather one that "*enters a dialogue with the 'real' and incorporates that dialogue as part of its essential structure*" (36). Reading this dialogue within fantastic literature through a psychoanalytical approach, Jackson concludes that it reflects deeper cultural issues, that it is concerned with unconscious desires within a cultural order (62–63). Thus, Jackson sees the subversive potential of fantastic literature in the undermining of cultural stability (69–70).

Lucie Armitt's *Theorising the Fantastic* (1996) highlights the influence of Jackson's expansions of the fantastic for feminist critics. Yet, Armitt further argues that neither a structuralist nor a Freudian reading allows for the

---

13 According to Peter Cersowsky in "Allegory and the Fantastic in Literature" (1982) allegory and the fantastic are similar in the assumption of two levels of expression, "namely the concrete image and the general meaning" (Cersowsky 141–42). Allegory, as Paul de Man defines it, is a sign that "points to something that differs from its literal meaning and has for its function the thematization of this difference" (Man 209). Paul de Man has introduced the temporal dimension of allegory because "it remains necessary, if there is to be allegory, that the allegorical sign refer to another sign that precedes it" (207). Allegory is therefore always already repetition: it refers to a sign with which it can never cohere, which provides a certain distance to its own origin. He, thus, emphasizes the destabilizing structure of allegorical figurations (Mailloux 265). If ghosts are read allegorically, they are rhetorical signs that point to something beyond their literal meaning.

Such an approach of ghost figures as allegorical, then, fits Derrida's deconstructive readings of these figures. They destabilize binary distinctions. Yet, the assumption of two levels of expression already establishes the ghosts as part of the imagery of the text: they are simply signs that refer to other, previous signs, in a chain of repetition. And although Cersowsky and de Man create a flexibility of reading the ghosts as destabilizing figures and as pointing to various signs, it diverges from the fantastic in that it places these figures – without hesitation – as part of the allegorical realm. For Todorov's fantastic to work, such a perception of the ghosts needs to be abandoned.

theoretical importance of Todorov's fantastic to fully emerge. With the fantastic basically subverting its own classifications as a genre on the borders and in-between natural and supernatural experience, Armitt calls for a "theorization of the fantastic as the discourse of the limit" (Armitt 6–7). Instead of reading a fantastic text as "an enclosed space or playground of fantasy as desire," Armitt suggests to foreground a poststructuralist reading to see how it "sets up a series of competing discourses or free-playing counter-structures that threaten to disrupt the very narrative they comprise" (81). In Armitt's view, the fantastic foregrounds the instability of its own grounds. Its fantastic figures – the ghosts included – appear as such border crossers, undermining the very differentiation into real/imaginary.

The direct transfer from such a Western and structural reading to Asian American literature appears problematic at least. This is certainly not what *The Ghosts Within* intends. But Todorov's approach and its rereading of the shifting nature of the fantastic helps to emphasize this same strategy in the Asian American novels that my project focuses on. All of them playfully engage with the ghosts' reality status, some more pronounced, others less obvious. Markus Oppolzer argues in his article "Todorov's Hesitation, Or: In the Reader We Trust" that what he likes about Todorov is his hermeneutical approach to ghosts: it is not the ghost as such, but the characters' as well as the readers' willingness to go along with the hesitation concerning the ghosts natural or supernatural being. And this demands a recognition of the "very specific socio-cultural and generic contexts [for] that makes all the difference" (Oppolzer 47). Moritz Baßler, Bettina Gruber, and Martina Wagner-Egelhaaf also read ghosts as discursive figures allowing significant insights into the construction of the world of its perceiver in the edited volume *Gespenster: Erscheinungen, Medien, Theorien* (2005) (Baßler, Gruber, and Wagner-Egelhaaf 9–10). According to them, ghosts are figures between the two poles of metaphor and 'reality,' with the special case of naturalized metaphors, which express otherwise unarticulateable aspects of a certain culture (10–11). In other words, if a character or reader approaches a text with the set belief that ghosts can merely appear as allegorical figures, this will inherently result in very different readings from someone who assumes that ghosts can be spiritual figures. This difference becomes a very important one in the context of Asian American literature.

Baßler, Gruber, and Wagner-Egelhaaf give a short but concise overview of the phenomenon across various disciplines and media. Most importantly, however, the editors emphasize a third pole: the mediality of these figures. Ghosts not only appear in different media – such as literature, film, photography, digital media[14] – differently, but they are, furthermore, self-reflexive figures pointing to their own mediality (11–12). This point emphasizes the importance of recognizing the specific medium with which one is working. Instead of a general application of psychoanalytical or sociological readings of the ghost figures, their status as literary ghosts in a certain ethnic tradition needs to be considered.

In case of the fantastic elements of Asian American literature, attention needs to be drawn to a cultural perception of how 'reality' and fantasy/ imagination are related. I argue that the distinction in 'real' and imaginary works differently in this context because of its combination of Asian and American traditions and therefore the category of the fantastic does not apply one to one here. While Western traditions certainly oppose easy binary differentiation of real versus imaginary, for example by focusing on the subjective perception of 'reality,' Asian traditions are grounded more thoroughly in supernatural beliefs accepting ghosts as spiritual embodiments of ancestors. Formulations like these are always dangerous as they imply a binary conception of East and West that was too often used in essentializing ascriptions and in hierarchical conceptions that favored the Western side. Stuart Hall, for example, has theorized and warned of such conceptions in "The West and the Rest: Discourse and Power" stating that these appear as self-conceptualizations for a West that distinguishes itself favorably of an 'othered Rest' (184–227). In an analysis of the ghost figures that shape Asian American literary writings, however, the differences and overlaps of both the Western and the Asian influences need to be addressed. Furthermore, the terms 'Asia' and 'the West' need to be seen as paradigmatic formulations to emphasize general differences between these two poles of Asian

14 For detailed analyses of ghosts in other media than literature critics often refer to Walter Benjamin's *Illuminations*, especially his "Thesis on the Philosophy of History" and "The Work of Art in the Age of Mechanical Reproduction," although he does not explicitly discuss ghosts himself, his ideas of mechanical reproduction and the loss of the origin lend themselves to a spectral reading. Another reference point for many theorists is Roland Barthes, *Camera Lucida: Reflections of Photography*, New York: Hill and Wang, 1981. See, for example, Marjorie Garber (especially pages 16–17); Jeffrey Sconce, *Haunted Media: Electronic Presence From Telegraphy to Television*, Durham: Duke University Press, 2000; or for the Asian American context: Bliss Cua Lim, *Spectral Times: The Ghost Film as Historical Allegory*; or Jutta Gsoels-Lorensen, "le thi diem thúy's *The Gangster We're All Looking For*: The Ekphrastic Emigration of a Photograph," *Critique: Studies in Contemporary Fiction* 48.1 (2006): 3–18.

American writing. In no way are these terms supposed to neglect the importance and existence of the heterogeneity of what constitutes each term. The perception of a spiritual approach of ghost figures that dominates in Asian traditional beliefs needs to be contrasted with the allegorical approach that shapes Western perceptions. However, *The Ghosts Within* argues that the interrelation of these approaches appears as a special feature of ghost figures in Asian American literature and that the novels often play with these contrary conceptions.

In a similar vein, Pearl S. Buck warns in her Nobel lecture not to simply search for what is known and familiar and to adapt it to our own standards, but rather to take the influence of other traditions seriously into account. Accordingly, Buck reflects upon the differences that she perceives in Chinese novels:

> "These Chinese novels are not perfect according to Western standards. They are not always planned from beginning to end, nor are they compact, any more than life is planned or compact. They are often too long, too full of incident, too crowded with character, a medley of fact and fiction as to material, and a medley of romance and realism as to method, so that an impossible event of magic or dream may be described with such exact semblance of detail that one is compelled to belief against all reason. The earliest novels are full of folklore, for the people of those times thought and dreamed in the ways of folklore." (Pearl Buck np)

Other scholars and authors have put forth a similar argument. Ming Dong Gu, for example, argues in the article "Theory of Fiction: A Non-Western Narrative Tradition" that in Chinese narrative traditions the fantastic is not at all a deviation but is deeply in-built into the narrative structures at large (Gu 325). Another example is Susan J. Napier's *The Fantastic in Modern Japanese Literature* (1996), which establishes a specific Japanese fantastic that is nevertheless related to other fantastic forms. According to Napier, although the West has in recent years increasingly challenged its Judeo-Christian tradition of absolutes, the Japanese have had a longer tradition of a subversion of 'reality.' Most importantly, however, the Japanese fantastic works with the distinctive aspects of 'tabooed images' that subvert modernity and "offer a variety of unique alternatives in its place" (Napier 223–27). These references exemplify the different approaches of Chinese or Japanese literary representations and perceptions. And although they certainly do not reflect the heterogeneity of Asian perceptions of the fantastic, these examples suffice to highlight the important differences between Eastern and Western readings of this genre.

Shifting from the Asian side to the specific intermixing of both traditions, Chinese American author Laurence Yep works with the idea that fantasy and 'reality' are actually not two distinct things but that they overlap and influence each other. In his words, "assuming that our imagination is inferior to our sense of reality in dealing with our external world" (Yep np) is erroneous. Instead, "[f]antasy and reality both play vital parts in our lives, for we may grasp with the mind and heart what we may not always grasp with the hand. It would be a tragic mistake to insist upon a realistic viewpoint to the exclusion of fantasy" (np). As Yep's argumentation shows, while it is important to acknowledge and address existing differences, the Asian American novels would be similarly reduced if one ascribed them a purely Asian framework. They are driven, instead, by both traditions; and the ghost figures are a motif that highlights the dual influence and creates a newly emergent one.

Nicole Waller already observes such a shifting in Maxine Hong Kingston's *The Woman Warrior*. She argues in "Transpazifische und transatlantische Gespenster in Maxine Hong Kingstons *The Woman Warrior* und Toni Morrisons *Beloved*" (2005) that the ghosts appear not only as metaphorical references but also simultaneously demand a recognition as based in reality (Waller 267). Certainly, all of the novels that *The Ghosts Within* focuses on rely on both spiritual and allegorical readings of their ghost figures, sometimes these figures are separated, sometimes the duality appears with reference to the same ghost. In any way, a division and rational explanation is never complete. The Asian American ghost continues to haunt the literature and it remains as a reference to the field's constant negotiations of its status as both Asian and American. Thus, although the conception of the fantastic cannot be taken over uncritically in an Asian American context, it is still helpful in highlighting the ways in which Asian American novels employ the ghost as a shifting, ambiguous figure of instability and uncertainty.

In her seminal *Cultural Haunting: Ghosts and Ethnicity in Recent American Literature* (1998), Kathleen Brogan establishes the genre of 'stories of cultural haunting' as a pan-ethnic tradition. Her reading of the ghosts emphasizes the concrete function of ghostly presences in these tales as figures calling for a reworking of the past for the present. Drawing on psychoanalytical approaches and working with a conception of ethnicity as constructed via narrative processes, Brogan notes that ghost figures "in stories of cultural haunting are agents of both cultural memory *and* cultural renewal: the shape-shifting ghost who transmits erased or threatened group memory represents the creative, ongoing process of ethnic redefinition" (Brogan 12). Brogan's ghosts refer to repressed and recurring aspects of the past of a specific ethnic group that appear in order to establish new memories and connections to this past in order to rework it into usable aspects for the present and future. Or, again, in Brogan's own words, in

"confronting an obscure history and a tenuous present, writers across the spectrum of American peoples conjure ghosts to solve a single problem: how to reframe the narrative organization of ethnic experience. Ghosts are not the exclusive province of any single ethnic group; they figure prominently wherever people must reconceive a fragmented, partially obliterated history, looking to a newly imagined past to redefine themselves for the future." (29)

Both quotes show Brogan's indebtedness to narrative processes of constructing a people's communal identity via a common (hi)story.

Without referring to them directly, Brogan uses Jan and Aleida Assmann's concept of 'cultural memory.' According to the Assmanns, individuals become part of a group through socialization and transmission (Assmann, "Kollektives Gedächtnis und kulturelle Identität" 9). Expanding Maurice Halbwachs' seminal ideas of a collective memory, Jan Assmann lists six constitutive elements for cultural memory[15], of which three seem to have special relevance in relation to Brogan's conception of ghosts. Cultural memory is constitutive of identity. A group's consciousness of its unity and common roots is built upon this collective knowledge. And it draws from this knowledge to reproduce and re-articulate its cultural identity. It is driven by a wish for a common identity that clearly distinguishes 'us' from others (11–13). Furthermore, cultural memory is reconstructive, which means that it always refers to a present moment in its recollections. It moves back reflexively to shared memories in order to remember them in the current context. This way, it appropriates existing memories, negotiating their value for the present (13). Each cultural tradition reveals in its artifacts what its basic assumptions are and what it intends to become. In and through these, a group imagines self-portraits for the present and future by way of reframing their collective memories (Assmann, *Das kulturelle Gedächtnis* 18). Thus, in its cultural heritage a group becomes visible for itself as well as for others (Assmann, "Kollektives Gedächtnis und kulturelle Identität" 16). As all of this implies, memories are not simply the things that we remember

15 For further information on the constitutive elements see Assmann "Kollektives Gedächtnis und kulturelle Identität," 12–15.

from the past.[16] They are certainly not reflections of a past 'reality.' Rather, they are subjective and highly selective constructs that are in a close relationship with the context during which a person or a group remembers (Erll 157). Assmann's concept of 'cultural memory' is therefore a perfect fit to Brogan's conception of ghosts as inherently referencing an aspect of a repressed or lost past.

Kathleen Brogan's influential study on ghosts as pan-ethnic phenomena serves as a reference point for my project. As already outlined with reference to Assmann's concept of cultural memory, her engagement with the ghost's link to memory provides a detailed analysis of the ghosts' function as constitutive of identity and as reflexive. In Brogan's work, the ghosts appear as active figures that link the past to the present in order to create a workable and livable future. *The Ghosts Within* builds upon her findings, but moves out of her rather limited context of identity formation. While this function is certainly still prevalent in contemporary figurations of ghostliness in Asian American literature, it is just one among many functions that these ghosts embody. While Kathleen Brogan's reading of ghosts remains bound to the earlier constructions of ghosts as carriers of an ethnic identity that is carried via a family's tradition into diaspora, my project foregrounds the complex interconnections that shape the construction of postcolonial ghostly identities. The literary ghost figures always conceive of and provide a (cultural) framework for an Asian American self-conception. But at the same time, they playfully trouble any categorization.

In this sense, I suggest to look at the highly interesting interconnections between all influences on a certain tradition, instead of simply turning the exclusive tendencies around, In the Asian American context, this includes the American, the general ethnic, as well as the respective Asian traditions that all shape and influence the ghostly figures haunting this literature. With this reading I am in line with Roger Luckhurst. While Luckhurst is working on the British Gothic, I agree with his general demand concluding his article, that critics need to go beyond the current meta-discourse of liminality, which means "to forget

16 The seminal work by Michel de Certeau as well as Hayden White on the close connection of history and fiction plays into this. Their stance on the fictionality of history has not only been highly influential in their field of expertise – history – but also for sociological and literary approaches (see, for example, Hayden White's *Metahistory: The Historical Imagination in Nineteenth-Century Europe*, Baltimore: The Johns Hopkins University Press, 1973 or Michel de Certeau's *Das Schreiben der Geschichte*, Frankfurt/Main: Campus-Verlag, 1991). This is, of course, also related to the New Historicist development of the late twentieth century in literary criticism, of which White was an instructive part.

the other cultural convention about ghosts: that they appear precisely as symptoms, points of rupture that insist their singular tale be retold and their wrongs acknowledged" (Luckhurst 542). Following Derrida's call for a re-politicization, he argues that critics "have to risk the violence of reading the ghost, of cracking open its absent presence to answer the demand of its specific symptomatology and its specific locale" (542).

In a similar vein, Andrew Weinstock proposes in the introduction to the edited volume *Spectral America: Phantoms and the National Imagination* (2004) to emphasize the diachronic existence of the ghost figure in American culture. However, he also argues that "particular ghostly manifestations are always embedded within specific historical contexts and invoked for more or less explicit political purposes" (Weinstock 8). I very much agree with Luckhurst and Weinstock in their call for more critical attention to the very specificity of a certain ghost appearance. Instead of simply reading these figures as deconstructive self-referential tropes, they need to be placed in their respective contexts. But to 'risk the violence of reading the ghost' also means not to try to squeeze these figures into categories or preconceived political or moral messages; it is an invitation to actually look at the figures' inherent ambiguity in all of their reference points and traditions. It means to combine psychoanalytical, historical, social, cultural, and allegorical approaches to these figures in order to unearth all of the nuances that these figures offer – and to be open to the diverse and playful functions that they take on in the literary imaginations of Asian America. *The Ghosts Within* hopes to follow this invitation in its readings of the very specific ghost figures that haunt the contemporary Asian American novels it discusses.

2 Postcolonial Melodramatic Ghost Figures: Signs of *Dis*-ease in Lois-Ann Yamanaka's *Behold the Many*

"'Look,' Ezroh said, […] 'Every time your wounds began to heal, new gashes appeared. They thought you were hurting yourself.' […]

Her eyes opened slowly. She surveyed the scratched and torn flesh on her arms. 'I did all of this to myself?'

'No,' he said. […]

'Who is doing this to me?' She looked past Ezroh to the corners of the room. Leah looked at her from one, her face concerned.

Little Leah?

[…]

But as she gripped his hand, she saw Aki. She stood in another corner, her hand over her mouth stifling back her laughter.

Aki!

[…]

She saw Seth crying in another corner, his finger pointing at his chest: 'Me. It was me.'

Aki clutched at her belly, her body bent over, laughing. 'No, me!' she squealed.

'Seth?' Anah winced in a painful delirium. 'You? No, it was Aki.'

'Seth? Aki? Stop it, Anah. My brother is dead. And your sister is dead.'

'I know, but—' She started, noticing Ezroh's face confused. […]

'Tell them, Anah.'

'They would not believe me.' She searched for Aki. But she was gone, her trill giggling on a gusty breeze. 'You would not believe me.' Seth followed her, a mournful wailing wind.

[…]

His fingers moved across her forehead, then down to her cheek, and slowly over her lips and chin. 'You do not let them cut your face anymore,' he said, his eyes searching hers for acknowledgement and promise.

Them.
She nodded, a tear slipping down her face, Ezroh blending it into her scars with another dab of turtle oil." (Yamanaka 126–29)

Even if a reader is not familiar with Lois-Ann Yamanaka's novel *Behold the Many* (2006), she would immediately recognize certain motives in this excerpt. Anah, the protagonist, is being haunted and hurt by ghosts. Two of the ghosts that appear in the quote are her dead sisters, Leah and Aki. Another is Seth, Ezroh's brother, – a ghost figure that provides one of the main puzzles of the novel. Hurt and confused, Anah questions her own perception. Only under Ezroh's loving care does Anah allow her tears to flow. And only with Ezroh's cautious affirmation of the existence of the ghosts, 'them,' does Anah realize the deepness of their mutual understanding. The ghosts take up center stage in this novel. Furthermore, when focusing on the style and narrative mode of this short scene, a reader might recognize a melodramatic and, especially with relation to the ghost figures, Gothic mode. In the tradition of these modes, the novel plays with the imagery of black/white or good/bad. The frightening ghost figures appear as the stark counter-image to Ezroh's loving care; their hurtful haunting counteracts with Ezroh's unconditional love. But *Behold the Many* develops a new kind of postcolonial melodramatic mode: although the reader certainly knows in each scene how to feel towards the characters in terms of a binary moral judgment – Ezroh the good one, the ghost of Aki the bad one –, these terms become increasingly destabilized in the course of the story as the reader is being pushed by the narrative to constantly revise earlier judgments and feel differently about the characters.

The sisters Anah, Aki, and Leah all suffer from a fatal illness, the younger two dying because of it, and the novel's progression implies that such a disease exists as a result of colonial encounters. Yet, most centrally, the novel emphasizes and stages the overarching *dis*-ease of its setting and its characters. This refers to Janice Radway's term as she uses it in the foreword to Avery Gordon's *Ghostly Matters* (2008), stating that some authors "use imaginative fiction […] to diagnose the political *dis*-ease of our historical moment" (Radway xi). In this sense, the ghost figures appear as references that emerge uneasily from the pages of this novel in order to express such *dis*-ease without, however, allowing for a conclusive reading of their function or offering solutions to the problems that they reference. Avery Gordon perceives of the ghost as a social figure, arguing that it is in forms of the ghostly that history and subjectivity meet to create social life. Via the ghost's haunting, something lost or almost absent, something that educated people do not belief to exist, demands recognition. With her approach, Gordon broadens the Freudian conception of the uncanny from that which haunts an individual to a whole society: exposing its structures as being haunted by its repressed aspects. Such a social figure allows for a political engagement with these haunting presences.

But Gordon also emphasizes the affective response to haunting (Gordon, *Ghostly Matters* 2004, 8). And it is this desired affective response that the postcolonial melodramatic mode strives for: *Behold the Many* creates this via the shifting, paradoxical nature of the ghosts. Instead of presenting easy solutions, *Behold the Many* in general, and the ghost figures in particular, attempt to reconnect the readers to intuitive responses to binary categorizations such as colonizer/colonized, Asian/Caucasian, historical/fictional, or allegorical/spiritual. It reframes these terms via melodramatic tableaus and various intertextual references for the ghost figures, yet, refrains from offering a morally or politically conclusive alternative. The ghosts' defiance of easy categorizations makes them troublesome because they do not follow a politicized postcolonial resistance narrative; instead, they expose the paradoxical interconnections between seemingly opposed systems and approaches.

SETH: AN UNREADABLE GHOST FIGURE

Yamanaka's *Behold the Many*, set in Hawaii in the early twentieth century, revolves around the protagonist Anah, who is being haunted by various ghost figures during her life. As one review pointedly puts it, this "dark yet luminous novel flows between the ghost world and mundane reality with an impressive flexibility of style" (Wakatsuki Houston np). The novel is about three sisters of Japanese Portuguese descent, who are infected with tuberculosis and are sent away to a German Catholic orphanage. During their time at the orphanage, each sister makes the acquaintance of Seth, the ghost of a young boy who died before the sisters arrived. One after the other befriends this ghost as they approach their deaths. Leah and Aki, the two younger sisters, die at the orphanage, while the oldest, Anah, survives, only to be haunted by the ghosts of her siblings throughout her life. Anah is also haunted by 'the many' that already appear in the title: these are the ghosts of all the children who died during their time at the orphanage, now looking for a way 'home.' When Anah finally leaves the orphanage to begin her new life as the wife of Ezroh, Seth's brother, she is cursed. Seth's friendship has turned into one-sided love and he cannot accept his brother's engagement to her. This curse follows Anah, complicating her life as a member of Ezroh's family even further, as it adds to his family's suspicions concerning her racial background. His family is of Portuguese Cape Verdean descent and looks down on what his aunt calls 'Orientals' – to which they count Anah, who is the daughter of a Portuguese father and a Japanese mother. Due to the curse, Ezroh and Anah's children are all born with disabilities, and the curse can only be lifted by the death of Anah's first-born daughter, Hosana. In the final scene of the novel, Hosana, turned into a ghost after being raped and murdered, calls all the ghosts to her – Leah, Aki, Seth, and 'the many' – to take them 'home' with her, to God.

While the plot foregrounds this "magical story," it "is also an uncompromising depiction of a hard immigrant life in Hawaii, of Chinese opium dens and Japanese laborers and Portuguese cowboys and whites eager to tame the lot of them" (Kirkus Review, *Review* np), as another review has it. Although this tension is central to *Behold the Many*, Yamanaka's novels in general are controversial. One of her novels in particular, *Blu's Hanging* (1997), initiated a huge debate in the field of Asian American Studies about the field's self-conception as either politically or aesthetically engaged. These questions of a representative status have been part of the field from its very beginnings – as expressed in the earlier debate between Frank Chin and Maxine Hong Kingston that revolved around similar problems.[1] In the writing of Japanese American Lois-Ann Yamanaka, this debate is particularly charged due to its setting: Hawaii. Her 'uncompromising depictions' of the harsh life on the islands add further fuel to an already emotionally charged discourse. Breaking with the conception of Hawaii in general and its Asian American community in particular as ethnic paradises, Yamanaka forces her readers to engage more honestly with the history and set-up of this part of the United States.

Hawaii's colonial history has not been particularly "sudden or bloody" but "Hawaiians have nevertheless suffered its 'violence' and also resisted and protested it," as Cristina Bacchilega writes in *Legendary Hawai'i and the Politics of Place* (2007) (Bacchilega 3). The nineteenth century was dominated by sociopolitical and cultural changes, such as the continuous depopulation of Native Hawaiians due to epidemics, the spread of alcoholism, a general orientation towards Christian morality – which resulted in the introduction of new laws and a devaluation of Hawaiian religious and cultural traditions, the division and privatization of land, the change to a representational political system, all of which culminated in the overthrow of the Hawaiian monarchy in 1893 and the annexation of Hawaii as a territory of the United States of America

1 A more extensive overview of these two debates and their central function within the field of Asian American Studies is given in the Introduction to *The Ghosts Within*.

in 1898 (3–4). Noenoe Silva states in *Aloha Betrayed* (2004) that "[o]ne of the most persistent and pernicious myths of Hawaiian history is that the Kanaka Maoli (Native Hawaiians) passively accepted the erosion of their culture and the loss of their nation" (Silva 1) and it is this myth that *Aloha Betrayed* challenges in documenting Hawaiian language sources of resistance. Silva highlights a process of "strategic accommodation to the Western ideas of nationhood and government, combined with an insistence on the value of Kanaka cultural identity" (10). Such a process of accommodation and resistance also structures Yamanaka's *Behold the Many*, especially in its portrayal of the children's perception of the missionaries at the orphanage. Thus, the novel neither depicts a successfully assimilated population nor follows a logic of heroic resistance, it rather offers an emotional engagement with the interconnections of both cultures and systems.

The imagination of Hawaiian history as particularly tension-free and non-violent is directly linked to the stereotypical conception of Hawaiians as particularly tolerant and peaceful. In this sense, Hawaii is often referred to as a 'multicultural model' or 'ethnic paradise,' in which harmonious ethnic relations and a high rate of intermarriage are common (Okamura 11). Although Jonathan Okamura acknowledges in *Ethnicity and Inequality in Hawai'i* (2008) that Hawaiian history has seen only a little number of collective racial violence in comparison with the continental United States, he still emphasizes the problematic and unequal ethnic relations that structure Hawaiian society (15). He documents the interethnic tensions that result from the privileged status of whites, Chinese Americans, and Japanese Americans in contrast to the lower social status of Filipino Americans. With this, Okamura also challenges the idea of a pan-Asian Asian American community on the islands (7).

Yamanaka's *Behold the Many* features these inter-ethnic tensions.[2] In the words of one reviewer, Yamanaka sets her novel in "Hawaii, but not the one tourists see" by giving "unflinching depictions of Paradise's darker side" (O'Briant np). Written after the controversy, *Behold the Many* takes up such

2 Okamura was one of the very outspoken critics against Yamanaka in the debate surrounding *Blu's Hanging* and so would not be satisfied with this connection. For him, every novelist's writing should follow a clear moral and political purpose in its depictions of ethnic groups and so he was outraged at her representation of Filipino Americans (James np). This chapter does not strive to either defy or support Okamura's criticism. Instead, it offers a reading that foregrounds the inter-ethnic tensions with which Yamanaka does engage in *Behold the Many* and focuses on the limits that a morally and politically preconceived approach to ghost figures entails.

controversial issues like inter-ethnic tensions once again, albeit consciously further fictionalized with the constant magical appearances that drive the story.[3] This "fascinating melding of reality and the spirit world" (Gaines np) is linked by reviewers of the novel to the depiction of "a powerful, three-dimensional portrait of an unfamiliar culture" (O'Briant np). Such an exoticizing shapes many of the reviews: Wakatsuki Houston, for example, praises the novel for showing that "yin qualities of subtlety, constrained passion, and beauty cannot only co-exist with yang outbursts of wild energy and over-the-top expression, but give a reading experience that is all the more powerful because of it" (Wakatsuki Houston np). Working with a similar mixture of fact and fiction, Maxine Hong Kingston's memoir *The Woman Warrior* (1977) already established the figure of the ghost as a central character in Asian American literature. In her article "Cultural Mis-readings by American Reviewers," Kingston voices her astonishment and anger at being measured "against the stereotype of the exotic, inscrutable, mysterious oriental" (Kingston, "Cultural Mis-Readings by American Reviewers" 95), forcing her into the position of an alien to American culture at large. Such exotic appeal is also attributed to the figure of the ghost in general as it appears in contemporary ethnic literature.[4] A seemingly obvious link between 'exotic,' 'mysterious' and 'spirits' reveals a self-fulfilling prophecy attributed to ethnic writing. Reading the ghosts in this literature as simple ethnic ornamentation not only locks ethnic writing in a self-referential circle, it also ignores possible other readings which might be more troublesome to America's or, in this case, Asian America's self-conception.

In fact, the four reviews I have cited so far ignore the most puzzling ghost figure that appears in *Behold the Many*. While some at least mention Seth's

---

3 For a reading that directly links the ghost figures of *Behold the Many* to this debate, see my article "A Haunting Controversy: Yamanaka's Fictionalized Melodramatic Ghost Figures," *Crossing Boundaries in a Post-Ethnic Era: Interdisciplinary Approaches and Negotiations*. Ed. Astrid M. Fellner and Simone Puff, forthcoming.

4 See, for example, Kathleen Brogan's *Cultural Haunting*, which reads the ghost figure as a pan-ethnic phenomenon that allows for an engagement with an almost lost past to re-make it for a useable future. This process, according to her reading, appears in a similar vein in all ethnic literatures. Another, less prominent example is Bonnie Winsbro's *Supernatural Forces*, which argues that ethnic authors work with a conception of the supernatural to emphasize the existence of various and diverse realities (Winsbro 6–10). Although I have reservations about such a limited reading of ghosts as solely linked to ethnicity, following Sladja Blazan's critique (Blazan 138), these examples are highly prominent in the field at large.

existence, most reviewers avoid his central position in the novel. Strikingly, they misinterpret the curse that haunts Anah throughout her life, portraying her sisters as the ones who curse her. Only one out of these four otherwise engaged reviews gives the correct source of the curse, which is Seth. Why does this mistake happen so frequently?

My answer is that a curse by the sisters is much more agreeable to our common readings of ghost figures, and that Seth troubles assumed notions of what a ghost is and does. Many conceptions of the Gothic postulate the existence of supernatural entities, historically in order to give expression to repressed anxieties connected to sexual taboos, religious fears, or guilt feelings as in *Beloved* (Hogle, "Introduction" 2–4). As Allan Lloyd-Smith argues, the Gothic generally is "about the *return* of the past, the repressed and denied, the buried secret that subverts and corrodes the present, whatever the culture does not want to know or admit, will not or dare not tell itself" (Lloyd-Smith 1). In his explorations of 'the uncanny,' Freud assumes the uncanny to be something repressed that recurs (Freud 241). He argues that "we should differentiate between the uncanny that we actually experience and the uncanny that we merely picture or read about" (247). As already pointed out in chapter one of *The Ghosts Within*, Freud himself seems troubled by his definitions and distinctions. Still, such a conception of literature helps to understand the ways in which Gothic literature can be read: because the reader knows that she is only engaging in a fictive story, she can lift the ban and acknowledge the repressed.

Jerrold E. Hogle argues that this is the social significance of the Gothic mode. In Hogle's words, "the longevity and power of Gothic fiction unquestionably stem from the way it helps us address and disguise some of the most important desires, quandaries, and sources of anxiety, from the most internal and mental to the widely social and cultural, throughout the history of western culture since the eighteenth century" (Hogle, "Introduction" 4).[5]

5 The first text to be termed Gothic was Horace Walpole's *The Castle of Otranto* (1764), but the literary Gothic exploded at the turn of the eighteenth to the nineteenth century with novels by various authors in England, Europe and the United States (Hogle "Introduction" 1). These early novels were extremely popular and established a certain set of features or characteristics of the Gothic mode. Literary Gothic has seen resurgence at the turn of the next century with classics such as Charlotte Perkins Gilman's 'The Yellow Wallpaper' (1892), Bram Stoker's *Dracula* (1897) or Henry James's *The Turn of the Screw* (1898). It spread across a wide range of media during the twentieth century, the Gothic mode certainly influences contemporary writings (Hogle "Introduction" 2).

Precisely this distancing in terms of place or time – this highly fictionalized othering –, enables the Gothic to address those voices which otherwise struggle to be heard. Under the disguise of surreality, the Gothic delivers the "world in an inverted form" (Punter 17–18), but the world nevertheless.

A curse that is uttered by the dead siblings could easily be linked to various worldly references that appear after they have been repressed. For example, with the sisters, a psychoanalytical reading of the curse as repressed survivor's guilt seems obvious. Anah, the oldest sister, who wanted to protect her siblings, has failed and is haunted by her guilt especially when she herself begins the new life she always tried to console her sisters with. The sisters' ghosts also neatly follow a postcolonial resistance narrative: the cause of their death – tuberculosis – refers to the many epidemics that Hawaiians had to suffer in the course of the islands colonization. Such a reading is similar to the process that Renée Bergland observes for the haunting presence of Native Americans in *The National Uncanny* (2000): the sisters as references to colonial losses haunt the colony and the ones who began to make a new life for themselves within this new setting from which they have been excluded.

But what of Seth? Applying classical theoretical reflections of ghosts, the reader soon encounters serious difficulties. Seth's ghost defies any attempt of clear-cut categorization or conclusive readings. He allows for a variety of associations, intertextual references, and even contradictory interpretations. Freud's reading of 'the uncanny' as something familiar that has undergone repression and recurs from it links ghosts to primitive beliefs that we have seemingly overcome (Freud 245–249). His theory of repression thus only works up to a point. Seth might symbolize such a repressed guilty conscience for Anah, reminding her constantly that she should have died along with her sisters. Or he might point to her anger and self-alienation, representing those aspects of herself that Anah represses. However, once seen in the larger picture, this explanation is not all there is to this figure. Seth also appears to other characters throughout the novel and therefore cannot be limited to Anah's very personal feelings. Thus, following a psychoanalytical approach, he could also be conceived of as embodying a universal 'guilty conscience' of Hawaii's colonial society. Yet, in contrast to Leah and Aki, the cause of Seth's death was an accident. He fell off a tree when he was playing at the orphanage. He was neither suffering from an illness brought on by colonization nor an orphan living at the orphanage. A general 'postcolonial guilt' is therefore not the most convincing reading of this figure. Instead, Seth's ghost also functions as a reference to those aspects that the Hawaiian American culture at large has seemingly overcome at this point in time: the lingering presence of traditional Hawaiian and Asian beliefs.

However, a reading of Seth as solely symbolizing ethnic cultural memory is also unsatisfactory, thereby challenging the most established explanations of these figures in ethnic literatures. For example, Kathleen Brogan explains the ghost figure as a pan-ethnic phenomenon that refers to a lost ethnic past that needs to be refigured for a livable future (Brogan 12). Seth haunts various characters with very different ethnic backgrounds. So, following Brogan's reading, Seth would function as a general reference to the characters' various ethnic backgrounds. In this sense, Brogan's and the reviewers' seemingly self-explanatory link of fictional ghosts to a certain exotic, ethnic background becomes just one out of many possible readings for this ghost figure.

I argue that Seth, then, defies a straightforward narrative within the classical conception of a ghost as referring to concepts such as a never ending past, guilt, or as a clear-cut reference to a certain group's memory. Instead, this ghost figure takes up all of these references, yet adds another, new dimension: he highlights the unruly, unmanageable aspect that the ghost figure in itself inherently demands. As neither absence nor presence, this ghost remains, up to a point, unreadable. Maybe this is the main reason why Seth's central position in the novel tends to be ignored. What is Seth's ghost, then, all about, instead?

Seth's ghost is introduced in the first few pages, when Leah is the first to be taken to the orphanage. When Leah is sad, lonely, and scared, Seth greets her at the bridge that leads to the orphanage and begins to console her. Although he sometimes causes trouble for Leah – because he advises her to use white ginger to protect herself, for which Leah is punished by the nuns – she experiences him as a loving protector, telling her not to be afraid for he is by her side (Yamanaka 19). In the beginning, Seth appears as a presence who haunts Leah, but as the reader meets him via her perception, he is not placeable. The reader learns his sad story only later on, when Aki and Anah also begin to see him. Leah introduces him in this way as a sad, loveable child. The reader feels pity and awe for this sad boy who still cares for and consoles other children.

This image is soon to be changed. At the central turning point of the novel, Anah's final escape from the orphanage, Seth's curse is uttered. Returning to the source of confusion for most reviewers, the centrality of this curse for the whole narrative cannot be overstated. It is articulated in the moment in which Anah leaves the orphanage, about to begin her new life as the wife of Ezroh and as part of his family. With his curse, Seth is also the only one of the ghosts in the novel who can follow Anah to her new life, while the others helplessly stay behind at the orphanage, crying. In that sense, Seth is the most powerful of them. His curse haunts Anah and her new family until it is finally released by Anah's first-born daughter, Hosana. The curse very clearly links Seth's frustration and his ill-will against Anah as the one returning to the place to which he should have returned himself:

"Curse your life for leaving me. Your home is here, turn around, come back. Curse my love for you. How I loved you those many years, passing myself from sister to dying sister. […] Curse the ground you walk on. […] Curse the food you cook. […] Die. Die soon. Curse your womb. […] Curse what issues forth. […] Curse the ones you love. […] There is no light here, dark the tunnel through which we come. […] I came to you whenever you called, through the dark tunnel, so cold, so scared, I came. […] Why have you left me here? It is me. Seth. It is cold here, Anah. I want to go home, too." (Yamanaka 212–213)

In this instance, Seth very openly reveals his feelings toward Anah. Consoling patiently each of the dying sisters until the end, he waited for his favorite of them all, Anah. But when she did not die and did not join him, his jealousy turned his love into hatred. In a way, the sad and lonely boy ghost still raises pity in the reader as his curse is so deeply connected to his own hurt feelings; yet, at the same time, his curse is also troubling this first reader reaction: the ghost suddenly gains powers that no longer fit the image of a suffering, lost boy.

As Seth's curse haunts Anah in her new life, his presence becomes more and more that of an evil ghost. A repetition of his curse induces each child birth – often way too early or too late.

"The morning appeared through the dark.
'Anah,' a voice rasped behind her. 'Anah.' She turned her head slowly to the corner of the room, a small figure standing there, weeping.
Seth?
He stared straight at her:
'Curse you, whore.'
Anah screamed and her water broke." (Yamanaka 233)

In this first example, Seth remains rather passive, staying in the corner of the room, repeating his curse without touching her, reduced to his earlier presence as a sad boy. And yet, already in these birth-inducing scenes, Seth seems to have some ominous power over Anah's body, her water seems to break when he gives the signal. Suddenly, in the next birth scene, his emotions turn into revengeful hatred.

"Anah lifted herself again, Ezroh supporting her back, the baby's head finally crowning. Anah pushed and pushed in a kind of stunning delirium she had known only in childbirth, screaming at the faces of unseen wraiths and demons.
Seth.
He stood there between her legs, pressing the baby's head inward. [...]
'C'mon, Anah, you can do it,' Ezroh said, Seth smiling right at her." (Yamanaka 260)

In this scene, Seth becomes not only the inducer of the birth, but rather hinders it by pushing the baby back into Anah's body. This, finally, does not happen simply due to his will or curse. He becomes an active force, having the ability to touch the baby in order to hurt Anah. Furthermore, he is no longer depicted as crying; instead, he smiles at Anah, as if in triumph. Although Anah finally wins this fight with the help of others, Seth holds an extremely powerful position in relation to Anah's body. While Seth himself is depicted in terms of a small figure in a corner, reminding the reader of his height and age, remaining a small boy throughout Anah's growing up, his increasing supernatural powers and his sadistic tendencies stand in stark contrast to any favorable picture a reader might have of this ghost figure.

In contrast to Seth's, Aki's ghost remains bound to a standard narrative. While the reader's feelings toward Aki and her ghost also change repeatedly, as we will see, her presence is more clearly connected to Anah herself as well as to a general postcolonial haunting. With Seth's ghost, this change appears more complete, even though they all finally depart peacefully at the novel's ending. Both ghosts represent a form of evil spirits whose anger is misdirected at the flawless Anah. Both appear as references to Anah's survivor's guilt. Although both defy categorization along the lines of psychoanalytical/allegorical or spiritual interpretations because they play with the continuities and connections between both readings, Seth's ghost highlights this more prominently. His disconnected existence – in terms of the general postcolonial setting and Anah's personal bad conscience – creates a certain distance to a standard postcolonial resistance narrative. As such, they both, but Seth especially, become unruly, unreadable presences that haunt Yamanaka's novel.

Taking a closer look at the figure of Seth, one perceives a conglomeration of various aspects combined, all of which are references to non-human or inhuman characteristics.[6] His name refers to a mythological figure of old Egypt. Seth is a

6 I take the term 'inhuman' from Juliana Chang's *Inhuman Citizenship*, as a reference to that which is neither human nor non-human. Like the term 'undead' – which refers to something being neither dead nor alive, but rather something that is a living dead –,

highly ambiguous figure also known as the god of confusion, disturbing the order between life and death (te Velde 27; 95). Seth is the anti-social god, "cut off from the community of gods" (31–32); he is also seen as the foreign god. Moreover, the name Seth is that of Adam and Eve's third child, the forefather of all humans. Throughout the novel, religion and ghosts constantly engage, sometimes opposing each other. In an interesting twist on the currently fashionable vampire story, Seth leaves behind fresh garlic everywhere. With its general indebtedness to fantasy, the novel takes on currently well-selling popular literature aspects, reminding the reader of examples such as *Harry Potter* or the *Twilight* series.

Moreover, as I have pointed out above already, the ghost theme has been a very famous one in Asian American literature ever since Maxine Hong Kingston. Thus, Yamanaka combines various sources, genres, and probably marketing aspects in this novel and especially in this one character. Keeping these references in mind as links to a conglomerate of associations is important for this chapter, for these are all part of what the postcolonial melodramatic mode intends: to allow for different associations, to break free from conclusive conceptions and to engage in spontaneous and emotional responses. In sum, these cultural and intertextual references underline the most important function of Seth for the narrative and for the ghosts in general: despite – or rather because of – these various references they remain unreadable and unplaceable. But the ways in which the ghost figures refer to, engage with, and rewrite existing genre traditions helps to understand them as intertextual figures that reconnect to various stories and beliefs.

One very concrete intertextual reference is directly linked to the name of the ghost. 'Seth' is a reference to *the* classical contemporary ghost story, namely Toni Morrison's *Beloved* (1987). *Beloved* tells the story of Sethe, a runaway slave who kills her daughter to protect her from being taken back into slavery. This daughter reappears in the figure of Beloved, haunting the lives of her surviving family members. This is one, psychoanalytical reading of the figure – as a very personal ghost coming back for retribution. Another, however, views Beloved as a social figure in referencing all those "Sixty million and more," to

---

'inhuman' refers to those areas in-between, that threaten "the very foundations of human identity," being "the alien that permeates the human, and the human that finds itself alien" (Chang 14). Arguing that inhumanity is most central to racial constructions, Chang criticizes current attempts at re-humanizing racialized, colonized others because with such a move, one remains within the framework that poses humanity against non-humanity (12–13).

whom Morrison dedicated the book, referring to the dead of the Middle Passage. This ghost figure has often been read as black cultural memory and thus in line with Kathleen Brogan's claim.[7]

Not only this fictional novel but also Morrison's academic publications call for a politicized reading of the ghost figure Beloved.[8] In her seminal essay *Playing in the Dark*, Morrison focuses on the Africanist presence that haunts American literature at large. In the classical literature of white Americans, she states that what "became transparent were the self-evident ways that Americans choose to talk about themselves through and within a sometimes allegorical, sometimes metaphorical, but always choked representation of an Africanist presence" (Morrison, *Playing in the Dark* 17). This self-construction of an idea of 'America' built on the haunting presence of African Americans has been transfigured in her novel *Beloved* into an actual haunting character.

Yet, what makes *Beloved* – both the novel as a whole and the figure especially – so interesting for readers and critics, is the impossibility of arriving at a conclusive interpretation.[9] In my view, the best articles on Beloved as a ghostly figure make this inherent ambiguity their main point, stressing, for example, the fantastic aspects of the figure which prohibit both a realistic and a marvelous reading, or emphasizing the multiplicity of meanings of this figure in leaving the contradictions intact. Beloved is, thus, many things at once: a disruption and a healing, a personal and a public ghost.[10] She embodies the impossibility of narrating this story of suffering, but is also an indication of the necessity to engage with this (hi)story. In this sense, Beloved and Seth are rather

---

7 See, for example, Solomon, Barbara H. "Introduction." *Critical Essays on Toni Morrison's* Beloved. Ed. Barbara H. Solomon. New York: G. K. Hall & Co, 1998, 1–35.

8 Toni Morrison calls for what Carl Plasa terms a "fully politicised aesthetic" (Plasa 5). This combination of political intent and beautiful art is probably the most central aspect about Morrison's writings as both an author and a scholar. With reference to *Beloved* in particular, its publication was a "conscious act" in that it was supposed to be "a studied memorial to the great social wrong of the enslavement of Africans," to use Nellie Y McKay's words (McKay 3).

9 See, for example, Solomon "Introduction" 13.

10 See, for example, Krumholz, Linda, "The Ghosts of Slavery: Historical Recovery in Toni Morrison's *Beloved*," *African American Review* 26.3 (Autumn 1992): 395–408; or Cutter, Martha J. "The Story Must Go On And On: The Fantastic, Narration, and Intertextuality in Toni Morrison's *Beloved* and *Jazz*," *African American Review* 34.1 (Spring 2000): 61–75.

similar figures: both defy conclusive readings and instead, indicate various possibilities. As such, they challenge a moralizing and politicized approach that many critics wish to highlight. Without neglecting such a political or moral function, these ghost figures simply offer more than one-sided readings.

The character Seth in Yamanaka's *Behold the Many* establishes interesting reference points to this ghostly precursor in contemporary ethnic American literature. Not only is he a ghost figure that intrudes with a similar force and intensity in the novel, he also remains as unreadable as Beloved, haunting the reader after finishing the book. Both ghost figures address complicated social settings and emotionally charged situations that result from unbalanced social structures. Both, thus, highlight the intricate interconnections between the personal and the political. With the close connection of the names, Seth and Sethe, the intertextual trace indicates such a politicized reading of *Behold the Many*. And yet, although both novels certainly critique existing systems of hierarchical power relations, they do not offer simplified overly positive pictures of their respective ethnic communities. They rather address the uneasy relationships among African Americans in *Beloved*'s case and in the inter-ethnic communities so typical of Hawaii in *Behold the Many*.

With the interesting reversal of the ghost figure and the name – in Morrison's novel the ghost haunts the character with the name Sethe while in Yamanaka's novel the ghost itself is called Seth – the later novel creates a certain distance from the original. Although, yet again, a conclusive reading seems inappropriate, one effect of this reversal is a questioning of the significance of haunting and being haunted: does it really matter whether a ghost is the center of the narrative or its haunting of a certain character? Are these two things to be separated? Jacques Derrida reflects upon the idea of possession:

> "One must possess it [the ghost] without letting oneself be possessed by it, without being possessed of it [...]. But does not a specter consist, in forbidding or blurring this distinction? in [sic] consisting in this very undiscernability? Is not to possess a specter to be possessed by it, possessed period? To capture it, is that not to be captivated by it?" (Derrida, *Specters of Marx* 132)

He ultimately demands recognition of the interlinking of the one who possesses the ghost and is possessed by it. For the readers of ghost stories this implies that they will begin to own the ghost, but only when they become haunted by it themselves.

In summarizing her various readings of Beloved, Linda Krumholz also argues that with the many possible references, the ghost "is also everyone's ghost" (Krumholz 400). And in this idea, Krumholz also includes the readers of the novel: "Beloved is the reader's ghost, forcing us to face the historical past as a living and vindictive presence. Thus Beloved comes to represent the repressed memories of slavery, both for the characters and for the readers" (400). Morrison herself gives a similar explanation for her use of such a haunting presence in her novel, stating that one of the purposes of including Beloved "is to keep the reader preoccupied with the nature of the incredible spirit world while being supplied a controlled diet of the incredible political world" (Morrison, *Unspeakable Things Unspoken* 161). Such an emphasis of reader reactions also shapes *Behold the Many* in its postcolonial melodramatic mode, albeit without delivering a clear-cut political or moral message.

Both *Beloved* and *Behold the Many* employ Gothic aspects to narrate their stories. Placing the ghost figures in this framework helps to conceive of these figures as part of various genre traditions in their intertextual reference points. Teresa Goddu argues that "the American gothic is haunted by race" (Goddu 7). Focusing on "specific sites of historical haunting, most notably slavery" (10), Goddu claims that American Gothic literature deals critically with America's conception of itself as a pure and equal society. Drawing on Kristeva's concept of abjection, Goddu explains how "the gothic serves as the ghost that both helps to run the machine of national identity and disrupts it" (10). The Gothic, in her view, exposes the contradictions underlying American national identity even as they are being repressed, telling of the historical horrors that formed the nation as closely tied to racial issues, yet keeping them at a safe distance (10). Basing her argument very much on both Toni Morrison's critical works (*Playing in the Dark* and "Unspeakable Things Unspoken") and her novel *Beloved*, Goddu argues that the United States is haunted by its racial history and that the Gothic mode offers a vehicle for starting an engagement with this repressed part of America's construction as a nation (159). With her strong emphasis on Toni Morrison's work, Goddu also engages a certain politicized discourse within the field, criticizing the still ongoing neglect of this racial history. The close connection between *Beloved* and *Behold the Many* already mentioned supports such a politicized reading of the ghosts in Yamanaka's novel. Following such a conception of American Gothic, the ghosts stage those aspects that the idea(l) of America needs to suppress. Exposing America's colonial engagements on the islands and destroying the picture of Hawaii as a perfect ethnic paradise, the novel in general and the ghost figures in particular, address those aspects that are hurtful to an American self-conception as a free, democratic nation.

Hogle gives specters a specific function because the Gothic mode "locates and focuses our longings and fears as though they are *and are not* ours, allowing them to be visible as part of our present, fearfully threatening us and yet making them either a relic of the decaying past or perhaps the avatar of a mechanistic or racially other future. […] The Gothic has lasted as it has because its symbolic mechanisms, particularly its haunting and frightening specters have permitted us to cast many anomalies in our modern conditions, even as these change, over onto antiquated or at least haunted spaces and highly anomalous creatures. This way our contradictions can be confronted by, yet removed from us into, the seemingly unreal, the alien, the ancient, and the grotesque." (Hogle, "Introduction" 6)

For Julia Kristeva, inspired by Jacques Lacan's re-readings of Freud, ghost figures are products of what she calls abjection. In the process of abjection, a person throws off any aspects that appear as contradictory to his or her self-construction (7). According to Hogle, the Gothic symbolizes this process of abjection and does so especially in its cross-generic mode. Classified as inherently in-between – high and low, serious and popular – the Gothic mode represents this blurring of levels, while it also questions opposed conditions such as life/death, natural/supernatural, unconscious/conscious. Turning these crossings into abjections, the Gothic creates deviant others that both "attract and terrify" (9). Ghosts such as Seth's embody this process of abjection: it stages the in-between spaces between those seemingly exclusionary opposition pairs.

As such, the Gothic mode engages with the abjected aspects of an individual or a society. These abjections are fundamental constituents of whatever they used to be part of and from which they are now being excluded. Thus, the greatest horror in the Gothic comes from the culturally constructed oppositions that are being exposed to be haunted by the negation of their inherent connection to each other. Hogle argues that the

"reason that Gothic others or spaces can abject myriad cultural and psychological contradictions, and thereby confront us with those anomalies in disguise, is because those spectral characters, images, and settings harbor the hidden reality that oppositions of all kinds cannot maintain their separations, that each 'lesser term' is contained in its counterpart and that difference really arises by standing against *and* relating to interdependency." (11)

Such psychoanalytic readings of Gothic novels allegorize the ghosts and turn them into figures of subjectivity. They can be productively applied to *Behold the Many* and to Seth in that these figures highlight the personal and cultural conflicts between the sisters and the orphanage, between the colonial missionary project and the lingering indigenous and Asian ghost beliefs in early twentieth century Hawaii. The ghosts address and simultaneously disguise these conflicts. But they also – Seth in particular – stage the inconclusiveness of such readings.

Seth's unreadability establishes a productive link to Jacques Derrida's conception of hauntology. According to Colin Davis, Jacques Derrida's specters are deconstructive figures *par excellence*, "hovering between life and death, presence and absence, and making established certainties vacillate" (Davis, *Haunted Subjects* 11). With his concept of hauntology, Derrida demands a radical critique of our conceptions of time and being. Arguing that the ghost as revenant always refers to another time and another place, he sees it as constantly showing its own deferral. Thus, a ghost gives reasons "to doubt this reassuring order of presents" (39) because "one has to realize that the ghost is there […] *before its first apparition*: […] *Two times at the same time*, originary iterability, irreducible virtuality of this space and this time" (163). With reference to the ghost figure Seth, this implies the necessity to read his appearances as closely related to a certain time and history – as well as to a certain space.

This link to very concrete historical sites is often taken up in postcolonial writings. As Alison Rudd argues in *Postcolonial Gothic Fictions* (2010), postcolonial writers

> "utilize a range of narrative strategies in order to express the experience of postcolonial conditions, to articulate the unspeakable history of colonialism and to uncover the obfuscation, silences and omissions inscribed by postcolonial discourses. The Gothic as a mode of writing can provide one such strategy, furnishing these writers with a means, in narrative and idiom, to expose and subvert past and continuing regimes of power and exploitation, and to reinscribe histories that have been both violent and repressed." (Rudd 1–2)

While a focus on the resistant potential[11] of the Gothic is a welcome correction, an over-emphasis of this aspect also locks postcolonial Gothic in a resistance paradigm.

11 Jennifer Lawn suggests that Gothic offers Postcolonial Studies a way to address achronological temporality, and vice versa, that Postcolonial Studies enriches Gothic in its demand to consider local aspects in terms of geography, history, or culture (Lawn 146). Early assessments of a postcolonial Gothic – like Patrick Brantlinger's *Rule of Darkness* (1988) or Gayatri Spivak's essay "Three Women's Text and the Critique of Imperialism" (1985) – emphasize the ongoing support of colonialist agendas even though they detect a questioning of Imperialism in postcolonial Gothic

Andrew Hock Soon Ng has dedicated a book to the study of postcolonial and Asian American Gothic.[12] Ng foregrounds the ambivalent status of the Gothic mode in a postcolonial or Asian American setting. He states that the Gothic in general defies binary oppositions and that its postcolonial variations further extend this aspect (Ng, *Interrogating Interstices* 31). In a postcolonial setting, the Gothic mode enables "to deconstruct the grand-narrative within which it is embedded" (30). However, as it is embedded in such grand-narratives, it simultaneously supports and questions these, so that the Gothic has come to be seen as critiquing an Imperialist agenda, yet also participating in its logic by constructing a framework in which the criticism is disguised as a spectralized figure. And it is this paradoxical move of the Gothic that makes it transgressive: "not in the sense of 'challenging' or 'resisting' the establishment, but that of

---

texts. Shifting the focus towards resistant readings, Judie Newman rather perceives a "duplicity of Gothic – its propensity for crossing boundaries, violating taboos, transgressing limits, together with its sense of blockage, privation and prohibition against utterance – makes it the perfect means to dramatise the horrors of the [(post)colonial] relationship" (Newman 98).

12 Treating the Gothic as a mode of writing, not a genre that is solely indebted to a Western literary tradition – although the Gothic delineates from this very tradition, Ng immediately refutes possible critique of his work as imposing a Western concept on literary productions from other cultures (Ng *Interrogating Interstices* 25–26). He argues that Asian traditions also use features that would be grouped under the label Gothic, simply without calling them by this name. Charles Inouye makes a similar claim in his study of Japanese Gothic, when he states that Japanese culture and writing is inherently Gothic as long as one uses the term 'Gothic' as not only grounded in its modern reaction to the Enlightenment. Inouye establishes the term 'pangothic' in order to address such a wider social significance of the mode (Inouye 443). This claim is also supported by Katarzyna Ancuta, who distinguishes three kinds of supernatural Asian Gothic: the first being inspired by classic Asian folklore, the second mainly following English models, and the third one being the modern Asian ghost stories written in English that capitalize on the exotic (Ancuta 431–435). Such a staging of the exotic points in the direction of Asian American re-writings and especially the interpretation of these works only as references to an exotic tradition. Even though these sources offer a potential link to the Asian traditions that certainly also inform Asian American Gothic literature, my readings focus instead on the significant re-writings and combinations of American and postcolonial traditions that Yamanaka's novel offers.

stretching the boundaries of the establishment to its limits, and there, fissuring with its own limitations" (19).

Zooming in on Asian American Gothic, Ng sees a close connection between Asian American literature and the Gothic mode because both generally question a white American identity and history that neglects what seems troublesome and that shies away from otherness (36). In this construction, attention needs to be paid to the material and historical dimension as well as the discursive and fictionalized dimension. In Ng's words, "aesthetics and history must be concurrently heeded; art must meet life" (37). Asian American literature lends itself to a Gothic reading due to its conception as being written against the dominant discourse and with its engagement with problems of assimilation, cultural haunting, and hyphenated identities (38–39).

With his conception of the Gothic as a highly ambivalent mode, Ng hopes for an opening up of criticism in Asian American Studies in that the Gothic aesthetics will lead to new critical insights that offer alternatives to the postcolonial-materialist tradition of the field (11). This wish is in line with Viet Nguyen's call for greater methodological flexibility in Asian American criticism, as I outline in the introduction to *The Ghosts Within*. Both demand an engagement that diverges from resistance/assimilation narratives. Linking this controversy back to Ng's approach to the Gothic emphasizes the importance of 'fresh' readings that allow for the ambiguities to emerge, that address the concurrent staging yet disguising of the most troublesome aspects that the strange figures of the Gothic embody. Therefore, my reading of the ghosts is indebted to such ambiguity and discursive openness in order to broaden long-established readings of American Gothic as *only* criticizing a white American construction of history through the lens of racialized ghost figures such as Beloved's or Seth's.

Ghost figures such as Seth's stage Gothic's inherent interpenetration of opposed conditions – life/death, natural/supernatural, modern/ancient, or allegorical/spiritual –, which is the reason for their unruly place within post-colonial Asian American literature. As Seth's paradoxical status in-between defies moral or political categorization, he becomes an unreadable presence for Asian American criticism. His central place within *Behold the Many*'s colonial setting, yet his ultimate disconnection from this overarching narrative, enhance his engaged but distanced function: he stages the paradoxical interconnections between seemingly opposed interpretations that his various reference points offer.

According to Hogle, Gothic fictions, "have been extraordinarily suited both to helping us deal with a modern world dissolving more and more into 'spectralizations' everywhere *and* to allowing us a safely-fearful posture that half-avoids and half-faces the multiple interconnections at the base of our cultural and mental lives" (Hogle, "The Gothic at our Turn" 158). As Stephen Bruhm states about contemporary Gothic[13]: "We seem to want these fictions from the inside out; we crave them not for their distance but for their immediacy, for they make our hearts race, our blood pressure rise, our breathing become shallow and quick, and our stomachs roll" (Bruhm 272–273). And we need these sensations so much

> "because the twentieth century has so forcefully taken away from us that which we once thought constituted us – a coherent psyche, a social order to which we can pledge allegiance in good faith, a sense of justice in the universe – and that wrenching withdrawal, that traumatic experience, is vividly dramatized in the Gothic." (272–73)

I argue that such emphasis on the immediacy of emotions also carries *Behold the Many* as its stages its melodramatic narrative. *Behold the Many*'s roller coaster of emotions – the ways in which Seth and Aki's ghosts make our breathing become shallow and our hearts ache –, however, ultimately neglects a sense of justice in the universe. It rather invites us to re-*feel* binaries such as good/bad or colonizer/colonized in every new scene or setting it provides. The polarized moral universe of the melodrama is, thus, employed but constantly undermined by the ghost figures that haunt the novel.

BEHOLD THE MANY AS POSTCOLONIAL MELODRAMA

In his influential study *The Melodramatic Imagination* (1976), Peter Brooks reads melodrama as a mode of "excess," that "at heart represents the theatrical impulse itself: the impulse toward dramatization, heightening, expression, acting out" (Brooks xi; ix). Furthermore, the melodramatic mode is associated in general with strong pronunciation of emotions, moral polarization of good and

---

13 Other scholars have also linked contemporary Gothic to our postmodern condition, as addressing a new kind of disorder that is, after all, comparable to the one after the Enlightenment and during the early twentieth century. See, for example, Lloyd Smith, Allan, "Postmodernism/Gothicism." *Modern Gothic: A Reader*, Eds. Victor Sage and Allan Lloyd Smith. Manchester and New York: Manchester University Press, 1996, 6–19; or Beville, Maria, *Gothic-Postmodernism: Voicing the Terrors of Postmodernity*, Amsterdam and New York: Rodopi, 2009.

bad, inflated expression and breathtaking final scenes in which the good wins over the bad (11–12). Among the most stylized and emotionally charged scenes in *Behold the Many* are those that revolve around the unconditional love between Ezroh and Anah. Right from the start, with these two, words are unnecessary. Ezroh understands intuitively who is hurting Anah. He simply knows how he can save her life. This strong emotional connection remains throughout the novel and is staged in many scenes.

"He did not let go of her hand, drawing it to his heart.
'I have nobody, too,' she said at last. 'No mother, no father, no sisters, no brothers.'
'We are alike, you and I,' he said, holding Anah's face, her gaze, her breath in the palms of his hands." (Yamanaka 141)

Another exemplary scene staging their unconditional love is their meeting after a very long absence from each other. Anah visits Ezroh's house because a family member is sick and they need her help. While she is staying there to help, the two of them meet secretly at night. And although they long for each other, they hold back their desires until they are properly married. Instead, they cherish each other's bodies and company.

"He slid his hands into her torn nightdress, his fingers over her breasts and then across her back, drawing her near: Anah moved her hands under his shirt and they held each other for what seemed an infinitesimal forever because forever would never be enough.
My Ezroh.
Warm skin, his hand on her head smoothing back her hair, petting her, she was his treasured one. They wiped the happy tears from each other's eyes.
[…]
Is it really you, my Anah?
He pulled Anah's hands to his face, wet with tears, and sobbed into her open palms.
[…] 'I want to stay with you,' he said to Anah." (Yamanaka 189)

These two scenes reflect the way that the melodramatic narration carries the mood. Connecting the rise of melodrama to the emergence of the modern novel and its effort to signify, Brooks argues that it serves "as a certain fictional system for making sense of experience, as a semantic field of force" (xiii). As such, melodrama is an essential drama: it is bound to the "desire to express all" and "to dramatize through the heightened and polarized words and gestures the whole lesson" of its moral absolutes (4–5). In this system, gestures become typically grand and metaphorical, the whole rhetoric excessive in its stereotypical "breathless pitch" (3). All of the typical features of melodrama – polarization, emotionality, intense moral claims, and artificial happy endings in which the good wins over the bad – are inherent to the logic of the genre. Such excessive posture is necessary because "every gesture [...] is charged with the conflict between light and darkness, salvation and damnation" (5). These gestures, then, provide the possibility to express and approach what could otherwise not be said (10–11).

Ezroh and Anah's love scenes follow such an excessive melodramatic mode. Not only is the melodramatic setting in both instances clearly given – the lost boy who finds his soul-mate; and the meeting of the lovers in-between their long periods of loneliness –, the stereotypical weeping into open palms then finally releases all emotions. But the general tone indicates a melodramatic mode as well: short repetitive sentences, emotional interjections, loss of words to express this all-encompassing love. The tableau-like scenes express pure emotions: this unconditional, unselfish, and over-boarding love is pure, chaste, immaculate, and incorruptable. It is a love that can save lives and that prevails, forever. Working with this mode of excess, highlighting some of the characters, such as Ezroh, as purely good and savior-like, Yamanaka takes up the classical melodramatic mode. Returning to the reviews and the scene depicting Seth's loving care at the very beginning of this chapter, this aspect, then, becomes highly pronounced. As Gaines puts it in his review, "Ezroh is the vehicle of Anah's salvation; […] he who offers unconditional love" (Gaines np) with Anah's "heart the repository of [everyone's] hopes" (np). Looking at the larger picture, other reviewers praise Yamanaka's creation of "a heartbreaking portrait of these ghost children" (Kirkus Review, *Review* np).

Thus, these scenes also follow the definition of melodrama that Linda Williams offers: "If emotional and moral registers are sounded, if a work invites us to feel sympathy for the virtues of beset victims, if the narrative trajectory is ultimately concerned with a retrieval and staging of virtue through adversary and suffering, then the operative mode is melodrama" (Williams 15). Both Ezroh and Anah have suffered severely – losing their siblings, facing problematic family conditions, lacking support for their love. As such, both are stylized as victims that invite the reader's sympathy. Through their virtuous behavior, they have demonstrated their moral incorruptibility even under the most severe victimization and pain, so that – in the moral universe of the melodrama – they deserve each other's unconditional love and a happy ending.

In *Playing the Race Card* (2001), Linda Williams focuses on the ways in which this sympathy for the virtue of some and antipathy against the villainy of others has been used as a modernizing force: while these opposed moral poles remain unchallenged in melodrama, the objects of this sympathy have changed (16). She argues that melodrama is not an aberration or simply an excess, but "the fundamental mode by which American mass culture has 'talked to itself'[14] about the enduring moral dilemma of race" (xiv). Playing the 'race card' on both sides, melodrama uses victimization as a means for gaining moral power.[15] As

> "[n]either an inherently racist nor an antiracist form, melodrama has effectively been utilized to both ends. Its key, however, is not simplistic, 'black' and 'white' moral antinomies, but what stands behind them: the quest to forge a viscerally felt moral legibility in the midst of moral confusion and disarray. Melodrama is organized around the paradoxical quest for a full articulation of truth and virtue at precisely those junctures where truth and virtue are most vexed." (300)

In other words, the key feature of the racial melodrama is sympathy for a suffering person; and this can be used in ever-changing contexts and applied to different suffering persons and thus with the intention of serving highly different social concerns (16). In order to illustrate this point, Williams focuses in her study on two main suffering characters: the victimized black male and the threatened white female. As a quest for moral legibility with regard to issues that appear most complicated and morally charged, melodrama has been and still is the most applicable mode to stage racial conflicts. According to Williams, even today melodrama meets

---

14 In *Melodrama and the Myth of America*, Jeffrey Mason argues that America performs itself in these dramatizations, enacting a cultural self-definition (1–2). Mason sees in the form of melodrama a central myth-making apparatus of what the shared idea of America is supposed to be (16). The certain key principles of the American tradition that serve as a basis for the social organization of American life, such as freedom and autonomy, are staged in melodramas. Ultimately creating an ideal of the American, as obediently following the American ideals, melodramas are constructed to explain the exclusion of everything that remains outside of this idea of America, excluding all others, representing them as threats to the ideal of America (191–94).

15 Williams emphasizes the "paradoxical location of strength in weakness – the process by which suffering subjects take what Nietzsche calls ressentiment, a moralizing revenge upon the powerful achieved through a triumph of the weak in their very weakness." She refers to what Wendy Brown calls "the overvaluation of the 'wound' in the political rhetoric of liberal identity politics" and Lauren Berlant's investigations of "the process by which pain and suffering confers moral power on 'wounded' subjects" (Williams 43).

"the entertainment needs of a modern, rationalist, democratic,[16] capitalist, industrial, and now post-industrial society seeking moral legibility under new conditions of moral ambiguity. In other words, the ongoing loss of moral certainty has been compensated for by increasingly sensational, commodified productions of pathos and action." (23)

Aki's death scene – another stereotypical feature within the melodramatic mode – can, at first glance, be read as staging such a moral empowerment of a racial victim. When she dies at the orphanage in the care of the missionaries from a disease that is typically associated with missionary encounters, Aki invites the reader's sympathy in her powerlessness against the larger systems that surround her.

"Anah pulled her [Aki] down from the sink. The door creaked open. She turned, her breath locked inside her chest. Leah's smoky white face peered in. She smiled at Anah, a cluster of rotten mangoes in the scoop of her dirty yellow dress.
Seth stood beside her, kind eyes, lonely eyes. The moment, a second a glance, then gone.
Anah felt the blood drain from her face, the skin of her forehead and cheeks pulling back into her skull. Her body weightless, stunned, a wave of nausea rising up to her gasping mouth.
Aki stepped toward their dissipating shapes. 'Take me with you,' she spoke to the darkness of the kitchen doorway. […] 'Maybe we can all go home.' Aki collapsed on the floor.
[…] Sister Mary Deborah moved quickly to tuck Aki into bed. […]
The quiet of the lamplight, the quiet of the night, Aki bolted upright in her bed, her eyes scanning the room. She did not panic, as her face filled with a kind of joyful knowing.
'Time is now,' she said. […] 'Time?' Anah asked Aki. […] She smiled and leaned toward Anah. 'Time is now, Anah.' She gazed in each corner of the second floor, her mouth slack open in fatigue and wonder. 'Time to go home.'" (Yamanaka 84–85)

---

16 Focusing on the beginnings of melodrama in America, Daniel Gerould argues that "melodrama became a direct expression of American society and national character" because it "has shaped the American popular imagination, molding our perceptions of self and country" (7). In its democratic, non-elite form, with the focus on technological skill and its general Weltanschauung, it relates to the American founding principles – such as the American Dream with its emphasis on equality, the power of innocence, and the idea of self-reliance – and preaches American ideologies (8–9). This idealization of America "offered audiences a perception of self that corresponded to powerful longings and imaginings about country and national character" (28).

Giving herself over to the ghost-world, Aki believes that they will show her the way home. Death becomes, then, not a fearful event, but something to look forward to because it finally fulfills Aki's wish to return home. She is not dying in fear but peacefully, 'with a joyful knowing.' This dramatized scene establishes clearly the opposites of light and darkness. Accepting one's death as a passing into eternal light and the high emotionality that is being dramatized, is certainly very suitable to the melodramatic mode. Again, the narrative implies the expected melodramatic reward for this suffering victim. Finally, after her physical and psychological trials during her time at the orphanage, Aki is relieved of all her burdens and allowed to go 'home.' Even though Aki's death is tragic and unfair, especially as it references missionary guilt, the reader is consoled by her peaceful passing.

Frank Kelleter and Ruth Mayer argue that melodrama "tends to interiorize, personalize, and excessively 'stylize' its subject matter" so much so that it is no longer threatening any existing social order. Indeed, "the specific achievement of literary and filmic melodrama might well be to symbolically enact conflicts and problems that seem irresolvable at the time of enactment, thus not so much mapping a way out of cultural predicament than rather staging it in the manner of a tableau" (Kelleter and Mayer 13). Aki's death scene also follows this logic: it enacts a culturally and politically charged moment at the turn of the century in Hawaii. But neither in this scene nor as a whole does the novel offer any solutions to these ideological and racial conflicts and focuses instead on the ghost figures. And yet, in the staging, the clash between differing cultural orders in this colonial setting becomes highly pronounced and explicit. Aki's death shifts this theme onto a very personalized and stylized terrain. The reader is preoccupied with Aki's and Anah's immediate situation and then consoled by the peaceful resolution that the scene offers.

However, the reader's sad but comforted state is soon to be challenged as Aki's death scene continues somewhat unexpectedly. With the sentence that it is time to go home, Aki has not died yet, although a reader can certainly believe so in a first reading. As if to foreshadow what is to come, the next, very short chapter is a conversation between the girl's mother and the ghost of their father. Even as a ghost, Dai remains a threat to his children; calling for his wife, "Sumi-Chan. Where are you, my beloved whore? I am still here looking for your children, the dead ones you made with your useless body," asking her to "[c]ome closer and spread your legs so I can smell you" (Yamanaka 86). Threatening to continue as he has done during their lifetimes, Dai tells the girls' mother that Leah's ghost "wants me to touch her. And I will. The way I touch you at night, put my hand over your mouth, put my weight on your struggling body, then put my long flesh deep inside you until you bleed" (Yamanaka 87).

With this three-page interlude, the tone has completely changed. The idea of a peaceful death and resurrection are suddenly replaced by the permanent threat of a ghost world in which the girls will continue to be harmed. Although a reader might think Aki is already dead, her actual death scene is influenced by this changed mood.

"Aki was feverish, her body shaking with chills, her neck red and swollen. And every breath she managed to pull into her body entered as if she were pulling air on a thick sennit rope, pulling it down her small throat. She coughed up ribbons of heavy blood. There were tears in her eyes, her mouth open and gasping.
'Open your throat, Aki. Don't die.'
'Anah.' She coughed, flecks of blood spotting her face. 'He *is* coming.'
'Yes, Charles coming.' Anah told her.
'Liar,' she said, wincing with her next breath. Then she opened her eyes and stared at the ceiling just as Leah had done and took in a labored breath. […] 'Dai, no!' she cried.
[…]
Aki's body stiffened. 'Go, go 'way, Dai,' she said, her words extinguishing the candle on the bed stand. She took in a final breath, held it, then exhaled one last time. A single tear fell from her eye. Anah took her limp hand to her lips and kissed her sister's fingers. […] Anah listened for the holy sister's footsteps, then quickly raised a small paring knife to cut a strand of Aki's hair. But Aki returned to struggle one last time against the threat of knife and the coming of death. She scratched at the air and then at Anah's face.
'Mentirosa,' she hissed at Anah in their father's Portuguese.
And then she left, calling Anah with her last word:
Liar.
Her mouth was open, her eyes horrified and stunned." (Yamanaka 91)

This scene is overshadowed by the danger that Dai's ghost implies. Gone is the idea of a peaceful, quiet death; instead, it is replaced by horror and fear. Aki's death no longer indicates a passing from darkness to light, but rather a passing into an eternal greyness, an in-between ghostly state in which she is permanently threatened by her father's ghost. Her 'joyful knowing' is replaced by labored breathing, bloody coughing, and tears. Aki's love for her older sister is darkened by her anger and frustration because Anah could not keep her promise of finally taking the sisters home.

Illustrating the sudden change of tone that dominates the whole novel, Aki's death scenes are indicative of its specific postcolonial melodramatic narrative mode. According to Brooks, melodrama works with

> "the sense of fundamental bipolar contrast and clash. The world according to melodrama is built on an irreducible manichaeism, the conflict of good and evil as opposites not subject to compromise. Melodramatic dilemmas and choices are constructed on the either/or in its extreme form as the all-or-nothing. Polarization is both horizontal and vertical: […] The middle ground and the middle condition are excluded." (Brooks 36)

Behold the Many also constructs polarized, fundamental conceptions of good and evil, as, for example, in the love story between Anah and Ezroh, in the character Dai or the final calling home of all ghosts by Hosana. And in each melodramatic setting, the novel offers unquestionable identification of good and bad, light and darkness. But – just as Brooks notices in his readings of Henry James – the ascriptions of good and bad constantly undergo changes and challenges, presenting the reader with a "melodrama of ethical choice" (157). While some characters in *Behold the Many* follow a classical binary conception of the melodramatic universe, the two most central ghost figures Aki and Seth challenge such clear-cut distinctions. *Behold the Many*, thus, engages in a melodramatic mode, but it diverts from the original in the ongoing changes that dictate the reader's surges of emotion. As a result, the emotional reaction of the reader is constantly re-framed, she is being pushed into new directions, forced to re-evaluate earlier feelings and ideas. This emotional re-positioning is the main difference that the novel employs in its postcolonial rewriting of the melodramatic mode.

Sheetal Majithia argues that due to changed conditions, postcolonial melodramas demand a rethinking of melodrama's uses and value (Majithia 1). She emphasizes what she terms postcolonial melodrama's "affective reason" as a "questioning through feeling" (19). She sees postcolonial melodrama's paradoxical potential in its ability to make its audience feel a certain history – in ways that contradict official versions of this history (3). The

> "focus on affect and temporality, expressed as interruption and simultaneity, reframes melodrama's failures as potentially critical of linear, progressive time and productive of a secular understanding that opposes conventionally championed identitarian politics. Through affective reason, which often generates counter-intuitive and unexpected relations between individuals or communities that do not need a reason to affiliate" (4)

postcolonial melodrama suggests an "ethics of relationality" and an "ethics of openness" (4). It is also driven by a shifting and changing of community (14). Majithia sees its potential for resistance in the possibility for each subject to employ various sites and points of view in order to question a narrative of progressive, linear time and a unified subjectivity or history (16). Reading *Behold the Many* as such a postcolonial melodrama helps to emphasize its focus on emotional reader reactions, especially how it drives readers to *feel* memories of a history in new and surprising ways. Yet, where Majithia sees primarily a resistant potential, *Behold the Many* rather stages these multiple reference points and subject positions as intricately intertwined and connected: while it implies resistant potential, it also simultaneously implies accommodation and interaction.[17]

Such instability and uncertainty dominates *Behold the Many*. The constant shifts in how the reader feels toward a certain character makes this instability graspable on a bodily, immediate level. The changing responses to Aki's character illustrate the reader's emotional rollercoaster. The three sisters spend the first year together in the orphanage, hoping against hope that on Visitation Sundays – once a month – their family would visit them. Aki is the troublemaker from the start. She refuses to partake in Sunday Mass rituals, refusing to eat the Communion wafer or the wine, and screaming "'Mass is ended!' […] before the priest" (Yamanaka 57). Anah tries to console her sad and disappointed sisters. When she herself almost breaks down under this emotional duress – for they are forced to stay outside and watch the other childrens' happy reunion with their families –, Aki steps in to console little Leah, who is at this point already very sick.

"Aki comforted Leah with the slow stroke of her hand over her sister's hair. 'Still early,' Aki whispered to Leah. And then she spoke in Japanese. 'I think our mother is making some of her special tonic for you so you can get better. You are her akachan, remember? It takes a long time to make that tonic, right, Anah?'

'It is rude of you to speak a foreign tongue in front of me, Aki,' the sister began.

---

17 In a similar vein, Lindsey Green-Simms analyzes West African video-film as 'occult melodrama.' She builds her argument along the lines of what Linda Williams calls 'body genres,' in that viewers are physically stimulated by these films. Green-Simms also draws on Brian Larkin's *Signal and Noise* (2008), in which he foregrounds an 'aesthetics of outrage' that is designed to "provoke reactions in the audience by sensationally depicting religious, social, and moral transgressions that contribute to everyday instability and uncertainty in the postcolony" (Green-Simms 28).

'Right, Anah, our mother loves our little sister best,' Aki continued in Japanese. 'Right?'" (Yamanaka 58–59)

In the beginning, Aki's anger and frustration turns against the missionaries and their dominance and force. She rejects their religion and tries to keep the connection to her sisters. When Aki acts cruel and scares her little sister, for example, when she tells one of the sisters in Leah's presence that Leah is about to die and that their well-meant medicine will not help, such acts are framed by Aki's own inability to help. Even though her emotional break-outs can be understood as psychological overwhelming of her own fears, these already trouble the reader's feelings toward her, especially in comparison with Anah's love, strength, and resilience.

After her death, Aki's ghost haunts the orphanage and her vicious acts are clearly directed against Anah. She releases all the animals during the night and does other forbidden things; convincing the sisters that these are Anah's doings. And

"Anah did not even try to tell them that it was Aki. Anah smelled her […]. Aki spiraled her earthy hands about her sister's face, then breathed her phlegmy, bloody wheeze. Anah smelled her hair, the sweet sweat of her neck, the spaces between her dirty fingers and toes. […] She giggled in Anah's ear." (Yamanaka 100–101)

Aki becomes a ghostly presence of cruel and hurtful actions, punishing her sister for her seeming betrayal. Strikingly, her presence is often indicated, as in the example just cited, by only partial appearances: smells or sounds, and always laughter. The tone, however, clearly charges these situations as frightening and threatening – the laughter, not friendly or a relief, but a revengeful, mocking sound of mischievousness. Locked in a situation that Anah cannot share with anyone, she is severely punished by her sister and thrown out of schooling because of Aki's hauntings.

But Aki soon also begins to physically hurt her sister, when Anah fails to respond to her callings.

"But on that night, alone in the nativity shack, she [Anah] heard *them* calling her name.
'Anah.'
These were different voices.
'Anah.'
She would not answer.
'Look, Anah.'

She would not look.
'In the trees, all around you.'
She shut her eyes and ears.
'We are many.'" (Yamanaka 106–107)

Anah then recognizes Seth, Leah, and Aki's voices among these many. But she also refuses to listen to them, trying to hold on to her improved life at the orphanage. Aki is pressing her on:

"'Behold Anah.'
But even then she did not.
'Behold the many, Anah.'
But she did not.
'Mentirosa.'
And for refusing to heed her command, Aki began scratching at Anah's arms, catlike with thin, razored claws, translucent pink, a trinity of talons that pierced her flesh again and again, moving under her skin like a reckless trio of maggots. […]
Aki bit Anah's cheek as she wrangled with air. Aki had no form, she who laughed as she bit her sister's neck, back, belly, and then buttocks, leaving the mark of her purple teeth all over Anah's body. […]
And in her vicious, consciousless child's anger, Aki slashed the thin membrane over the orb of Anah's eyes, red and blue veins spider-webbing inside, filling her eyes with bloody tears. She sliced open the delicate skin of eyelids with the precision of light, each cut intended for Anah to see no more what she did not want to see until the weight of skin and tears, blood and pus, sealed her eyes shut, blood issuing from every hole on her face.
'Behold, mentirosa,' she commanded.
But Anah could not." (Yamanaka 108–109)

The short, repetitive sentences, calling Anah to listen, see, and behold the many, reminding the reader once again of the typical breathless pitch of melodrama, finally turn into the extremely detailed and descriptive narration of violence. Having 'no form,' Aki holds unbelievable powers – especially due to her position in-between life and death, in which she is locked. Aki becomes a haunting, frightful presence, but she remains Anah's beloved sister. The reader is torn – with Anah – in her emotional reaction to this ghost: although her anger is directed at the wrong person, Aki has every reason to be mad. This suits a reading of Aki's ghost as an expression of Anah's survivor's guilt. Anah loves her sister unconditionally and projects her own anger and fear onto this ghostly presence. Even though Aki only haunts and hurts her sister, she remains confined to the spaces of the orphanage. With this, her appearance becomes deeply entangled with the colonial situation that caused her death. Her presence therefore always already indicates a haunting of the missionaries and the (post)colony. Although in this sense Aki appears to follow common readings of ghost figures, she remains a puzzling presence especially with regard to her unfair violence.

The general layout of the narrative mode establishes Aki as a figure that needs to be recognized in its full force.[18] In general, it is hard to place her on either side of a good-bad dichotomy, as it is typical for this postcolonial melodrama. The reader feels with her, experiencing her own suffering, but within a few pages, the reader is surprised and angry at her for her spiteful actions against the ones who tried to protect her. This emotional rollercoaster is furthered by the constant shifts of the novel's narrative perspective. The main story is set in the past, in the early twentieth century. It is narrated by an omniscient narrator. But this narrative is constantly interrupted by short chapters that provide close-ups of certain characters or letters. These short chapters are narrated in the first person and the present tense and switch from one sister to the next as they experience their first days at the orphanage. The reader's emotional identification with the suffering sisters – which includes Aki – contributes to the general uncertainty of whether Aki is good or bad, to be pitied or to be scolded.

These intermediate chapters also often feature the ghost figures as they talk to Anah, for example, as Seth curses her, or later as the ghosts talk to Anah's daughter Elizabeth. The ghosts are not banned from the rest of the story; they appear as haunting presences throughout. But in these short first-person chapters, their appearance is experienced as immediate by the reader. The switch from omniscient to first-person narrator enhances the emotional reactions to these figures. The breathless pitch that characterizes these chapters – which often only present dialogues or monologues – highlights the urgency with which these presences haunt the narrative. As a result, the reader is drawn into the story's growing tension, experiencing the haunting first hand along with Anah. The emotional immediacy and the close identification that these chapters provide also stage the insecurity that drives the larger narrative. These chapters function as mirrors for the reader in that she directly experiences the haunting presence and the confusion that this produces. That not all of these chapters feature the

18 This may also be at least a partial explanation why the reviews focus on Aki's ghost instead of Seth's. Still, their lack of acknowledgement of Seth as the central figure that he clearly is, remains a puzzling fact.

ghost figures even fuels the reader's feeling of insecurity and thus reproduces the characters' turmoil.

These shifting emotions create an anticipation of something bad to happen, for one can neither trust happiness and peace nor one's evaluation of a certain character, which results in insecurity in categorizing. This links the novel back to Hogle's analysis of the Gothic mode as concerned with the interpenetration of seemingly opposed systems. In this re-writing of the postcolonial melodrama, *Behold the Many* invites the reader to reconnect to intuitive approaches of binary categories such as colonizer/colonized, good/bad, or Western/indigenous. These neat categories are broken apart and become entangled in the course of the novel.

Such deconstruction of clear-cut terms shapes the novel from the beginning where it attaches its narrative closely to its location: "The valley is a woman lying on her back, legs spread wide, her geography wet by a constant rain. Waterfalls wash the days and nights of winter storms into the river that empties into the froth of the sea" (Yamanaka 3). This valley is the general setting for all the major events: it is the location of the orphanage and the family home, and it is the place where Anah's daughter Hosana dies. With this close connection of the land and its history established from the very beginning, this opening refers very directly to female sexuality. This image seemingly signifies Hawaii's landscape as a fertile place, buying into the mythical construction of the islands as an erotic Edenic space[19], only to be replaced by the close connection to Hosana's rape and death in this exact valley. Such distancing from the paradise-like picture of an ever blossoming and nurturing Hawaii foreshadows the critical deconstruction of other myths surrounding this part of the United States and it establishes close ties to postcolonial melodrama.

And this regional social milieu requires a rethinking of Peter Brooks' claims concerning the post-sacred. Linking the origins of the melodramatic mode to the French Revolution and its aftermath, Brooks argues that it expresses "the beginnings of a modern aesthetic" (Brooks 14). At a time that is marked by the decline of the traditional Sacred and its representative institutions, throwing ideas of truth and ethics into question, people were in search for a new ethics that could fill this void. And melodrama was one mode by which this void could be filled. As Brooks has it, melodrama "becomes the principal mode for uncovering, demonstrating, and making operative the essential moral universe in a post-sacred era" (14–15). He reads melodrama as a reaction to the Enlighten-

19 See, for example, Parikh, Crystal. "Blue Hawaii: Asian Hawaiian Cultural Production and Racial Melancholia." *Journal of Asian American Studies* 5.3 (2002): 199–216.

ment with its "desacralization and pretensions of rationalism" (17).[20] In contrast to Brooks, who links melodrama to modernity and the post-sacred, Sheetal Majithia rather sees 'postcolonial melodrama' as "characterized [...] by divergent histories of secularism and a multiplicity of religious traditions" (Majithia 7).

In a way, the time, place, and history in which *Behold the Many* is set mirrors the political and cultural struggles of the origins of the melodramatic as Brooks establishes them. In both cases, the cultural world-order is being re-thought. However, with the end of the Enlightenment, as Brooks argues, a post-sacralized world view had become prominent, to which the melodramatic mode was a reaction that stylized remnants of myth. In early twentieth century Hawaii, colonial aspirations were being set against traditional Hawaiian and other ethnic beliefs. This curious intermingling of religion and civilization on the one hand, and the polarization of traditional forms of worship and civilization on the other hand, is one of the central conflicts being staged in *Behold the Many*. Like the original melodrama, *Behold the Many* stages a moral conflict between light and darkness, in which, however, the two sides become not only personalized but also deeply interconnected, just like Majithia observes for a postcolonial melodramatic mode.

Behold the Many engages in the representation of such an intertwining of religious beliefs, which it stages most clearly in the scenes at the orphanage. Read as an allegory of the nation,[21] this haunted house points to the haunting legacy of colonial history along with its missionary impulses. Not only is the orphanage led by German Catholic nuns, but the sickness of the children in the first place is a reference to the mass diseases and deaths that the early colonizers brought to Hawaii (Silva 24–27). The missionaries, however, saw themselves as "bringers of light" (30): they were on a civilizing as well as Christianizing mission, helping these backward 'savages' to adjust to modern life. Thus, the

20 In their connection of Gothic to the postcolonial, Andrew Smith and William Hughes argue in *Empire and Gothic* that both want to challenge "postenlightenment notions of rationality," and in Gothic fiction this "challenge was developed through an exploration of the feelings, desires and passions which compromised the Enlightenment project" (1).

21 For example, Juliana Chang argues in *Inhuman Citizenship* for an "uncanny domestic," by linking the home and the family to the nation. The concept of the nation is, thus, linked to the domestic in allegorical fashion: home and family are not only metaphors for the nation but they are also sites of cultural and subject formations central to the nation (15–17).

orphanage holds the clash of two cultures: one posited as modern and progressive, the other as archaic, primitive, and superstitious.

Drawing on postcolonial critique, Bliss Cua Lim argues in *Translating Time: Cinema, the Fantastic, and Temporal Critique* (2009) that such a binary conception is typical of a colonial setting. In order to devalue the otherness of the colonized and their beliefs, the colonizers linked modern historical time to the ideology of progress. By way of a temporal exclusion, anything that does not fit the colonizers' model is perceived as primitive, anachronistic and about to vanish (Lim 12–16; 82–83). Lim sees in the mode of the fantastic a resistance to such a 'homogenous' time: drawing on Jacques Derrida's conception of spectrality, she argues that the supernatural allows a spectral temporality which accepts various presents at once and challenges any narrative of coherence and linear progressive development (149, 152).[22] According to such a reading, a ghost figure such as Aki's offers the possibility to express those aspects that run counter to common conceptions of 'being' and 'time.' This specter is both present and absent at the same time. And it belongs neither solely to the past nor to the present, defying a linear conception of time as progressing. Instead, Aki references Lim's spectral temporality, challenging the binary construction that the colonizer's model relies upon.

Another exemplary character highlighting this struggle between the colonizer's and the colonized's beliefs is the Chinese cook of the orphanage, Aunty Chong Sum. The short chapter called "Aunty Chong Sum's Comfession" is a prayer by the cook to God, confessing her sin: "I think I sin a bad one. The girl, our Anah, make me see the ghost again. I try change since I accept the Lord Jesus Christ in my life as Lord and Savior, but I see all the ma-ke keiki again" (Yamanaka 97) and continues "I know it is sin in the holy word when I listen to ghost" (97). Aunty Chong Sum's conflict manifests her continuing struggle of accepting the rules of the missionaries and the ghosts who "scratch[…] my face when I no listen them" (97). The title of the novel, *Behold the Many*, is itself a reference to such a struggle: 'the many' refers in the novel to the many children who have died at the orphanage and who continue to haunt the place. This, in turn, is a biblical reference – 'my name is Legion: for we are many' – which refers to the demons Christ needed to exorcise (Gospel of Mark 5:9). As Aunty Chong Sum's struggle highlights, the missionaries perceived of themselves to be

22 A famous example for a novel that works with such a strategy of having different temporal layers appear right next to one another would be Gabriel Garcia Márquez *100 Years of Solitude* (1967).

on a similar mission: they felt like they needed to exorcise the old beliefs of the different ethnic groups living in Hawaii.

The melodramatic pitch of this short chapter cannot be overstated. Referring to Seth, Aunty Chong Sum asks "You was there, hah, Father? You seen all this, hah? You seen the boy, Father? That one is another sin of mine" (Yamanaka 98). Trying to relieve her bad conscience, she continues her prayer: "Oi Virgin of virgin, my Mother, to thee I come, before thee I stand sinful and sorrow! [...] Ai-ya, my God, I am so sorry I offend thee, [...] I firm resolve with the help of you, I no sin no mo' and pass the near sin" (Yamanaka 99). The highly stylized language merges her Chinese accent with words and tone used in scripture. Interjections like 'oi' and 'ai-ya' further emphasize her emotional turmoil. While Aunty Chong Sum resolves to behave herself by ignoring the ghosts that surround her, the struggle also shows her resistance to simply accept a rational explanation for these figures. The presence of the ghost figures, Aunty Chong Sum assumes, is also known to God. This intertwining of Christianity, traditional ghost belief, and a certain idea of becoming civilized and educated, is one of the unresolvable conflicts central to the novel. Christianity is represented as a relief for all virtuous victims in the moral struggle of the melodramatic mode between good and bad. And yet, it appears also as a belief system totally at odds with the traditional beliefs, a system that is imposed from the outside, something that remains ungraspable and alien to many of the characters.

The confusion that this project of the missionaries creates is especially evident in Leah's perception of the ghost Seth and the nun's actions. When Leah arrives at the orphanage alone as the first of the three sisters, she encounters Seth right away. Having no idea about Seth's history, she immediately connects him to what she heard about Jesus: "Jesus stay with me now. He the boy with white hair. The one was waiting for me on the bridge. 'Be not afraid,' he say to me" (Yamanaka 19). As her only companion and consolation, Leah perceives of this ghost figure as a representation of Christian religion, although it should be the nuns at the orphanage who wish to Christianize the sick children. The nuns, however, "scrub me with pig soap. 'Filthy filthy full of the krankheit,' the big one [nun] say. [...] Then she do the head stomach shoulder shoulder. Owee Owee. Jesus come. Jesus watch" (20). Instead of reaching out to this hurting child, the nun appears as distanced and inaccessible. The sign of the cross appears as a weird movement of the hands that is associated with the pain of the scrubbing. And it is, again, Seth, the specter, who appears and offers consolation. With this, Seth's appearance refers also to common Catholic narratives of Marian appearances to which the Catholic authorities have reacted with reservation. Although they have approved of some such appearances – for example the famous Lady of Lourdes, the phenomenon has been highly controversial.[23] The ignorance of the nuns thus references this internal struggle of the Catholic Church and its believers, emphasizing just another layer of cultural and religious associations that Seth's character offers.

Similarly, an orphanage – a place with no parents, no orientation, no traditions except the foreign Western ones – calls to mind the state of Hawaii at the turn of the century. Aunty Chong Sum even refers to "[o]ur poor Queen Lili'uokalani" (Yamanaka 99), the queen whose overthrow at the end of the nineteenth century, ultimately resulted in the annexation of the Republic of Hawaii as a territory of the United States (Bacchilega 4). In this confusing set-up, the characters of the novel desperately look for ways of building meaningful communities. One such bond is created between the Chinese cook and Portuguese Cape Verdean Ezroh over the care of Anah. As Anah is repeatedly attacked by Aki's ghost, the orphanage is at a loss how to help her, since they cannot accept this supernatural explanation. As the scene from the very beginning of this chapter already shows, Aunty Chong Sum and Ezroh believe Anah and offer cures: Ezroh explains to Anah that "what I put on you, I put inside you" (Yamanaka 128) while he feeds her a broth the cook prepared and massages her scars with oil; Aunty Chong Sum instructs her "to wear the sennit-knotted rosary around her neck, sprinkle Hawaiian rock salt, and splash ti leaves dipped in holy water around her bed" (Yamanaka 134). With this curious mixture of Catholic and indigenous cures, Anah survives. In this sense, the three create a community that bridges cultural differences through their shared belief in supernatural appearances. They borrow from Catholic beliefs what they deem right – a rosary and holy water –, but they adapt this to fit their own ways of approaching ghosts. In the production of such fleeting communities and following an 'ethics of relationality' – to use Sheetal Majithia's terminology for postcolonial melodrama –, *Behold the Many* emphasizes the ongoing adaptation and intertwining of existing belief systems. Yet, these interconnections produce not only resistant potential but also accommodation.

Both Ezroh and Aunty Chong Sum appear as successful figures: they found their respective positions within Hawaii's colonial set-up. The key to this success – as their shared struggle to save Anah's life highlights – is an ongoing

23 See, for example, David Blackbourn. *Marpingen: Apparitions of the Virgin Mary in Nineteenth-Century Germany*. New York: Knopf, 1994; Andreas Fuchs. *Mariologie und „Wunderglaube". Ein kritischer Beitrag zur spiritualitätstheologischen Valenz der Mariophanie im Kontext humanwissenschaftlicher Fragestellungen*. Regensburg: Pustet, 2009.

negotiation between the existing religious and cultural traditions that surround them. Christianized Asians such as Aunty Chong Sum or Anah, thus, follow a mixture of both traditions. As the reader experiences the ghosts through their eyes, she evaluates these figures – along with Anah and Aunty Chong Sum – as both allegorical references in line with psychological readings of the Gothic and as spiritual figures, embodiments of ancestors in line with traditional Asian beliefs. This mixture shapes not only the plot of *Behold the Many*, but also its narrative mode. The novel employs these seemingly contradictory approaches, indicating the intricate interconnections and showing how they cannot and should not be separated.

Such paradoxical interconnection also shapes what Linda Hutcheon calls "historiographic metafiction." In her own words, such fiction "asks us to recall that history and fiction are themselves historical terms and that their definitions and interrelations are historically determined and vary with time" (Hutcheon, *A Poetics of Postmodernism* 105). Its close connection of history and fiction creates paradoxical movements: "it installs totalizing order, only to contest it, by its radical provisionality, intertextuality, and, often, fragmentation" (116) so that it "problematizes the very possibility of historical knowledge" (106). In its framing of the prominent ghost figures as referencing various traditions, *Behold the Many* stages the impossibility of separating or neatly summarizing this particular past. To use Hutcheon's words, historiographic metafiction produces "a loss of faith in our ability to (unproblematically) *know* that reality" (119). The novel offers an engagement of the past that questions the separation between colonizer and colonized and instead foregrounds the ambiguous crossings between these categories and worlds.

But instead of what Hutcheon sees as a parodic re-writing of history in historiographic metafiction,[24] *Behold the Many* rather employs an 'affective historiography,' to use Jeremy Maron's term. Maron argues that melodrama serves as an alternative mode of history writing in that it works with the viewer's emotional reactions to connect to history, sounding "emotional rather than intellectual registers" (Maron 93). Just like the postcolonial melodrama, then, such 'affective historiographies' re-write a past as it branches into the present, and they do so in emphasizing emotional reactions. *Behold the Many* follows

24 For Hutcheon the "collective weight of parodic practice suggests a redefinition of parody as repetition with critical distance that allows ironic signaling of difference at the very heart of similarity. In historiographic metafiction [...] this parody paradoxically enacts both change and cultural continuity" (Hutcheon "The Politics of Postmodernism," 185).

such a narrative mode as well. But it does not re-write this history in terms of an uncomplicated resistance narrative. Instead, it narrates the shifting and changing emotions and relations that shape this (post)colonial setting.

When Anah finally leaves the orphanage to build her new life with Ezroh, this does not result in the expected freedom. Although Anah escapes the confines of the orphanage and their missionary and colonial baggage, her new life is dominated by inter-ethnic tensions. Her new family might appear at first glance as a happy adoption into an ethnically diverse community of Portuguese, Cape Verdean, and Japanese Hawaiians, calling to mind the (tourist) image of Hawaii as an ethnic paradise (Bacchilega 5). However, the novel is frank in its depiction of the harsh inter-ethnic tensions that result from the marriage and that dictate the life of this family as well as the nation as a whole.[25] This tension, then, shuttles us back to the reviews and the lack of academic sources on *Behold the Many*. Maybe – and this is also what Crystal Parikh argues in relation to the controversy surrounding *Blu's Hanging* – Yamanaka's novels "are interested in countering the exotic/erotic fantasy of Hawaii as Edenic space of escape by figuring the history of traumatic loss that such a fantasy disguises" (Parikh 201) and this is simply not selling well. Parikh also argues in this article, that "Hawaii is itself a haunting figure of loss in the American experience" because "the U.S. is haunted […] by its own imperial and military history" (213). Even though this is certainly true, *Behold the Many* invites an emphasis of the internal hauntings of this society and not a singular focus on the ghost figure as only resisting Western homogenizing tendencies.

Even before they get married, Ezroh's Aunty Tova very directly voices her doubts about this interracial marriage, although Anah has both a Portuguese, like Aunty Tova herself, and a Japanese heritage: "She looked at Anah, shaking her head. 'Half-breed orphan,' she whispered. 'Our mother warned us against inter-marrying, especially with the Orientals. You [she is addressing Ezroh's father] did not heed her admonition. Now look at what your son has chosen for a bride. Even worse than a negra portuguesa'" (Yamanaka 215). Just as she complains about Japanese meals as "horrible" in their smells and tasting "so primitive and ghastly" as if they were cooked with dirt in them (240), she also very openly states her general attitude towards 'Orientals' as a backward race. Talking to one of Anah's children, she rants:

25 For a detailed analysis of the different statuses of various ethnic groups and inter-ethnic conflicts, see Okamura, Jonathan Y, *Ethnicity and Inequality in Hawai'I*, Philadelphia: Temple University Press, 2008.

> "'It is not like the government hasn't been trying to Americanize you Orientals. […] What with half of the children in our schools being Japanese.' She made the sign of the cross and shook her head. 'These Orientals act as though it is owed to them. When will Governor Farrington realize that educating them will not make a lick of a difference. Look at them – their traditions, their appearance, their innate tendencies, their very blood is still so Oriental.'" (257)

With this rant, Aunty Tova very explicitly establishes a hierarchy of ethnic groups in Hawaii, counting the Portuguese among the dominant and well-established groups and denies this right to all 'Orientals.' Her justification indicates her self-serving racist attitudes. It also shows the way in which her classifications are linked to colonization and assimilation. According to Aunty Tova, Asians simply do not fit well into a Westernized, civilized new Hawaii because they remain bound to their traditions.

Interestingly, Aunty Tova is also the one to raise the possibility of Anah being cursed several times throughout the novel. Talking to her sister, Lydia, she claims to know: "'I tell you, Lydia somebody sure has a curse on her.' 'Do not talk like that, sister. We are not in the old country anymore.' 'And she has brought the bad luck here, I just know it. It is so clear that the girl is cursed. Do you think our nephew knows? How can he not know?'" (Yamanaka 248). While Aunty Tova disqualifies 'Orientals' because of their traditions, she refers to the possibility of a curse on the basis of her own beliefs from 'the old country.' She is, thus, shown to be a hypocrite. When this aspect is emphasized, Aunty Tova functions as a figure of selfish assimilation to the colonial setting. However, her hierarchical classification of ethnic groups also exposes the troubles and tensions that exist in-between the ethnic groups. Aunty Tova, thus, becomes the living embodiment of Seth's curse: highlighting not only the personal disadvantages that Anah has to suffer from in her new family, but also laying bare the larger interracial conflicts that divide the Hawaiian society.

This representation of Hawaiian interethnic conflicts undermines a resistance narrative that might be pronounced otherwise. As the novel offers both – resistance and accommodation – it once again produces confusing, paradoxical possibilities of identification. *Behold the Many*'s resistant potential also links itself to self-critical observations of Hawaiian ethnic groups and the potential of accommodation; and this results in the novel's unplaceability or – to use the term that refers explicitly to Seth's ghost – unreadability.

The reader's feelings toward Seth change again at the very end of the novel. Within the course of the novel, he appears first as a lonely, lost boy, who then turns into a frightening, evil spirit. But the end depicts him once again as a sad boy and in a reconciliatory frame. After Anah's daughter Hosana has been raped and murdered, Seth's curse is finally lifted. Hosana herself returns as a ghost and takes 'the many' ghosts of the novel home to God.

"The dark sky opens up with the first rays of this dawn. Anah sees Hosana in the threshold of that light, standing before her in a kind of indomitable radiance.
'Come,' she says to the many around them, 'I know the way home.'
There is rustling in the flower and herb beds, a trembling in the trees, the sound of little feet, many feet running on the gravel road. She turns away from Anah and heads into the light, the children in the wind following her.
[…]
'I want to be set free,' Anah tells her beloved daughter, her first blood relative when she had no one, the one whom she loved the most.
'I want to free,' she answers, her voice full and resounding.
The sunlight is warm.
Beatrix and Bertha's spirit bodies take flight [Anah's stillborn babies], becoming part of the sunlight. Little Leah in her pretty yellow dress follows, waving her hand at […] Anah as she goes. Aki hesitates at first […]. She turns to Hosana, who is softly saying her name, Hosana, her mother's mirror, her mother's child, keeps saying her name, beckoning to her *come, come home.* Aki follows her voice, dissolving into the light.
[…]
Seth lingers in the shadows of a mountain apple tree. Anah stands up and walks toward him, he who never aged, little towheaded boy, the quiet one who followed Leah, then Aki, then her, a loyal friend who never complained, his calm but sad presence in her most agonizing and unbearable moments. An angry wraith who believed she had betrayed him.
'Seth, my friend and brother in marriage.' Anah holds out her hands to him.
'I want to hear and I want to be heard.'
'Love – is – sweet,' he says, not moving.
'Remember always, brother,' says a voice behind her. Anah turns. It is Ezroh, who falls to his knees before the little boy who fell from the big tree all those years ago. Seth walks toward him and places both hands on his brother's head. His eyes survey the panorama of the valley as if placing the horses in the pastures, the green hills, his childhood home, a father, a brother, and a once beloved friend in the sweep of his memory. When fades the light behind an errant cloud, so fades he." (Yamanaka 335–337)

With only a few sentences, enhanced by the repeated quoting from scripture, Yamanaka creates an atmosphere of highly charged emotion and a scene so rich in its stereotypical images of light and darkness that it appears almost involuntarily as part of a film or theater scene that absorbs its viewer. This theatricality is furthered by the narrative representation of a tableau: the final scene of the novel is compositionally arranged; the images described not only absorb the viewer but force her to actually envision the characters as if on stage. They appear as frozen for a moment, a visual representation of the emotional ending of the novel as a whole.[26]

The end of the novel attempts a solution of the previous conflicts: the curse is lifted, the ghosts have finally found their way home and can stop haunting Anah and the orphanage, Seth has finally given his blessings to his brother and Anah's love, they can now begin to live a peaceful life. Still, the reader cannot trust this reconciliatory ending. The previous 340 pages have continuously undermined her feelings, drawn her in a certain direction only to push her into the exact opposite direction within the next few pages. She is exhausted from the overwhelming emotions, and the insecurity of her value judgments. Hosana's death and her final disappearance frame the larger narrative of *Behold the Many*. The novel begins in the present tense with Hosana's death and Anah's reaction to it in 1939. It then shuttles back to 1913 and tells the sisters' story from the moment Leah is taken to the orphanage in past tense. In the last few pages the novel moves back into 1939 and the present tense. Just like in the intermediate chapters throughout, this shift into present tense enhances the feeling of immediacy and unpredictability. The feeling of *dis*-ease that dominates the novel's plot has infected the reader. Although the story provides no reason to doubt this happy ending, the shuttling of emotions in this postcolonial melodrama is so present to the reader that a solution will always already give room to expectations of further haunting.

---

26 This is following Brooks' analysis of the use of a tableau in melodramatic representations (Brooks 36–48).

3 Traditions of Haunting: The Narration of a Ghostly Self and a Family's Ghosts in Heinz Insu Fenkl's *Memories of My Ghost Brother*

"That night, I dreamt of a wide, still river with banks of white pebbles, and a face that looked like my own looking up at me through the clear, rippling water, and when I woke the next morning, the magpie was dead. [...] Perhaps I had begun to understand at that moment, as I crouched in the rain and heard the whispering ghosts, that the magpie's death would go on and on forever like the endless sky." (Fenkl, *Memories of My Ghost Brother* 8)

From its very beginning, *Memories of My Ghost Brother* (1996) establishes its narrator's world as full of ghost presences. The novel is set in 1960s South Korea and tells the autobiographical story of the narrator's family. Insu[1], the son of a Korean mother and a German American GI father grows up in the shadows of the camptown world. Engaged with ghosts while playing in his backyard, continuously dreaming of a ghost boy who is suspiciously familiar, he is reminded again and again that the dead and death surround him. All of these ghosts connect him to a past that seems threatened by silence and erasure. And yet, the ghosts also appear as distinct figures, each with its own history. Some of them are quite public ghosts – referring to the history of a certain place, for example. Others like the ghost boy from his dreams, are highly personal ghosts – referring to his specific family history. However, all of the ghost figures are intertwined with both a public and a personal story. And this connection is one of the driving forces of the novel. Through its various ghost figures, the novel emphasizes the different traditions of haunting that shape the narrator's life

1 I call the narrator Insu in order to distinguish him from the author Heinz Insu Fenkl.

because his parents offer him differing perceptions of these figures. *Memories of My Ghost Brother* exposes the interconnections between the parents' cultures in the narrator's life, questioning the basic differences between spiritual and allegorical hauntings, highlighting the public as constantly interfering with the private.

Although his parents are married, his father remains a distant figure, living either on-base or fighting for extended periods in Vietnam. Insu grows up between the Korean world of his extended family, with its ghosts from the past and present, and the American camptown world that shapes almost every aspect of his family life. Not only is his father a GI, his mother also works secretly as a black marketeer. This coming-of-age novel narrates Insu's growing up in between his parents' two separate but overlapping worlds. It spans from Insu's birth to his family's emigration to the United States about 12 years later. During this time, Insu is not only attached to his parents' worlds but also to his extended Korean family and his friends. The novel narrates episodes from the boy's life: the struggles of his relatives, glimpses into the father's military life, Insu's own education at a Catholic Sunday school and later an American school, and the friends he makes who disappear one after the other – some die, others go to America. The reader learns by the end of the novel that Insu's father would not accept a stepchild, so that his mother gave up his older brother for adoption in order to marry Insu's father.

The motif of an Asian American child that is forced to go to America is an established one – for example in Puccini's opera Madame Butterfly (1904) that depicts the Japanese Geisha's suicide, when she learns of her husband's plan to take their son to America, or the musical Miss Saigon (1989) that follows the reverse logic of a heroic suicide of the Vietnamese mother of an American Vietnamese son in order to offer her son a better life in America with his father. Yet, *Memories of My Ghost Brother* addresses this motif from a new perspective: it links it to ghost figures and thus references a specific Asian American tradition that dates back to Maxine Hong Kingston's *The Woman Warrior*. Just as in Kingston's memoir, Insu's experiences are framed by the ghosts that accompany his growing up, especially by the ghost brother from the novel's title. This family secret is only revealed towards the end of the novel, but it is foreshadowed from the beginning and haunts every relationship. Fenkl's use of the ghost figures differs from Kingston's, however, in that the ghosts appear as distinctly referencing and oscillating between two different, yet interconnected approaches to these figures: Korean spiritualist beliefs and American psychoanalytical explanations. The novel, thus, negotiates on a thematic, fictional level what the theories about these figures struggle with. With this, it reflects upon questions that have driven discussions about this motif from its inception in Asian American literature.

Although its autobiographical dimension is obvious, *Memories of My Ghost Brother* is published as a novel, playing again with the intertwined conceptions of private and public, personal and historical. *Memories of My Ghost Brother* is Heinz Insu Fenkl's first novel and was a Barnes and Noble "Great New Writer" pick as well as a PEN/Hemingway award finalist. The author is a writer, editor, translator, and folklorist, who studied and taught in various institutes in the United States and Korea (The Creative Writing Program at SUNY New Paltz np). Born in the 1960s, he grew up in Korea and moved to America, just like the narrator of his first novel, opening his personal life to narrate a larger history of Korean American relations.

Betty Ann Bergland summarizes the specificity of narrating such a life pointedly: "Autobiography constructs a life; ethnic autobiography constructs a life and a community" (Bergland, "Representing Ethnicity in Autobiography" 87). This simple fact emphasizes the intricate interconnection between a personal life and a public history of an ethnic community, explaining both the fear to overgeneralize a universal immigrant experience and the requirement for representative status. Read as a representative text of the Korean American community, *Memories of My Ghost Brother* raises troublesome questions about Korean America's self-conception. Intertwined with the construction of this biracial self is the construction of a Korean American history. Following Grace M. Cho's analysis in *Haunting the Korean Diaspora* (2008), Fenkl's autobiographical novel exposes a history that has often been neglected and silenced. And this silence has not only been an imposed one by the American mainstream, but was also upheld by the Korean diasporic community itself. Participation in the erasure of a shared history of sexual relations between Korean women and American soldiers meant participation in the positive picture that was painted of happy interracial couples, when the soldiers took these women home as their wives (Cho 12–15). Breaking this silence, *Memories of My Ghost Brother* exposes the ghosts that haunt the Korean American community. While the secondary literature has focused on the negative depiction of the American imperial designs in Korea,[2] a focus on the ghost figures in the novel calls for a rethinking of Korean American participation and the current rewriting of this history.

2 See, for example, Remigio, Myra. *Adolescent Empires: Identity, Liminality, and Advocacy in Contemporary American Literature*, Dissertation submitted to Collumbian College of Arts and Science at The George Washington University, 2008, (esp. chapter 2); or Kim, Jodi. *Ends of Empire: Asian American Critique and the*

Memories of My Ghost Brother highlights the need to address ghosts of the past that haunt the present constructions of both self and community. As Grace Kyungwon Hong convincingly argues,

"[i]n this context, any binaritic schema of colonizer and colonized, perpetrator and victim, complicit and blameless, is rendered impossible. Accordingly, such complex relationships to sovereignty demand a narrative form organized around a complex and divided subject unlike the possessive individual at the center of traditional autobiographies, a divided subject formed around an ethics in which no one is blameless and everyone is complicit." (Hong 50)

At the center of *Memories of My Ghost Brother* is, thus, a subject that struggles with basic questions of identity formation, a subject that is haunted by a partially erased personal and public history and that needs to position itself within the available cultural traditions. These beliefs are implicitly connected to his Korean mother and his German-American father. The strength of the text lies in its rather simple point: the questionable morality of some acts actually is not an inherent feature in any of the characters, but results from neocolonial forces that reach far beyond each individual. The parents serve as representatives of their respective cultures, drawn and pushed by larger forces. Set against the background of the Vietnam War and referring back to the Korean War, the novel also exposes the interconnections between these cultures in their shared histories of violent conflicts.

The camptown world that *Memories of My Ghost Brother* depicts in its cruelty and its alluring promise of riches emphasizes the interconnections of larger public forces with the characters' very personal lives. The novel presents this struggle not only on a thematic level, but also in its generic ambiguity. Neither autobiography in the strict sense, nor a cultural history, it breaches these genres in order to tell its specific story on the borders of the private and the public, the personal and the historical, the fantastic elements of the fictional and the horrific depictions of the factual. For, in the end, what the novel finally narrates is a haunted self.

Corld War. Minneapolis and London: University of Minnesota Press, 2010 (esp. chapter 4).

LIFE WRITING: NARRATING A GHOSTLY SELF

"I belonged out there. I should have been watching this bus go by, running alongside in my white rubber shoes, my feet squelching inside from their own sweat. [...] But I was on this bus, sitting behind freckled GIs who spoke with accents from places I had only imagined, whose sweat smelled thick and nauseating, whose eyes were the color of the sea and sky, whose boots and tanks trod the earth of this country to bitter dust. [...] Earlier that week some boy had dug out a shell and dropped it on a stone, and he had blown himself to pieces, scattering fragments of himself so far they could not gather him together again to hide under a straw mat. He had died so suddenly they said he didn't have time to realize it and his ghost was still drifting back and forth across the range wondering why no one could see him or speak to him. But sometimes they would hear his voice whispering in their ears or feel his breath on their necks, and they would have to say, "Tong-su, go away, go away," and listen to his weeping. That afternoon I had found scraps of cheap clothes black and stiff with dried blood and I had walked gingerly back to the road, carrying my armload of brass all slippery with my sweat as I followed my own footprints back and counted my breaths to keep calm." (Fenkl, *Memories of My Ghost Brother* 248–249).

While Insu feels that he should have belonged 'out there,' he remains seated in the bus with the GIs. He is torn between the outside with its 'bitter dust' and the inside with the strange smelling and looking men. He remembers the scary presence of death, the immediate threat that waits in the dust outside, and he recounts how the people encounter and narrate these threats in the form of ghost figures. The passage shows how the novel is build around this child's perspective: the reader can easily imagine the sweat that should squelch in the rubber shoes or the child's fear that is kept at bay by counting breaths, sensations that adults certainly remember from their own youth. The GIs belong to one half of his world, the unspecified 'they,' who talk about and to the ghosts, belong to the other half. In a way, these worlds overlap for Insu, but again and again they appear as sharp contrasts. The passage highlights the way in which the self is torn between fact and fiction, between his own autobiography and the larger story of his country, and between the cultures that surround him.

The narrating self is also torn between this child's perspective and a grown-up perspective throughout the novel. In a way, the story is being told by two Insu's; although most of the story is focalized through the eyes of the young Insu, from the beginning, this perspective is presented alongside or even undercut by shorter chapters in italics which seem to tell parallel storylines from the perspective of a grown man. This narrative set-up creates and enhances the tension that is central to the novel. The story becomes a larger one than that of a small child, but it remains for the most part in this perspective.

A child will – of course – perceive and reflect upon his surroundings and relationships in a way that differs markedly from that of an adult. This fact shapes the logic and the drive of the narrative immensely as it allows the narrator to narrate his stories as he experienced them. As a result, the novel shifts around a number of troublesome questions and exposes the confusing world of a young boy, who only begins to grasp the larger forces that shape his family's lives. Insu reflects upon the ghost of the young boy who died so suddenly. He does not address the scary fact that it could easily have been him. Instead, he presents this horrific story as part of his own experience – finding bloody clothes – and as part of a larger cultural frame: ghost stories. He participates in the tradition of telling these stories by referring to what 'they say' about this young boy's ghost. The narrative format, thus, mirrors the torn self of the narrator – he is presented by a ghostly subtext that runs alongside his own narrative.

Strikingly, *Memories of My Ghost Brother* begins with a description of the narrator's birth:

> *"A giant serpent, thick as a pine tree, dangles its head from atop the palace gate and whispers to her in human speech, "I have something to tell you" [...] My mother takes a cautious step forward. But before the serpent can speak again, she returns to consciousness and, enduring the last contractions of her day-long labor, she gives birth to me."* (Fenkl, *Memories of My Ghost Brother* 3)

In terms of autobiographical writing, this opening concedes with the genre's expectations of telling an author's life.[3] It begins at the beginning. And yet, from the start, *Memories of My Ghost Brother* undermines this very expectation on various levels. Not only is it published as a novel instead of an autobiography, it also breaks with the idea of realistic depictions of the author's memories in that the narrator of the story cannot remember the moment of his own birth or know what his mother experienced at the time. The unreliability of the narrator in terms of the autobiographical pact is further enhanced by the introduction of a dream serpent. The appearance of the serpent has been read as a "cross between Eve's temptation in the garden of Eden and the Annunciation of Angel Gabriel

3 Roughly following Philippe Lejeune's classic concept of the 'autobiographical pact,' which states that a pact between autobiographer, reader, and publisher secures that the author, the narrator, and the protagonist of the text are identical and that a first-person narrative of this person's life is given (see Lejeune 193–222).

to the Virgin Mary" concluding that "[c]onceding that Korea was not known for poisonous snakes, Mr. Fenkl as cultural anthropologist locates the childhood teaching that snakes were dangerous and bad in family stories" (Uchmanowicz np). The beginning of the novel thus already establishes its specific Korean German American mix: it presents the Christian myth of origin as part of a Korean folk story that is directly linked to its narrator's life. Playing with the readers' expectations, *Memories of My Ghost Brother* forces its readers to shuttle in between autobiographical and mythic elements, referencing a tradition of such generic mixing in Asian American and postcolonial writings.

In a way, autobiography as a genre[4] always already exists on the fringes of literary productions: its existence in-between literary artwork and historical documentation marks both the reason for its relatively recent discovery as an object for literary studies and its contemporary boom. Autobiography stages the struggle between referentiality and performativity (Wagner-Egelhaaf 1–2). Linda Anderson argues in *Autobiography* (2011) that it is "always a complex matter involving both the subject's discursive position *and* material/historical location"

4 While earlier critics such as Philippe Lejeune, Karl Weintraub or Georges Gusdorf – to name a few of the classic references of autobiographical studies – are still preoccupied with an essentialist or Romantic notions of a unified self, recent studies have moved away from this approach especially in the aftermath of poststructuralist redefinitions of stable categories (Anderson 1–6). Sidonie Smith, for example, states in her Presidential Address in 2011 that in the last twenty years, "[t]he central concepts of a stable genre, a monolithic I and a bounded life have come undone. [...] The contemporary diversity in narrated lives confronts us with different understandings of what constitutes three key concepts: the I, the life, and the narrating of lives around the globe" (Smith 565). Inherent in the shift of theoretical approaches to the genre is a shift in the canon and reception of autobiographical texts. As Linda Anderson observes in *Autobiography* (2011) how the deconstruction of the genre's original protagonist – white and male – opened it for new social groups. She further explains how these groups also began to employ the genre's political potential (Anderson 96). Anderson argues that not only did the objects under scrutiny change to include women or ethnic autobiographies but that this shift opened up new possible applications and readings of the genre. As representative for a certain group, the text becomes empowering in a political sense in that "autobiography becomes both a way of testifying to oppression and empowering the subject through his/her cultural inscription and recognition." However, such an overly positive reading elides the problems inherent to such an approach because "this politicization of the subject [...] can also elide further differences under an assumed representativity" (Anderson 97).

(97). Keeping this instruction in mind, what is the discursive position and material/historical location of *Memories of My Ghost Brother*? Its existence in-between genres as an autobiographical novel, already locates it as a text that is not easily categorized. It is set in South Korea, yet written by a Korean American author, it features the life in the shadows of the Korean camptown world, the maturing of its biracial narrator, it references the Japanese colonization of Korea and exposes the troubling history of Korean-American relations. Autobiography – as it is centrally concerned with the question 'Who am I?' and 'How did I become what I am?'[5] – offers a way to address the complex development of a narrator in his or her personal and public environment. Inherently, these questions emphasize not only the personal family situation, but also reference the larger framework into which the narrator is born. In the case of Heinz Insu Fenkl, these questions echo the larger questions of 'What is Korean America?' and 'How did it become what it is?' As such, *Memories of My Ghost Brother* needs to be read as both an Asian American and a postcolonial narrative that situates itself on the borders of the autobiographical. In short, the characters' intertwined life stories exemplify the ambiguity of conflicted identifications which dominate the camptown world. In contrast to a traditional novel, *Memories of My Ghost Brother* "is organized around the impossibility of resolution" (Hong 56).

This complex and ongoing mediation of one's positionality between cultures echoes in all postcolonial autobiographies, as Alfred Hornung has it in his introduction to *Auto/Biography and Mediation* (2006) (Hornung xii). Since postcolonial autobiography exposes not only the conflicted identifications of the colonized but also of the colonizers, it renders the Western subjective self unstable. Postcolonial autobiography has therefore been "increasingly recognized as a powerful counter-hegemonic practice" (Boehmer 756). In order to highlight this aspect of resistance, many postcolonial studies scholars favor the term 'life writing' over 'autobiography,' conceiving of the latter term as referencing a Western, paternalistic tradition (Carballal 285). Although this chapter also uses the term 'life writing,' it does not follow such a politicized and positive reading of the genre. Rather, life writing exposes the constant intertwining of conflicted identifications, foregrounding the ambiguity that the postcolonial situation creates for all sides. The term is used here not as a

5 These questions as basic to the genre of autobiography were originally posed by Karl Weintraub in *The Value of the Individual: Self and Circumstance in Autobiography*. Chicago: University of Chicago Press, 1978.

celebratory reference, but because of its broadness and openness. As Susheila Nasta has it,

> "[t]oday, the idea of life-writing is often summoned up as a broad brush label to cover a wide range of literary forms, emanating from across the globe and ranging from autobiography to memoir, to personal letters, diaries, essays, testimony and travel journals. Increasingly too, and perhaps as a consequence of the contemporary acceptance of a more transcultural vision of global modernity, life-writing has come to be seen not only as a recognisable Western form of authorised *belles lettres,* but rather as a dynamic and democratic force for change, a hybrid vehicle which can stretch and reshape the often unstable boundaries between genres, interrogate questions of subjectivity and open up the symbolic borders of new or previously contested national histories." (Nasta 1)

In a similarly cautious reading, Elleke Boehmer argues, that it is often assumed by postcolonial critics that by writing a self, the postcolonial subject automatically secures identity and agency for herself, but "how such difficult constructions and claims might relate to the continuing hegemony of Western individualist humanism [...] these are questions that are by and large only obliquely addressed" (Boehmer 757). *Memories of My Ghost Brother* narrates a subject that is torn between different forces and cultural traditions. The young Insu on the bus, who feels like he belongs outside of it, but still remains seated among the GIs, is one such reflection of positionality in the novel. The passage continues with Insu remembering what he had done that afternoon: selling his brass to a dealer in small dark back alleys where he encountered young girls and boys prostituting themselves. He recounts how

> "we were all doing our best to get money from the yellow hairs [...]. The *yang saekshis*, the slicky boys, the hustlers, the pimps – all after the same things – skulking through narrow alleys running with sewage and piss and wafting with a stench so awful that it gagged you." (Fenkl, *Memories of My Ghost Brother* 249)

The novel constructs a self that positions itself in the neocolonial framework, but refrains from depicting this position as resistant or overly positive. It rather emphasizes the intricate interconnections of the Western and the Korean conceptions of this positionality.

In a review of Bart Moore-Gilbert's *Postcolonial Life Writing* (2009) David Huddart summarizes that postcolonial selves are "[d]ecentered, relational, and embodied" and that this fact influences their approaches to life writing (Huddart

550). The same could be said about Asian American subjects.[6] Rocío G. Davis summarizes that

"Asian American autobiographies generally highlight the protagonist's growing comprehension of the meaning or value that society places on questions and attitudes

---

6 In order to place themselves in an American tradition, immigrants often used the genre of autobiography. Autobiography has been seen as a central part of the American literary tradition, for, according to one of the earlier critics, James Craig Holte, "the American question is a question of self" (Holte 25). In "The Representative Voice" (Summer 1982), Holte argues that the genre provides a ground for constructing an (American) self in giving structure, coherence, and causality. Moreover, as America is perceived as "a country where individuality is professed to be the height of virtue, autobiography makes the individual the source of authority" (30). In Holte's conception, autobiography is especially suited to cater to the needs of immigrants to the United States for they have a special interest in imposing order on their fragmented and disrupted lives (28). He differentiates two patterns of ethnic autobiography: the transformation from outsider to insider in the form of a successful assimilation story and the opposite story that remains at a distance and resists the homogenizing tendencies of American culture (34–35). William Boelhower even argues in "The Making of Ethnic Autobiography" (1991) that the immigrant autobiography was the "corresponding new text type" to the shift in American culture between 1880 and 1910 to address new modern versions of the American self (Boelhower 139). Although Holte's and Boelhower's conceptions of autobiography clearly remain within a framework that still features Romantic notions of selfhood, they identify the strategic use of the genre for immigrants to reinscribe themselves as belonging to a newly diversified America.

Boelhower's concept of immigrant autobiography has been critically commented upon. Paul John Eakin, for example, highlights Boelhower's focus on the "reciprocity of influence in the relation between mainstream and ethnic cultures, a salutary corrective to any simplistic, one-way construing of cultural influence" (Eakin 9). Sau-ling Cynthia Wong, on the other hand, criticizes Boelhower for making universal claims about the immigrant experience and immigrant autobiography, charging him with a Eurocentric approach that furthermore ignores generational differences. Focusing on the example of Chinese Americans, Wong emphasizes the striking differences in immigration history as well as cultural and religious beliefs to the European immigrants that Boelhower refers to (Wong, "Immigrant Autobiography" 159). Such critical evaluation of the existing literature exemplifies an emotionally charged and politically engaged approach to the topic.

about ethnic differences, historical reconstruction, and the place of their communities in American societies. This approach recontextualizes earlier notions of both the self in autobiography and the life writing process, stressing the complex representation of the ethnic subject's self-awareness and self-inscription. Issues of representation in life writing – and its concerns with identity politics, the rewriting of history, and the attempt to claim validity of personal and social experience – characterize the narrative strategies employed by Asian American writers." (Davis, "The Self in the Text" 41–42)

Following Davis' analysis, Asian American life writing centers on the field's core aspects and questions: the need to create a space for themselves in America, to correct the writing of history, to represent the community via the self. Davis, one of the leading voices for emphasizing formal features of Asian American writing, reads the autobiographical as an inherently performative text, emphasizing the ways in which form mirrors content:

"The self *of* the text frequently becomes the self *as* the text – the narrative strategies used reflect particular forms of perceiving and/or performing subjectivity. Selfhood in life writing is thus understood as a narrative performance and the text often exhibits the writer's process of self-awareness and struggle for self-representation through the narrative structure itself." (42)

Thus, focusing on the way a narrative is being told enhances the general understanding of the text. Although this certainly applies to any kind of writing, life writing's purpose of consciously representing a life and a self calls for a special engagement with its stylistic features.

According to Davis, Asian American memoirs have an important historical dimension. They construct personal narratives that narrate also, at the same time, collective and cultural memories of a certain group (Davis, "Mediating Historical Memory" 491). In this sense, Asian American life writing is highly political. To use Betty Ann Bergland's words, "[b]ecause that 'I' is perceived generally to represent the ethnic community, what the 'I' speaks and how it speaks become critical" (Bergland, "Representing Ethnicity in Autobiography" 78). Referencing Ien Ang's conception of autobiography as staging a public self – one that can be put to work –, Davis argues that Asian American life writing provides cultural memory for the communities in the United States, explains their presence in the United States, and forces readers to reexamine the presence of the US in Asia (Davis, "Mediating Historical Memory" 503).

Davis emphasizes the relational status of Asian American life writing. She sees Maxine Hong Kingston's *The Woman Warrior* as a revision of the paradigms of life writing. In this, she highlights the postmodern dialogue that Kingston's work allows with readers, different traditions and communities as well as a relational approach to constructions of the self in narration, referring to Paul John Eakin's work. To Davis, these Asian American texts exhibit an intersection of biography and autobiography (Davis, "The Self in the Text" 44–45). Deborah Madsen concludes that

> "Kingston's work exemplifies the subversive power of the entire genre of Chinese American autobiography. She uses the assumed competence of a white readership to subvert Orientalist images of Chinese America, even as she undermines the stable racial identity of mainstream white America. Like the Chinese American autobiographers who preceded her, Kingston does this in order to question the adequacy of specific racial discourses to represent ethnic authenticity and thus to undermine hegemonic definitions of racial authenticity." (Madsen, "Chinese American Writers" 270)

And the idea of undermining hegemonic constructions of racial authenticity can go both ways: to the white mainstream as well as to the Chinese American community itself. Thus, in presenting a relational self as part of an ethnic community, but writing this story within a new stylistic form, Kingston's memoir – just like Fenkl's – invites controversial discussions of genre.

Memories of My Ghost Brother also uses such a mixture of genres. Published as a novel, but clearly autobiographical, it builds on the Asian American tradition of rewriting existing genres. Just like Kingston, Fenkl blends fact and fiction. Just like Kingston, Fenkl moves in between the two modes without clearly instructing readers in which realm his narrative currently moves. Referencing the most widely known memoir of Asian American literature is not something unique to Fenkl's novel. Many Asian American novels that have been published since Kingston's *The Woman Warrior* refer back to it in terms of theme or genre or both. However, Fenkl also populates his autobiographical text with ghost figures, just like Kingston. This curious mixture of a seemingly factual narration of one's life with the haunting figures of ghosts breaks with the conception of autobiography as a referential discourse. In this sense, then, Kingston's text presents another revision of the genre.[7] How do ghosts fit into life writing? What do they add?

---

7 Donald C. Goellnicht even reads Kingston's work as 'autobiographical theory' or 'theoretical autobiography,' crediting her with a theoretical questioning for the need of dichotomous genre distinctions (341).

The secondary literature tends to read these ghosts as metaphorical, as psychoanalytic references to repressed aspects of a personal and cultural identity. In her essay "The Ghostly Rhetoric of Autobiography," Carol Mejia-LaPerle examines "the relationship between memoir and ghosts, the possible reciprocity between the telling of memory and the evanescent shapes that haunt the telling" (108). In response to the critical reading of Kingston's ghosts as catering to the wish of a white audience for exoticized elements in life writing, Mejia-LaPerle argues that these ghosts rather emphasize the inconsistencies of any view of cultural authenticity, be that white American or Asian American (113). She summarizes,

> "[g]hosts represent not just the unknown and unrepresentable in the world, but also the unrepresentable in the self, expressed through the reappropriation of a repressed personal history. [...] Indeed, ghosts show us that both the past and the self are knowable only through the tenuous creation, rather than recollection, of memory. Ghosts emphasize what is constructed – therefore fleeting, undependable, ephemeral – yet this constructedness is proof of, and perhaps the only tenable foundation for, one's identity." (119)

In Mejia-LaPerle's reading, ghosts function as allegorical references to the instability of cultural subjectivity in their curious position in-between absence and presence.

In a similar vein, Belinda Kong focuses on the changes that have occurred in the application and reception of ghosts in Asian American literature. Comparing lê thi diem thúy's *the gangster we're all looking for* (2003) with Maxine Hong Kingston's memoir (1976), she concludes that today Asian American literature has moved away from earlier conceptions of American nativity and othering of Asia, in that the gaze goes equally in both directions: Asia and America. Therefore, both locations are haunted, just as the Asian American hyphen itself is haunted by the memories that it includes and excludes. To Kong, the ghosts are "metaphors, finally, for Asian-America's own internal strangers" (Kong 137). The ghosts of Asian American autobiography, thus, expose the troubled self-conception of Asian American subjectivity and, in the representative terms of ethnic literature, the troubled construction of Asian American history.

In my view, *Memories of My Ghost Brother*, as part of and reference to this psychoanalytic tradition, exposes the ghostliness that pervades the camptown world and the subjects that this setting calls forth. In Grace Kyungwon Hong's words, "[t]he memoir is rife with ghosts of all kinds. [...] Rather than emphasize only a simple causality, the memoir conveys a generalized sense of *deathliness* that pervades the camptown, with the backdrop of potential war and neocolonial militarism" (Hong 56–57). Hong refers here to the various deaths that occur throughout the novel, some of them directly related to an American military presence, others only indirectly or not at all. According to Hong, the ghosts embody the unsettling situation that the neocolonial presence creates. However, she stresses that the novel

> "undermines any Orientalist binary that might posit an essentializing definition of Korean culture as mythic and US society as rationalized, and indeed suggests a correspondence between the superstitions and symbols that camptown residents and soldiers alike deploy to articulate their proximity to death. The novel thus presents all of these populations as ghostly: physically alive, but ruled by death." (62)

Hong begins to address the different traditions of haunting that shape the novel. My own reading is indebted to hers as she sees the ghost figures as part of both a Western and a Korean culture, as both metaphorical and spiritual forms; and she emphasizes the connections between these two cultures in the forms of ghost figures in the all-pervasive presence of death. The ghosts, thus, function as metaphorical references to the ghostly status of all characters who live in the camptown world. With such a focus, *Memories of My Ghost Brother* reads as a text that unsettles the binaries of East versus West, while it does engage with existing differences in terms of the family members and their cultural distinctness.

In this neocolonial setting, the representation of a self surely mirrors such ambiguity. For Insu, as a biracial child, does neither belong fully to the Korean society nor the American one. He remains at a distance to both, shifting between yearning for a place to belong and distanced observations, puzzled by misogynist or racist aspects in both cultures. Hong continues with the argument that

> "[i]n this context, the narrator's divided condition, characterized by his split and inconsistent identifications, is not anomalous but representative. Here we see the second formal aspect of the novel: the production of a narrative subject based on contradiction." (62)

In Jin-Kyung Lee's words, the in-between status of such biracial children "can only be described as ghostly" (Lee, *Service Economies* 167). Such a ghostly self calls for new ways of narrating itself.

If one wishes to follow the traditional script of resistance narratives in Asian American or Postcolonial Studies, such a divided subject would not make a fitting protagonist. For, as Andrew Hock Soon Ng pointedly asks,

> "how is resistance possible when the resisting (postcolonial) subject is *also* the subject (interpellated by colonial inheritance) to be resisted? Here, we see the postcolonial subject as profoundly 'multiplicated' – a bricolage embodiment who is struggling to understand her own fragmented identity and to negotiate her multifaceted belonging." (Ng, *Interrogating Interstices* 33)

Following Hong, Lee, and Ng, I argue that the divided loyalties, the struggling characters, the moral dilemma and the resultant blame that is not centered on a single character but rather runs through the whole setting – all of this creates a narrator who remains ghostly to himself and to others. Fittingly, *Memories of My Ghost Brother* features ghost figures of both traditions, mirroring the shifting position of its narrator between these two cultures. The novel engages in a specific way of narrating this ghostly self and his surroundings by using the perspective of the child Insu. This way, some questions simply do not need to be answered conclusively. Instead of offering an explanation of the ghost figures as metaphorical – as the secondary literature often attempts – the child, and therefore the novel as a whole, accepts the co-existence of possible explanations for these figures. In terms of the ghost figures this perspective evades questions of the ghost's 'reality-status' – the novel narrates Insu's experience and this is what he remembers. It offers a combination of the father's psychoanalytical and the mother's spiritual explanations without the need to resolve this confusing co-existence. The child perspective helps to establish these ghost figures as credible: this particular perspective at once supports the material existence of these figures, while it also shows how they are coping mechanisms for the confused child. The ghosts are, essentially, a way to narrate memories. In the eyes of the child the world is confusing and this confusion can be kept in the narrative.

Such an approach to memories and remembering is also given in the characters' approach to storytelling. His uncle Hyongbu often tells Insu stories, weaving powerful threads to Korea's traditional folklore. His tales feature Korean women, who are either dutiful wives saving their husbands' lives or horrible threats to the men in the form of fox demons, they also feature Korean men outsmarting goblins – possibly a reinscription of Korean masculinity after emasculation through the American soldiers' presence. While these tales serve as guiding stories for the young narrator – especially since his father is often absent so that his uncle stands in for a Korean father-figure –, Insu is often rather puzzled by the misogynist tales. Asking for explanations, his uncle continuously scalds him and instructs him: "We tell stories because they're meant to be told. Just remember the story, and you can worry about the meaning later, understand?" (Fenkl, *Memories of My Ghost Brother* 228). Overall, Hyongbu's stories remain ambiguous and the narrator does not, finally, arrive at satisfactory explanations. While these myths tie Insu to his Korean folkloric background, he remains at a distance to this tradition. And yet, as the young Insu tells his own narrative, he follows his uncle's model of storytelling in that he also refrains from further framing or interpreting these stories. They simply exist – to be remembered, just like the ghost figures of the novel.

The child narrator approaches his father's American traditions with a similar attitude: he tries to understand his father's actions, but often becomes confused by what he perceives so that he neglects further explanations. Insu has fantasies about an adult life very close to his father: "I promised to myself that when I grew up and became a dark-haired GI, I would make lots of money and buy everyone everything they wanted to have so they would be happy always" (18). As a young boy, Insu sees no other option than becoming a GI himself. He associates with this American lifestyle a life of abundance and happiness. He imagines a closeness to his father that is not part of his life at present, thinking that "my father, by then, would surely be a great general with white hair and a beard instead of only his short yellow hair. He would tell me wise things and we would kill many enemies together" (18). Although the passage is driven by Insu's wish for a proud and instructive father figure, he is already acutely aware of the differences between his father and himself, underlined here by the distinctive hair colors. Insu's hope that these colors will someday fade into an indistinctive grey or white, expresses his wish for similarity and familiarity with his father. In his GI fantasy, Insu exposes the ambivalence of existing images about America. Although his fantasy feeds into the idea of America as a benevolent protector of a freed Korea, empowering him to make everyone happy by partaking of the American riches, this fantasy is already in itself undermined through the unbridgeable distance Insu feels towards his father. In the end – and this is also what the novel as a whole arrives at –, it remains exactly what it is: a fantasy, even though it is a powerful fantasy for the young boy.

Throughout the novel, Insu is almost obsessed with the physical differences he perceives in his father. In these descriptions, Insu remains very much at a distance, his tone moving far beyond that of any curious small boy closely inspecting a family member. For example, when he plays with his father, Insu notices that his father's sweat smells different, "filling the room with his strange animal smell" (123). On another occasion, Insu describes his father's face:

"The wrinkles around his eyes – cut deep from squinting into the Vietnam sun, from peering into the observation glasses at the 38th parallel, at the DMZ between Koreas – they fan out like the delta of a river, and he is smiling so hard, laughing his surprisingly

> *loud and barky laugh until tears stream from the corners of his cold blue eyes and are squeezed into those channels."* (63)

The connection Insu makes here between his father's wrinkles and his life in Asia, seems to invite a closeness between father and son. Noticing and acknowledging how Asia has marked his father's physical appearance, watching him laugh, the reader might expect a tenderness between the two. And yet, what follows is a surprisingly distanced description with the 'loud and barky laugh' and the 'cold blue eyes,' once again featuring the physical but also the cultural differences that distance them.

This passage is taken from one of the italicized short chapters that separate the usual child-like narration. The narrator's ambiguity towards both cultures, but especially towards America, is mirrored in the two narrative styles that the novel employs. Keith Ames Russel distinguishes in *Dislocated: Trauma and Narrative Distance in Korean American Literature* (2007) the two styles as "italicized, lyrical passages focalized through an adult Insu and simple, more direct passages from the perspective of his younger incarnation" (Russel 112). He argues that these intrusions are ambivalent, linking this ambivalence to the traumatic experience of the narrator. The adult narration, according to Russel, "undermines the trustworthiness of the child-like sections, which destabilizes that story" but the italicized passages themselves are not "seamlessly cohesive" in holding the narrative together (112).

An interview of the author with the *Spectator* highlights the ambiguous generic status of the novel, calling it an "intriguing mix of reality and the supernatural" which

> "give[s] many scenes an almost magical quality; as Fenkl explains, the book could just as easily have been called a memoir 'because everything in it is true – there is the usual condensation or rearrangement of chronology, but as for the events or stories in the novel – they all happened in exactly the way they're told.'" (Fenkl np)

In the same interview, the author explains the arduous journey of writing his first novel. He began by writing vignettes that did not seem to connect. Unable to face the tragic losses of his childhood, he tried to avoid writing those difficult passages at first. Over a time span of 11 years, Fenkl worked on his book, spending some time trying to write 'the generic American novel' – in an attempt to rebel against writing the expected ethnic novel that his life called for. Finally, during a visit back in Korea, he realized that he needed to adapt the format of the novel. In his words, "I think what I started to see was that this was not just going to be a book about me" (Fenkl np). This realization, then, gave birth to the peculiar format of *Memories of My Ghost Brother*.

In an interview with Piya Kochhar, he describes his changes to the original format:

> "I had an entirely transformed attitude towards what my writing should be. […] And although most of the material is very, very similar to the original manuscript and a lot of the language is the same, the architecture of the book, the addition of the italics, entirely changes what those original stories mean." (Fenkl np)

Russel's observations are, therefore, quite fitting. According to Fenkl himself, the italicized passages reflect a differing viewpoint from a matured narrator, and they place the story into more of a historical and public realm. At the same time, these passages do not cohesively ground the story in this realm. In their stubborn resistance to be placed definitively, these passages give the novel as a whole a ghostly feel: they invite a description as a ghostly subtext.

As Russel states, much of the novel "oscillates between nearness during the childlike narration and farness during the interruptive adult voice" (Russel 120). The immediacy and simplicity of the depicted events in the childlike passages creates a nearness both between the narrator and his narrated life and the reader with the narrator. His style is straightforward, the flow of the narrative smooth. In the italicized passages, the narrator often depicts singular moments that seem disconnected from the rest of the storyline. The style is lyrical, the flow of the narrative is interruptive. These passages create a farness between both the narrator and his material and between the narrator and his readers. These different passages mirror, on a stylistic level, the ambiguous relationship that the narrator shows towards his parents, their cultures, and the ways in which history has been told. Especially with relation to a fantasy of America, the difference is highly pronounced. In Russel's words, "[w]hile Insu's narration from childhood is eager to accept American ways, his adult reflections are bitter and resentful toward the charms of America" (140). And through this stylistic set-up, the ambivalence that runs through the novel remains intact. The conflicting images that the novel depicts are never resolved.

> "What remains for me are the resonances of memory and nostalgia, the initially-imagined narrative, the world of my childhood over-written by the darker meanings of the world as I know it today. In the language of emotion and imagination, those are the ghosts that haunt my writing, and those are the things which I am trying to invoke with *Memories of My Ghost Brother*." (Fenkl, *A Few Notes on Memories* np)

These explanatory words of Heinz Insu Fenkl's concerning *Memories of My Ghost Brother* explain the centrality of the ghost figures for the author. His narrative is driven by lost places and persons, and for him, remembering them is vital. And the most applicable form to remember those who have almost vanished is via the concept of haunting. Sociologist Avery Gordon writes in *Ghostly Matters* (2004) how haunting describes the ways in which a ghostly presence makes itself known and it should be recognized as 'a social figure.' As a result, no matter which traditions, beliefs, or explanations one associates with ghost appearances, the central point that connects all of them is the call for an investigation of something that is barely visible and that has social roots. Haunting figures are 'seething presences' that force those they haunt to take closer looks at the issues that they raise and that remain in order to be finally acknowledged. Fenkl's novel attempts such acknowledgement.

The child's fantasies and hopes are taken seriously, but they are also presented alongside the older narrator's more distanced descriptions of his family and 1960s South Korea. The child's initial confusion is conveyed, but the older narrator's reflections and interpretations of these memories also frame the child's narrative. Memories and realities are, thus, constructed and undermined, created and challenged in an ongoing engagement with the past.

Eventually, the stylistic choices echo the impossibility of narrating this ghostly self. As part of a neocolonial setting, in which – and I refer to Grace Kyungwon Hong once again – 'no one is blameless and everyone is complicit,' the contradictory subject that emerges needs to find new arenas to perform itself. *Memories of My Ghost Brother* strategically constructs this self as ghostly, foregrounding the ways in which it remains ambiguous and unfinished, structuring itself around the ghosts of its past. In Fenkl's own words, "[o]ver the years I've come to believe that literal and figurative hauntings can be the same: memories are ghosts of the past and ghosts are those memories embodied" (Fenkl, *A Few Notes on Memories* np).

FAMILY HAUNTINGS: FOLK KNOWLEDGE AND PSYCHOANALYTICAL GHOST FIGURES

Memories of My Ghost Brother rather emphasizes the complexity of the situation than pointing fingers at singular specific agents. And yet, as it tells its story from the perspective of a child, the confusion, sadness, and helplessness is conveyed throughout for the complexity of the situation and the larger systems are above the child's ability to grasp. Insu perceives, instead, the various haunting ghost figures. These are presences in his daily life, his sad memories, figures that reference what remains too abstract otherwise. They give his world some kind of structure, offering a way to engage with memories and the different approaches to these figures that his parents embody.

In its focus on a typical Korean American family, *Memories of My Ghost Brother* refers to various traditions of haunting. In doing so, the novel presents approaches to the topic of haunting that seem opposed to each other, yet brings them uncannily close to each other. While the narrator explicitly states his own closeness to the particular Korean ghost beliefs, the novel refrains from predetermined judgments of Western or Eastern, postmodern or traditional, psychoanalytical, allegorical, or spiritual approaches to the topic. Rather, *Memories of My Ghost Brother* shows the entanglements of these approaches for this young Korean American boy. In his gendered world structure, his Korean mother and his German American father each stand in for their specific cultural traditions and their particular conceptions of haunting presences, but both are haunted by their shared secret of the narrator's ghost brother. Thus, the novel plays with and mixes folk knowledge and psychoanalytical approaches to these figures; the shifting between its child perspective and the italicized passages underlines the narrator's struggle with his memories and his perception and framing of the ghost figures.

In order to grasp the characters' specific struggles, the larger history in which their stories are embedded needs to be understood. Overall, the whole family is shaped and haunted by the history of Korea-U.S. relations. The Korean War is often referred to as the "Forgotten War."[8] Historian Bruce Cumings describes the war in *The Korean War* (2011) in its origins as a civil war, enhanced by lingering fury over the Japanese colonization of the country from 1905 until 1945. By the end of World War II Korea was liberated due to the surrender of the Japanese forces, but it was then divided along the 38th parallel, with the North occupied by the Soviet Union and the South by the United States. All sides hoped for a reunification of Korea under their influence after having finally thrown off the Japanese imperial power (Cumings 64–66). Although it was part of the Cold War, with North Korea supported by communist China and the Soviet Union and South Korea supported by the UN, mainly the United States, this war does not appear prominently in Western history writing. The reasons for this amnesia are probably to be found in its unsatisfactory outcome: after 3 years of fighting (1950–1953), an armistice agreement was signed and the

8 See for example, Clay Blair. *The Forgotten War: America in Korea*. New York: Anchor Books 1987.

Demilitarized Zone (DMZ) was created to separate the North from the South. The country remains divided along this line and conflicts along the border have not subsided, so the US holds its military presence in the South to this day (Liem 114).

The setting of Fenkl's novel refers to the dominance of this history and the shadows it still casts on Korea in the 1960s and early 70s. But the timeframe of the novel and the father's continuing absences also highlight the importance of the Vietnam War as the ongoing struggles of the United States in following its containment strategy towards communism. Furthermore, it shows the close entanglements between Korea and the United States with South Korean participation in the Vietnam War as a stepping stone towards more power. It emphasizes the constant presence of a United States military dominance in Korea even before and long after the Korean War, exposing not only the neo-imperial status of Korea, but also referring to Korea's own economic and strategic gains from this ambiguous relationship.

Due to this presence, marriages between Korean women and American GIs were common at the time. Especially the military bases and the camptown world offered various meeting points for these couples. In general, these relationships are stained, however, by referring back to a history of military prostitution. With the United States taking charge in 1945, the sexual slavery system set up for the Japanese Imperial Army in the comfort stations was exchanged with the system of camptown prostitution set up for the US military (Cho 8). The Japanese colonial government in Korea used people in positions of authority to promise young, pretty Korean girls jobs in factories in Japan, where they were forced into prostitution for high-ranking military officials before they were sent to war zone brothels. About two hundred thousand women and girls were recruited or simply kidnapped and forced to work as sexual slaves for the Japanese military (Yuh 18–19). These brothels were later used by American military camptowns. As Ji-Yeon Yuh puts it, "[t]hese women are America's comfort women, the victims of a system of militarized prostitution that is supported and regulated by the U.S. military for the benefit of its soldiers" (16), emphasizing the way that both the Korean government and the US military had a part in maintaining such easily accessible prostitutes for their troops. Even though Yuh focuses on the dynamics that shape relationships between Korean military brides and their husbands once they move to America, her argumentation also holds for the time they spend in Korea: the linkages she makes

"between the imperialist nature of Korea-U.S. relations and husband-wife dynamics, between pressures to Americanize and Orientalist images of Asian women and family relations – demonstrate that even the most personal of relationships are deeply rooted in and shaped by historical and social circumstances." (7)

In other words, the family relations resulting from this military history in Korea are constantly framed, evaluated, judged, and dominated by forces far beyond the reach of the family itself.

Because of this background, the scant secondary literature that exists on *Memories of My Ghost Brother* reads the novel primarily in terms of its imperial setting. Kun Jong Lee, for example, views the novel in his focus on the ironic references to Rudyard Kipling's *Kim* as essentially a critique of the troubling US presence in Korea and their centuries old imperialist projects in Asia at large, stating that Insu "contraposes the West and the East as enemies" (Lee, "Heinz Insu Fenkl's *Memories*" 329). While this chapter also addresses the centrality of this historical setting – for the novel depicts all of its characters as deeply influenced if not chained by these larger forces –, it argues that the novel as a whole does not work within a framework of categorizations in terms of colonizer/colonized, perpetrator/victim, as Lee has it, but highlights instead the inherent interconnections in the historical and political setup of South Korean and American relations in the life of the narrator's family and friends. Just like Yamanaka's *Behold the Many* in its rewriting of postcolonial melodrama's affective potential, Fenkl's autobiographical novel offers a rethinking of such binary terms and classifications. Both novels employ the characters' approaches of the ghost figures to address and undermine such dual thinking.

Even though Insu's mother is not a prostitute, the parents' marriage is framed by the stereotypes that surround such connections between Korean women and American soldiers. In this framework, the father's world serves as a reference to the ambiguous presence of the United States in Korea. While it brought liberation from Japanese colonialism, the US took over as another dominating presence. Thus, the attitudes towards this presence fluctuate between awe, gratitude, anger, frustration, and fear. Images of the American Dream are presented alongside the nightmares of the Korean camptown world. The mother's world serves as a constant reminder of this ambivalent relationship to the United States. I argue that instead of buying into an empire/colony imagery, *Memories of My Ghost Brother* highlights the complicated relationship that Korea and America share. As Grace Kyungwon Hong argues,

"South Korean sovereignty as a nation-state cannot be characterized only as subsumed or dominated by the United States; while this is certainly the case, South Korea has wielded its own forms of subimperialist power, gaining economically and politically through its position of power relative to Vietnam." (Hong 54)

And even though the novel does not explicitly cite South Korean privileges from the Vietnam War, this war provides the background for its setting and shows the family's connections to it.

The parents' relationship is tightly intertwined with the setting. In the gendered logic of the novel, the parents appear not simply as parental figures for their son but as representatives of their cultures. Jin-Kyung Lee argues that biracial children like Insu have a specific relationship to their cultural backgrounds in that their

"subjectivity is negatively constituted, through their very distance from both societies and cultures, while at the same time this very distance itself is what provides them with an intimate knowledge of two cultures, knowledge acquired from the margins of both." (Lee, *Service Economies* 164)

The mother is very close to her son, taking him along even to her black market activities, connecting him to his extended family and his Korean roots, including its spiritual and ghost beliefs. That the father remains a puzzling figure to his son is spotlighted in various aspects: his looks and smell, his American background, his GI life away from the family, his spontaneous and sporadic visits with the family, as well as his religious beliefs. The mother's world is full of ghost presences, but it is the father's world that appears as ghostly and frightening to the narrator.

However, the proximity or distance Insu feels towards each parent reflects his familiarity with the respective culture and especially its religious beliefs. And yet, even though Insu obviously favors his mother's Korean beliefs, he does not completely denounce the Christian traditions which he associates with his father.

Just like Insu's father himself, Christianity remains at a puzzling distance for Insu. Exposing the tragic irony of the gap between words and action, he states,

"I imagined Christ in dusty robes and dirty sandals walking through the desert, but in church there was the priest in a gold-trimmed, pure white cassock telling men – whose job it was to kill other men – that they should be Good Samaritans and build their houses on stone." (Fenkl, *Memories of My Ghost Brother* 240)

While Insu does know Christ's stories of healing and wonders and can understand their wisdom, he struggles to place these stories in the neocolonial world in which he lives. And yet, even when he criticizes the Christian priests' hypocritical references to brotherly love when these men are supposed to kill in the next hours – he criticizes not Christianity as such, but the framework in which its teachings are (ab)used because he does sees the value of the stories from the bible.

Without proper explanations, Christ's dead body on the cross evokes horror in the child and makes him wonder:

"How could they [the Catholics] line up under his body and eat the white disks that were supposed to be his flesh, sip the red wine that was supposed to be his blood, and go away healed? How could I worship this man with the unbearable agony in his eyes or the father who sent him to earth to be tortured to death?" (240–41)

To Insu, the Catholic religion remains unclear and illogical. The father's abandonment of the son appears to him very cruel, and might unconsciously stir memories of his own father's absence and the abandonment of his brother. For Insu, Christianity is a religion of stories – some beautiful, some frightening, but it achieves nothing more.

All of this is posited in stark contrast to traditional Korean beliefs, which are often closely connected to specific places or situations.

"I understood the way each Buddhist temple up in the Korean hills had a separate shrine dedicated to the old man of the mountain, how Buddhists prayed to nature spirits and honored their ancestors, how Korean Christians often lapsed and called upon a mudang to perform healings [...] – but the American religion I could not understand. [...] But I also understood that my father's religion was one whose miracles were old; they were in the stories of healing, the walking over water, the multiplying fishes and loaves; there were no miracles now. My father's priest could not lead the souls of the restless dead into the other world [...]. He could not bring luck to a family whose house was full of tragedy or bring sons to a woman who could bear only daughters. My father's religion wallowed in stories and pictures of tragedy and suffering, but it could not heal what happened every day outside the gates of the U.S. Army post. And so I could not worship his God or the murdered son – I believed in ghosts and ancestors and portentous dreams of serpents and dragons because those were the things I could touch in my world." (240–41)

To Insu, the American religion stays out of touch with everything. It does not follow the hands-on approach to which he is used from the Korean shamanist tradition. His mother's ghosts and dreams appear as strong forces that actually shape Korean lives. The references to the Korean tradition of shamanism pronounce its healing potential. Instead of telling old stories, shamans face the remains of what appears to be past but continues to haunt the present. In this direct contrast, I see the ghost figures function in making graspable what is otherwise abstract, they allow Insu to 'touch' upon what would otherwise remain untouchable. Although ghosts are usually rather perceived as fleeting and shifting, the child narrator experiences them as concrete, material presences. The Korean spiritualist ghost figures appear in stark contrast to an ungraspable Christianity.

Insu not only misunderstands or questions the authenticity of the priests and believers, but also associates an unnamable fear with this religious presence. When his father forces him to attend Sunday school – so that he will not become a 'heathen,' as his father explains – Insu feels highly uncomfortable, just like his mother. "The nun made Mahmi uncomfortable – the big American MPs with their rifles and pistols didn't scare her, but the woman in the black habit seemed to frighten her, and I felt the same strange fear in my heart" (76). The 'strange fear' that is opposed to the more threatening presence of rifles relates to the overarching presence of an America that wishes to dominate. While the open, obvious power through the military has become part of everyday life to the narrator, the subtler cultural takeover that is anticipated evokes fear and raises barriers. Insu's father is part of this world and tries to force him into it, yet fails to explain or convey his religious beliefs properly.

That these passages about the religious differences are part of the italicized parts of the novel – the ones in which an older Insu frames his childhood memories – underlines the importance of the ghost figures for his recollections throughout. Even though he has matured and begins to grasp the larger forces, he still needs the ghosts to address these tragedies. In *The Location of Culture* (1994), Homi K. Bhabha notes the hierarchical set-up inherent in such colonial settings, yet focuses on the complexity of cultural formations, exposing their inherent ambiguity. To him,

> "colonial hybridity is not a *problem* of genealogy or identity between two *different* cultures which can then be resolved as an issue of cultural relativism. Hybridity is a problematic of colonial representation and individuation that reverses the effects of the colonialist disavowel, so that other 'denied' knowledges enter upon the dominant discourse and estrange the basis of its authority – its rules of recognition." (Bhabha 162)

Certainly, Fenkl's novel narrates differences in cultural and religious traditions, but, in the end, a sense of overlapping is what remains. The estrangement of such authority is directly related to Bhabha's conception of the unhomely. It is the haunting presence that always already challenges a supposed colonial authority from within. Yet, in contrast to Bhabha's unsettling of the hegemonic discourse, *Memories of My Ghost Brother* engages in a reversed haunting. For the young narrator, the Korean shamanist traditions shape the ways in which the novel's protagonists view and explain the attempted authoritative Christian discourse. But the effect of such an unsettling is the same: the traditions are seen as particularized yet intertwined. The novel emphasizes in this view that both traditions are carried on through stories and memories – sometimes in the form of ghost figures.

Instead of thinking in terms of binary oppositions, Bhabha describes the colonial situation in its complex web of interconnections. In his words,

> "[i]f the effect of colonial power is seen to be the *production* of hybridization rather than the noisy command of colonialist authority or the silent repression of native traditions, then an important change of perspective occurs. The ambivalence at the source of traditional discourses on authority enables a form of subversion, founded on the undecidability that turns the discursive conditions of dominance into the grounds of intervention." (160)

And it is exactly this undecidabilty that the narrator foregrounds again and again. The novel exposes the contradictory identificatory possibilities, the larger systems and their influence on personal lives and the resulting production of moral dilemmas. What emerges is not a clearly distinguishable set of categories with value attachments, but a lingering sense of overlapping in the discourses of haunting. The ghost stories of the novel provide a way of addressing the haunting memories that these larger forces create.

Many such ghost presences appear throughout the novel. It begins with the haunted house in which Insu lives with his extended family and ends with the revelation of his ghost brother. The novel charts Insu's growing up in South Korea alongside many different ghost figures. And in that, the novel once again foregrounds its specific Korean German American mix: while most of the ghosts who make appearances are consistent with Korean folklore, the actual ghost brother may not even be dead – so this haunting is clearly metaphoric (Laurel Kendall in email correspondence, 23.3.2012). Both Korean and Western traditions of haunting are, thus, presented throughout the novel as appearing side by side.

The literal ghosts that accompany Insu's mother's specific Korean world appear, to him as familiar presences. And even though some of them scare him, he usually takes their presence as taken for granted, as does almost everyone around him. A telling example of this omnipresence of the dead is a conversation between a shop owner, Insu and one of Insu's close friends, Jani. After a maid placed her baby on the lid of a well and it fell down and drowned in it, the area is supposed to be haunted, as the shop owner warns the boys:

"'The baby's ghost is calling people.' […] 'Even Jani – even if you believe in Jesus – the ghost will call you, too. Korean ghosts don't care what you believe in.' 'I still don't believe those things,' said Jani, laughing. Mr. Peak pointed across the street. 'The baby's mother doesn't believe in ghosts. She believes in Jesus like you,' he said quietly. 'But she nearly jumped in last night.' Jani stopped smiling and looked across the street with me. Though it was just past noon, the square around the well looked as if it were in evening light." (Fenkl, *Memories of My Ghost Brother* 184)

Simply because of his age, the shop owner has some sort of authority. His warning becomes even scarier due to its nuanced explanation by openly addressing existing differing beliefs of Christians. That 'Korean ghosts don't care what you believe in' makes them even more powerful.

And to be sure, in the following pages, Insu becomes haunted by this ghost presence. On his way home from the movies, Insu has an accident with his bike because he almost runs over a passing woman with a red scarf. Without being able to explain why, Insu is very frightened of this figure, only to learn the next day that the maid of the baby went to the well to drown herself and so far only her scarf could be found. Later that day, Insu flees from a couple of boys and, by chance, hides behind the well in the dark. While crouching behind the well for protection, he begins to fantasize:

"The bodies were still inside, under the cold, black water – the maid with her red scarf and the horribly bloated child. But they had taken the scarf, and now, with the wet dripping sounds, the maid would be climbing out to find it […]. She crawled up, bit by bit, dripping water from her soaked dress. She reached the top and pushed up at the pale wooden lid. 'Did you take the scarf? It's you. You've come to stay with us. It's so lonely down there.' The lid thumped as she reached out to grab me with her icy hand, and I felt the water drip against my neck. I screamed and looked up, but the cold water fell into my eyes and I couldn't see until I twisted to my side, crashed against the well, and heard a sound like the cracking of crisp paper." (196)

There is an interesting shift in the tense that the narrator uses. While in the beginning of the quote the maid is imagined to be doing something, the narration quickly shifts into the past tense, implying that this actually happened. The reader is drawn into this scary episode, fearing with the young Insu hiding behind the well, having escaped his pursuers only to be haunted by the ghosts of the well. In the daylight of the next day, Insu forces himself to remember this scene in minute detail, trying to convince himself that there was nothing ghostly happening at the well. Still, Insu is not entirely sure – and so is the reader. This episode ends with the finding of the bodies two days later, when a "rumor spread that the baby had been in the maid's arms when they dragged her up by her long, tangled hair" (200).

Left with this feeling of unease especially because a large number of accidents happen right there, everyone tries to forget. This erasure is enhanced by the opening of the Apollo Club. The incident happens while the Apollo Club is under construction, the well originally intended to be a part of the club's Apollo theme. Interestingly, the club is owned by a rich man from Seoul, offering "strip shows and all the latest drinks from America" (178). And when, a week later, cholera deaths start and a "*mudang* at a nearby exorcism rite said in her trance that the cholera had come because the Apollo Club had polluted the water and offended the guardian spirits of the well" (200), the haunting is ascribed to the clash between the two cultures. Instead of having a traditional Korean exorcism, the club owner opens its doors and soon begins to make a fortune there with the hordes of GIs coming to see its shows.

Insu also struggles to sort out his feelings.

> "Each time I passed the Apollo Club I became very uneasy. I thought, at first, that it was fear and sadness, that I was afraid of my memories and the ghosts that might dwell there now, that my sadness was for the Apollo Club; but then I realized that my fear was of the Apollo Club and my sadness was for the ghosts of the dead. 'It's so lonely down here. Have you come to be with us?' Everyone so quickly tried to forget. The ghosts of the drowned maid and the drowned baby, the ghosts of all my friends who had gone away forever – I often saw them in my dreams and they were always so lonely." (201)

Following the novel's logic, Insu here places himself on the Korean side of the incident. The shift from fear of the ghosts to fear of the Apollo Club, thus, indicates his maturation. Even though he was first scared of the ghost appearances – and probably still is, in some way –, he begins to understand that these sad presences simply belong to his life. The ghosts of the baby and the drowned maid force Insu to reflect upon the current situation: questioning the American presence and their ways to engage with such tragic incidents in contrast to Korean beliefs and rituals, Insu confirms his Korean roots. Yet, the scene also already indicates the complicity of Asians in foregrounding that the owner of the Apollo Club was explicitly not an American, but a 'rich man from Seoul,' furthering his riches by catering to the wishes of the American soldiers. Thus, highlighting the entanglements that the imperial American power calls forth in South Korea, the narrator emphasizes the participation of Asians in the ambiguous riches that the American presence offers, for once referencing the economic gains for South Korea very openly. Following the logic of the novel at large, reminding one once again of Bhabha's conception of hybridity, these puzzling interconnections are shown via reference to ghosts and haunting.

Memories of My Ghost Brother engages in a striking mixture of psychoanalytical and spiritual explanations for its ghost figures. The novel plays with the distinct ethnographic material upon which Insu's story is based: it emphasizes that Insu experienced what he did because of his growing up in post-war South Korea as the son of a German American father and a Korean mother. But in this larger cultural context, the novel also highlights that these are the narrator's own subjective memories. The ghosts of the novel reference both of these arguments: they are products of a specific Korean German American mixture, but they are also his personal haunting memories. The tragedy at the Apollo Club, for instance, highlights the economic gains and losses of South Korean American relations at the time. It also foregrounds the contradictory reactions that Insu perceives: the *mudang*'s warning and the GI's entertainment at the club. The reflections of the narrator emphasize the Korean ghost beliefs, but also allow a psychoanalytical approach in the idea of keeping memories of absent presences of his lost friends. Strikingly, some of his friends, who 'had gone away forever,' have not died, but vanish from the narrator's world, when they leave for the United States. As a result, America itself becomes a powerful frightening presence to young Insu. The American presence not only haunts his South Korean life, but is also experienced as a force that turns its immigrants into ghosts, foreshadowing Insu's own fear and sadness when he finally moves there himself. Following the dual logic of the narrative – that it relates a child's personal memories and a specific Korean German American tale – the ghost maid appears as if part of a traditional folkloristic tale, but also as part of Insu's very personal experience.

In these scenes, *Memories of My Ghost Brother* offers glimpses into the specific ethnographic quality of his stories. It shows how Korean spiritual beliefs are deeply anchored in accepting the presence of ghosts – foregrounding the constant presence of the dead – in everyday life. As such, Fenkl's fictional novel invites a reflection through an anthropological framework. Laurel Kendall's seminal work on Korean shamanism, for example, explains the reasons for ghostly presences that become vengeful in contrast to peaceful ancestors:

> "Those who died well are ancestors. They married, begat or bore children, and now receive ritual sustenance from sons and grandsons. Ghosts violate all of these conditions. Ghosts died badly: as bachelors or maidens, without descendants, violently, or far from home. These unhappy souls are filled with resentment and envy." (Kendall, "Wives, Lesser Wives" 217)

The ghosts' anger is mostly directed at the living who live their dreams or at children or siblings, basically at those who still have their lives to live. Even if good intentions might be driving the dead or the living to search for closeness, this proximity between the two is unhealthy (217). So that even ancestors "who hold any lingering emotional attachment or desire are restless and dangerous" (218). Studying how ghosts and ancestors comment upon areas of social life, Kendall argues that "[r]estless ancestors [who have become ghosts] beckon us to consider some of the murkier aspects of Korean family life" (222). One of these aspects, according to Kendall, are struggles between first and second wives (222). Without directly referring to it, this approach to ghosts calls to mind sociologist Avery Gordon's conception of the ghosts as 'social figures.' And although *Memories of My Ghost Brother* does not depict struggles between first and second wives, the ghosts refer to social aspects, some to what Kendall terms 'murky family aspects.'

Ghosts and shamans have been reviled as anti-modern superstition, especially in contrast to the image of the West as a modernizer of its colonized countries but also already during Japan's occupation in anti-superstition campaigns (Kendall, *Shamans, Nostalgias and the IMF* 8). Some Christians in *Memories of My Ghost Brother* also approach shamans and ghosts with such an attitude. But the novel as a whole engages with these lived Korean traditions in its narrator's every day life. In her recent book, *Shamans, Nostalgias and the IMF* (2009), Laurel Kendall focuses on the tradition of shamanism in modern Korea, which in no way belongs to a past but is very much alive, as she argues. With the vanishing of urban Korean villages, however, shamans have had to change some of the ways in which they practice. In her definition, shamans are "religious practitioners who engage the spirits on behalf of the community, either through encounters during soul flight or by invoking the spirits into the here and now of a ritual space, conveying the immediacy of these experiences with their own bodies and voices" (xx). Today, working in the big cities for mostly middle class clients, shamans still "interact with gods and ancestors by divining their presence and will, by doing a variety of small rituals to placate them and sustain their favor, and by performing *kut* to feast and entertain them" (xx) and sending the lingering dead on to paradise (3), but the problems that they are called to engage with are now often business related anxieties (xxvii). Today, shamans also appear as celebrated national icons. Glossed as cultural entertainment for the masses, even for tourists, these shamans offer a nostalgic view of things past. And even though they are often criticized for playing into a modernizing tale of the vanishing Korean tradition, they need to be recognized as public figures nonetheless. In her nuanced reading of these practices, Kendall emphasizes the shape-shifting presence of today's urban shamans (32–33).

Even though *Memories of My Ghost Brother* does not narrate a ritual performed by a shaman, it refers to these traditions repeatedly as part of what it offers as its specific ethnographic material. The novel begins with the haunted house of the Japanese Colonel. Nobody wants to move into this house because it is said to be haunted. The house "was built during the Japanese Annexation by a Colonel who tortured and murdered tens of thousands of Koreans for his amusement" (Fenkl, *Memories of My Ghost Brother* 5). Insu explains how the owner hired a "*mudang* to perform a day-long exorcism of the ghosts of the Japanese and their victims" (5), but that during the Korean War the house became a haven for refugees, many of whom died there, and for these victims the new owner refused to have a traditional exorcism offering instead to have a Christian one if any trouble with ghosts should occur. Having little money, Insu's extended family moves into the house nevertheless, so that Insu grows up in the vicinity of these ghosts. Insu relates that

> "I often heard whispers which I knew were the lamentations of the refugees who had died during the war. Sometimes when I looked towards the boulders, I would see the ghost of the Japanese Colonel standing quietly under the trees, gazing at me with his sad and lonely eyes." (7)

This ghost of the Japanese Colonel is one of the central ghosts of the novel, appearing repeatedly, even talking to and touching Insu at some point. The Colonel's ghost is a reference to the suffering that the Japanese occupation has caused Korea. The reader is spared the horrid details of the Colonel's 'amusement,' only being told that he "would gloat in his rock garden, pretending to meditate, and then he would have some tea before seeing to the next victim" (5). This senseless torture exposes the brutality of the regime. Insu, actually, has no personal connection to this part of Korean history and it also seems as if there is also no connection to the story as such. Set in a time long past the Japanese occupation, the novel seems to be removed from this history. The Colonel's ghost, then, serves as a reminder of the presence of this history, even if the Japanese forces have been replaced. This ghost's prominent appearance forces

Insu and the reader alike, to remember the time before the American takeover of the South.

Painting a picture of a murderous Japanese authority, one that works with senseless torture just for its own amusement, the novel begins to construct a familiar story-line: with the end of World War II, the United States freed Korea from its brutal colonization. In this version, America appears as the benevolent protector of a freed Korea. And yet, *Memories of My Ghost Brother* diverges from such a construction of Korea's history. While the Colonel's ghost surely references some of the gruesome aspects of Japanese occupation, the novel strives to present the harsh consequences of both the Japanese and the American dominance over Korea. In spite of the Colonel's dark history, there is little fear in the meetings between Insu and the Japanese Colonel's ghost. Indeed, the ghost appears as sad and lonely instead of frightening. One evening, for example, Insu looks out of the window while his family is eating and talking. "I could hear the refugee ghosts wailing because they had lost their homes in the war. Then, through the streaks of rain on the window, beyond our reflections, I saw the ghost of the Japanese Colonel watching us with his sad eyes," prompting the question for him: "Why was he always so sad [...]. Was it because his ashes had been scattered under the tree roots and he had no way of getting them back? Or was he just lonely?" (12). Just as in Insu's reflections about other ghost appearances, he arrives at the conclusion that the ghosts are lonely and sad. Rather than fear, the ghosts prompt a feeling of sadness in Insu, emphasizing a (tragic) loss.

Indeed, the ghost of the Japanese Colonel even consoles Insu once. After having fought with the bully Cholsu, Insu suddenly feels very exhausted.

> "I saw a purple ring around my vision, like afterimages of the sun, and when I tried to rub my eyes and blink them away, the rings grew brighter and wider until suddenly my vision went entirely white. 'Hello,' said the ghost of the Japanese Colonel. He had never spoken to me before, and his eyes had never been quite so sad. 'Hello,' I said. 'This is a beautiful place,' said the ghost of the Japanese Colonel. 'This is not a place you should be afraid of.' 'I'm not afraid,' I said. 'Good.' When I opened my eyes, he was gone and I was lying on my side on front of the boulder. I felt like I had just awakened from a long and restful sleep." (87)

The passage begins as if Insu is going to simply pass out, his vision blurring. But then, the ghost of the Japanese Colonel appears once again. This time, however, he starts talking. As if he knows that with the growing closeness he is about to disappear from Insu's life, his sadness is even greater than usual. But still, he reaches out to him, referring to the beauty of the place and unnecessary feelings of fear one might have there. This scene shows the way in which the child perspective of the novel helps in establishing these figures as forceful material presences. The child remembers this meeting and it is therefore part of what he narrates. Whether this happened as part of a dream or even unconsciousness or is simply a fantasy of the child that serves as a psychological coping mechanism or actually part of the narrator's reality is intentionally left open. The child's re-collections are all that matters for the selection and presentation of his material.

In their last meeting before Insu's family moves out of the house, the ghost finally touches him.

"Late one afternoon the ghost of the Japanese Colonel had appeared to me among the boulders in the old rock garden. He had gazed upon me, especially forlorn, anticipating a loneliness greater than what he already endured. [...] He looked at me, his eyes shimmering, the leaves behind him quivering with anticipation of something dire, and he had leaned forward, reaching out his left hand to touch me – I realize now – for the first time. Suddenly I could no longer see him, but I felt my back straighten, and then I had the oddest sensation – more like a knowledge than a sensation – that he had thrust his fingertip into my skull and run it all the way around the crown of my head. My eyes were closed – I knew. But somehow the top of my head had vanished, as if my skull were the cylinder of an open can, and I could see the blue sky receding to infinity directly above me. My body was hollow. I was empty, although it held my shape, and into the contoured vessel the sky came pouring like a bright blue liquid, and I felt that I had no outside and no inside, that the sky within me and the air outside me were the same substance and my self but a thin veneer that floated between them like some filmy membrane in water. I was breathing in the liquid sky through the top of my open head, and the air was cold with the freshness that lingers after a hard rain. I sat there for the longest time until, degree by degree, I realized that I was seeing again through my eyes. [...]
The Japanese Colonel was gone. [...] I would never see the House of the Japanese Colonel again. Never – not even in my dreams." (90–91)

Presenting the climax of their strange relationship, this meeting again follows the logic of ambiguity. With Insu about to move from this house and entering the American school, he is starting a new episode of his life; one in which his closeness to the American presence is more pronounced. The farewell from this most prominent ghost of his early childhood represents Insu's growing up. Its presence indicates the omnipresence of ghost figures in Korea, the constant presence of the dead and the past. The Japanese Colonel's ghost, however, remains a puzzling presence without offering its own history that would place him in the narrative. Rather, he appears as a reminder of something larger than himself: he is a figure of memory for the child narrator, bound to his childhood home, his first encounters with Korean folklore and ghost presences that he associates with his mother. Accordingly, this ghost's touch opens Insu's head, allowing the sky to enter. Insu becomes a 'vessel' – larger than life, yet containing his life. Without making it explicit, this scene foregrounds the main point of the novel: its characters are not only references to their personal lives, but their selves become 'thin veneers' that 'float' between the 'sky within' and the 'air outside,' exposing the larger forces that shape their lives.

The various ghost figures that are grounded in Korean folklore link the narrator to this side of his family. The ghosts serve as figures of memory, as references to aspects, characters, or events that should be remembered. They anchor him in a cultural context. And they serve as orientation points for him: they refer to blurry yet highly important aspects. Their appearances are shown to be part of Insu's everyday life and the way in which he conceptualizes his memories.

The story of Insu's cousin Gannan exemplifies the way in which his memories are deeply intertwined with ghost figures. It is but one example of the way in which the American presence causes death and suffering and the way in which Insu's parents keep a certain distance from each other. When Gannan becomes pregnant by a white American GI while working on the American base, she sees no way out of the dilemma and commits suicide. After her burial, Insu is preoccupied with the question of whether Gannan will come back as a ghost, asking his uncle: "[D]o you think Gannan's spirit is unhappy?" His uncle's evasive answer – "Don't worry and go have fun, *ungh*? It's too early for you to be worrying about things like that" – does not deny the possibility of Gannan's ghost coming back to haunt the family (26). Actually, following Korean ghost beliefs, Gannan has every reason to appear as a ghost: having committed suicide, killing her unborn baby, and having a vengeance against those who did not protect her. But Insu is already sure that "Gannan would never come back as a bad ghost, but if this was such a sad world like Big Uncle said, I thought it would be better if she didn't come back at all" (27). Along with grief, Gannan's death brings about financial trouble for her family. Insu's extended family tries to make up for the losses, but "to my father, they would say nothing" (31), although he would have attended Gannan's funeral if they had told him, underlining the distance that the parents keep between themselves. So, although

Gannan does not become a classic Korean ghost that haunts Insu, her story does haunt him.[9]

At one time, Insu visits his father at the military base when he sees his mother approaching in a taxi. Insu remembers that "Mahmi had explained to me many times about how my father wasn't supposed to know about how she bought things and then sold them to the black market people," fearing that if his father saw her, "they would argue all night and then she would be unhappy for a long time" (73). Taking sides with his mother, wanting to protect her from his father's anger, Insu starts making rude gestures towards passing GIs in order to make his father face him instead of the taxi in front of them. Beaten by his father for his behavior, Insu sees his mother leaving, unnoticed by his father. This scene highlights the way in which the family is haunted by various secrets. The ghost brother is one; a repressed knowledge that they all share. But Insu's Korean family also keeps many secrets from his father as well. Gannan's death is one example, the mother's engagement in black market activities, or the mother's miscarriage of twins towards the end of the novel are others. These secrets can be kept rather easily because the parents' worlds do not cross very often: on his sporadic visits, Insu's father remains at a certain distance. Insu seems to be the main part to connect his parents. And since he knows their secrets, he feels obliged to protect his mother. As he gives the following explanation for his behavior: "I did not want her [Insu's mother] to be sad the way Gannan had been" (73), he acknowledges the father's power over his mother. The parents' precarious relationship highlights the ways in which larger forces intrude upon his life and in which they all participate to a certain extent. For Insu, American soldiers have the power to turn his loved ones into sad ghosts. And since his father is one of these American soldiers, he is surely afraid of him at some level.

The contrast between the familiar presence of ghost figures and the frightening and distanced presence of his father and America becomes particularly pronounced throughout the novel, turning the father himself into a ghostly figure for the young child because he remains unreadable. Just like the mother, who represents a Korea that is haunted by various ghosts, the father refers to

9 Actually, Keith Ames Russel reads one female ghost who appears in the novel as Gannan's ghost, stating that "her depictions are multifaceted in recalling Korean myth and presaging American materialist influence" (Russel 126). In my view, the connection between the female ghost figure and Gannan is not explicit. Whether this link is made or not, Gannan's story becomes a haunting presence for the novel in any case.

America and specific Western traditions of haunting. In referencing this tradition, *Memories of My Ghost Brother* plays with psychoanalytical explanations of ghosts as references to the family's precarious relationships.

The communication between father and son is problematic throughout. For example, after Gannan has committed suicide, Insu breaks down while spending time alone with his father.

> "'Aboji,' I said.
> 'Hmmm?' My father looked down on me from his awful height, more frightening than comforting.
> 'Aboji,' I said again. My mouth twisted into a funny shape and my eyes filled with tears. 'Gannan die!' I said, bursting into tears. My father put me on his lap and held me while I cried.
> '*Genug, mein Heinzchen, genug, genug*,' he said after a while. '*Wir mussen nicht* – we shouldn't get too sad.' He rocked me back and forth, patting my back as if to make me burp. When I had calmed down enough, my father made me tell him everything I could in the English words I knew, but it took a long time before I felt any better because, when I was done, he didn't have the proper words to comfort me." (71)

Although Insu obviously hopes to be comforted by his 'aboji' – referencing his wish for more closeness by calling his father in the Korean style –, the scene prohibits the fulfillment of Insu's wishes from the beginning. The father's 'aweful height' already refers to biological differences that seem insurmountable to the little child. This distance is further enhanced by the language barrier that separates the two. Insu remains without the hoped-for paternal comfort because the father lacks 'the proper words,' indicating both of these barriers to their relationship: the lingual as well as the cultural. Neither can the father provide comfort by using a shared language, nor through shared belief systems. Even the last remaining area, physical comfort, is represented as fraught. Although the father tries to console his son by patting his back, Insu is only reminded of burping. Insu is not sure of his father's presence and readiness to respond, he is never entirely sure that he is welcome. So that, although his father may provide physical comfort, he remains emotionally distant to his son.

Still, both father and son reach out to each other sporadically. These attempts show their hope for intimacy. For example, Insu makes his father a leather wallet for his birthday, carving a buffalo into it. His father buys him a book on his eleventh birthday, Rudyard Kipling's *Kim*. Insu regrets not having read the book until his father passed away, reminiscing about the lost chance to talk about it with his father. In retrospect, Insu sees remarkable coincidences between this novel and their own lives, thinking that his father might have quoted from the novel in order to create a certain closeness and forgiveness between them (63). Here, the narrator clearly emphasizes his own lack of initiative. And yet, in the very next paragraph, Insu describes how his father reacted when he saw him for the first time after his birth. When his aunt

"held me out to him as he stepped down from the green U.S. Army bus, he had held me like a piece of wood, a rifle stock at present arms. He had held his son and turned bright red from the shame of having a mixed-blood child – or was it simply that he did not know how to hold an infant?" (63).

Although Insu leaves room for a less hurtful explanation of his father's behavior, the image is burned into his extended family's memory. Especially so, because the father later "*erupted at my mother for daring to let him be seen in public with a child presented to him by a Korean*" (63). Told right after Insu's own regrets of having let his father down, this episode appears both as an explanation for their distanced and awkward relationship and as a reference to his father's cultural framework. Knowing about the stigmatization of intimate relations between Korean women and American soldiers, the father needs to save his face in front of the other soldiers. The presence of his Korean family threatens to undermine his authority. So, a third explanation for the father's bright red color – that is only hinted at in this scene, but emphasized throughout the novel – is his own regret of being in this awkward position where he is not free to show his affection for his son openly. This episode is told in one of the italicized chapters, by an older Insu, looking back and reflecting upon his memories and the stories that his family told him. This older narrator has the age, knowledge, and distance to understand the forces that pushed and pulled his family. He reflects upon possible areas of connection and disconnection with his father. And although this passage frames the narrative of the younger Insu, the child's personal fears and disappointment is still emphasized even in the chapters that begin to provide answers to the child's puzzlement.

Even though the love that Insu's parents feel towards their child is not doubted, the family secret – as it is shaped by these larger forces – undermines their bond. As his parents have abandoned his brother, a dark stain remains upon the relationship between father, mother, and son.

"That night, when we were all asleep on the floor on our sleeping mats, I woke for a moment, feeling afraid, as if I were some stranger my mother and father would send away.

I reached across the mat and touched my mother's warm hand. She closed her fingers around my cold palm, and I slept." (79)

Like most children, Insu is haunted by fears of abandonment. And although his mother's physical closeness and warmth quickly console him and allow him to go back to sleep, the reader already suspects that Insu's fears have a specific source. Following John Bowlby's classic model of attachment theory, a child should feel his or her parents to be a reliable source of protection and love.[10] Even though Insu's mother is this source to her son – providing physical and emotional comfort when he is sad or frightened, ready to respond to his questions[11] – her protection is, from the beginning, unreliable. She has abandoned one of her sons before so that Insu is haunted by the question whether she would do this to him as well. The family's relationships – mother and son, father and son, mother and father – are haunted by the secret that connects and separates them.

Memories of My Ghost Brother narrates the life of a family that suffers from transgenerational haunting, to use Maria Torok and Nicolas Abraham's term. In the relationship with his father, Insu's haunted state becomes especially pronounced, so that the parents in general, but the father in particular, become ghostly presences to their son. Abraham and Torok's psychoanalytic approach focuses on how phantoms haunt one generation after another. According to Nicholas Rand, their theory "insists on the particularity of any individual's life story, the specificity of texts, and the singularity of historical situations" (Rand, "Introduction" 1). In Rand's view, their theory is driven by the term introjection, which he defines basically as "a constant process of acquisition and assimilation, the active expansion of our potential to accommodate our own emerging desires

10 Bowlby departs from traditional libido theory as represented by Freud, which treats various types of behavior as expressions of one single drive, in arguing that attachment behavior, like other types of behavior, serves a specific biological function. Whereas sexual behavior ensures reproduction, attachment behavior reinforces protection. As such, attachment behavior is partially preprogrammed and only the details have been learned. Bowlby strongly disagrees with the term 'dependence' because it calls for associations with regressive or childish behavior, which is a misinterpretation because the drive to be protected and comforted remains a vital part of human life regardless of someone's age (Bowlby 5–13).

11 Bowlby calls this a 'secure base:' a place from which a child can explore the world, knowing that she can return and will be nourished physically and emotionally (Bowlby 12).

and feelings as well as the events and influences of the external world" (9). This idea presents a life as a series of transitions, instead of focusing only on the changes that occur in early childhood. This process of introjection works similarly for all new experiences and is most important for crises like shock, trauma, or loss. Abraham and Torok identify obstacles to introjection, one of which is the 'phantom:' "an undisclosed family secret handed down to an unwitting descendant" (16).

The silence surrounding the secret[12], the older generation's own unconscious struggle with the secret – all of this is transmitted from one generation to the next in the form of a gap. Abraham explains how the

> "phantom is summoned therefore, at the opportune moment, when it is recognized that a gap was transmitted to the subject with the result of barring him or her from the specific introjections he or she would seek at present. The presence of the phantom indicates the effects, on the descendants, of something that had inflicted narcissistic injury or even catastrophe on the parents." (Abraham, "Notes on the Phantom" 174)

As the phantom is the result of someone else's problematic psychic development, but continues to haunt his or her descendants, the haunting becomes transgenerational. Acknowledging that they still have to determine how the phantom passes from one generation to the next, they rather focus on the "phantom's periodic and compulsive return" for the individual, stating that it "works like a ventriloquist, like a stranger within the subject's own mental topography" (173). The phantom/secret appears as a stranger within the self – even though the secret is not actually the self's own, but rather the parents' secret.

Similar to the processes in which attachment theory views the repression of certain unfavorable aspects of the parental figures,[13] Abraham states that the

12 Abraham and Torok's conception of the 'secret' diverges from every-day usage of the word. In their view, a secret is "a trauma whose very occurrence and devastating emotional consequences are entombed and thereby consigned to internal silence, albeit unwittingly, by the sufferers themselves" (Rand "New Perspectives in Metapsychology," 99–100). This definition is important in order to grasp that, in Abraham and Torok's conception, the parents do not consciously decide to keep something a secret from their children. Looking at the family secret at the heart of *Memories of My Ghost Brother*, it is hard to decide whether the parents made a conscious decision to keep the secret from their son. In either case, their own guilt and grief about this partially self-inflicted trauma has resulted in an internal silencing.

"horror of transgression, in the strict sense of the term, is compounded by the risk of undermining the fictitious yet necessary integrity of the parental figure in question" (174). For what is exposed in the parent's unconscious are their "unspoken fears, their apprehensions, the reasons for their enslavement, their hidden faults. Inscribed there is also the fact that the parents are not at all the gods of coherence and consistency, courage, and power that their young offspring would wish" (Torok 180). Torok calls that which is transmitted between parents and children a "story of fear" (180–81). This story transports not only the fear that the parents have felt, but also instills this fear in the children, enhanced by the frightful recognition of the parents' dissolved integrity.

The process of accepting one's parents as themselves instable, unsure, frightened, determined by larger forces, driven by fears and full of flaws can be rather frightful for a child. For, if parents cannot even protect themselves, how could they protect their child? As an adult and from a distance, it is only realistic to perceive one's parents' flaws and see them in their incomplete humanity, which is also the point that *Memories of My Ghost Brother* brings across throughout. But from the perspective of a child, these fearful parents become unreliable presences. And as such, they take on features of the uncanny – strange yet familiar – and ghostly. Following Abraham and Torok's logic that it is not the dead who haunt the living, but rather the gaps left within someone by the secrets of others, Insu is haunted by his parents' unbearable secret.

Even though Abraham and Torok's concept of the phantom assumes that the parents have already passed away and that this transgenerational haunting spans many generations, the logic that they follow applies to Insu's family as well. Especially in the relationship with his father – which foregrounds again and

13 Bowlby distinguishes three distinct categories that lead to such a shutting off of experiences in children: situations in which children have done something about which they feel utterly guilty, experiences that parents do not wish their children to know about or situations in which parents have treated their children in ways that the children find too unbearable to think about. According to Bowlby, children are aware of their parents' feelings and obey them by "excluding from further processing such information as they already have; and that, having done so, they cease consciously to be aware that they have ever observed such scenes, formed such impressions, or had such experiences" (Bowlby 114). This repression serves not only to obey one's parents' wishes, but also to protect the image that the child has of them. Children wish to see their parents in a favorable light and to ensure that they also see them in such a way (Bowlby 121).

again the power relations that inherently determine it – this haunted process is to be seen. The father himself becomes a ghostly presence for his son for he has given his son a gap to inherit. Embodying the secret through his presence, yet, shutting it off from reflections, the father restrains his son's introjection. Therefore, Insu is unable to cope with his loss, opting instead for a preservative repression of his memories. The father has not yet passed away and so cannot haunt his son from the grave, but he has passed on a secret to his son in the form of a phantom which not only works like a stranger within Insu's own mental topography, but also haunts the whole family. The father's presence, at the same time, calls forth and neglects the ghost brother. The ghostly father embodies the struggles that the novel wishes to highlight: he becomes a ghostly figure for his son not because of a bad character trait, but because he is himself caught in the cultural and political webs of power that surround him. And yet, the novel does not shy away from the moral dilemmas that this situation creates: it puts them center stage, exposing the ghosts that haunt the Korean American relationship as a whole.

On one day his father takes Insu to where he works and lives. On this day, father and son seem close, the father sharing military tricks with his son, telling him stories like his uncle does. So that, finally, Insu dares to ask his father about his brother.

"'Daddy,' I said after a moment, 'I had a dream I had a brother. His name was Kuristo and he was a ghost. Why do you think I had that dream?'
When I looked up, my father's face was red – I couldn't tell if it was from the beer or because he was angry with me. He sat there, swishing the beer around in his nearly empty can, glancing from the crossed swords on his partition wall to the pictures on his desk.
'What did Lee say?' he said finally.
'I didn't ask Mahmi.'
'Well, don't ask her. You don't ask nobody. That's just a bullshit dream, you understand? Sometimes we just have bullshit dreams where we appear and we think it's our own brother.'
'But he saved us. And his name was Kuristo.'
'Kuristo – what does that sound like to you.'
'Christopher.'
'It's Christ. Jesus Christ. Ha saved us all and you just saw him like he was your brother, nicht wahr? Remember the time I was sick with fever and I saw Maria when my mother had her church pray for me?'
'Yes.'

'It's like that but it's just a bullshit dream, too, and you don't need to tell anyone else about it.'
[...]
'We gotta get you out to the bus,' said my father. 'You want to get back in time to catch the last one back to ASCOM.'
We walked to the bus stop without speaking. I had said the wrong thing to him, something as bad as telling him why Mahmi was really sick, something as bad as asking Mahmi whether she had lost the twin babies or had aborted them.
[...]
He didn't know the schedules as well as I did – I hadn't told him I would reach Yongsan too late to catch the last bus home." (Fenkl, *Memories of My Ghost Brother* 257–59)

Having spent a rather long time alone with his father, reaching out to him seems easier, almost natural to Insu. So, he finally dares to breach the tabooed topic of his brother Kuristo. Interestingly, Insu asks his father first, not his mother. Maybe he simply wishes to spare her pain because she is sick at the time. Maybe he could not endure destroying the picture he has of her. Or maybe he senses that this ghost presence is not a typical Korean ghost, but rather associated with his father's Western conceptions of haunting. In any case, the conversation becomes the turning point. His father becomes angry and distant again and the general response is very clear: do not ever talk about this again with anyone, trying to push this secret back into the taboo zone of their relationship. His father struggles to respond to Insu's outright question, shifting between explanations from wonders to dreams. Following his own Christian upbringing, the father tries to explain this ghost away as simply a part of Insu's imagination. In Insu's experience, however, spirituality is concrete and direct, like the ghost maid from the well, who calls out to and tries to grab him.

In the end, the ghost brother becomes such a puzzling presence for Insu because he cannot place him definitively. He is not a classical ghost figure of his mother's Korean tradition; but Insu can also not grasp his father's explanations of imaginations. The ghost brother, thus, serves as a very direct example of Insu's growing up among diverse, even contradictory cultural beliefs. In *Memories of My Ghost Brother* this ghost takes center stage and it highlights the way in which the novel both merges and contradicts these traditions. The lack of clear-cut value judgments that the novel provides follows its specific child's logic. Such categorizations only partially reflect Insu's own experiences. The child emphasizes different aspects and follows his own priorities that differ markedly from those of an adult.

Driven from the very beginning by the haunting presence of this ghost brother, the narrator is on a quest to solve the puzzle to this secret. This ghost is bound up with his father in the same way that his mother is associated with the Korean ghost appearances, pointing to Western traditions of haunting. And surely, just as psychoanalytic theory argues, the narrator encounters his ghost brother in dreams as a repressed memory that resurfaces.

"I began to dream that I was looking down into a beautiful, clear river at faces that looked up at me from under the water. I knew these faces [...] and sometimes the face would be my own reflection, sometimes a subtle distortion that I took to be myself but knew, in my heart, was really an older stranger. I would know that stranger soon." (35)

After this first reference to his ghost brother, the novel only gives hints about the secret, for example when a nun at school refers to Insu's older brother and his father vehemently denies his existence (75). Towards the end of the novel, the dreams and references become more frequent and pronounced. With slight variations, Insu has the following dream:

"There is a shadow in front of the curtainless window. I look, moving only my eyes, and I see an old woman standing there, hunched almost double. [...] She turns, and in her hand I see a gleaming kitchen knife just sharpened on a spinning stone. I know with dream certainty that she has come to kill someone. If I cry out to warn the others, she will surely plunge the knife into my heart, but if I remain still, if I close my eyes into slits and remain silent, she will kill someone else. [...] Slowly and suspiciously, the crone turns toward me, raising the knife. I must decide. Now. Now. And her eyes turn toward the sliding door, open just a crack. Her eyes widen. She sees someone standing in the opening. She smiles, and without a sound, she steps between our bodies to follow the figure in the doorway.
I would always wake from the dream wondering who that figure was in the doorway. He looked so familiar – so much like myself – that I tried to imagine he was me. But he was not me. He was too old in that place to be me, and he was too thin, his ears a bit too wide, his face too narrow. He was a stranger in my skin, and each time I saw him I was terrified and unspeakably sad." (202–03)

Turning his brother into a savior, structuring the whole situation as if he had had a choice in it, Insu takes on some of the blame in his dreams. Interestingly, the threat that he encounters in his dreams is an old woman with a knife and the intention to kill someone. Jin-Kyung Lee reads this ghost as his mother's, referring to his matrophobia (Lee, *Service Economies* 169). But it is simply an old woman and therefore not clearly Insu's mother nor father. This disconnected strange woman rather points to the way in which the novel addresses the puzzling memories of the young child narrator and his older incarnation: she could be a Korean ghost figure, a ghost that has come back for some kind of retribution. But she could also be a disfigured memory, pointing to the blank that the family secret has left in Insu's conscience.

Even though Insu has had no active part in the abandonment of his brother, he does blame himself, when he finally realizes who that stranger from his dreams actually is. Dreaming the dream again, Insu suddenly knows:

> "He was the face I so often took for my own, and this time I knew his name – Kuristo, my ghost brother – and just then the crone's foot stepped in front of my face, and when it came up again, Kuristo was gone. The old woman was gone.
>
> And now I lay there with my soul full of silence, having passed from dream to waking without pause. I turned my head, and through the open door of our room, I thought I saw a smile on my mother's sleeping face, a smile formed in her dream; and at that instant I hated her, and I hated Kuristo for having saved us from the crone's gleaming knife. The hate was so strong that all the wooden stiffness in my body burst at once, with an audible *crack!* in my throat, and the hate splinters flashed like cold needles into every part of my body, back into my memories, and as the cold tears streamed from my eyes, one eye emptying into the other, then down to soak the sleeping mat, I knew that I would hate myself most of all." (Fenkl, *Memories of My Ghost Brother* 246–47)

With this realization, Insu needs to revise his picture of his mother. Finally able to understand the precarious relationship with his parents, Insu feels hatred towards her. How could she have done this? And yet, at the same instant, Insu states that he would hate himself most of all, taking on the blame for a situation that is far beyond his reach. And yet, the 'hate splinters' do exist and reach back into his family history, poisoning his memories.

Since his father evades Insu's outright questions about his brother, he also talks to his cousin Haesuni about his memories, when he finally gets home that night. She tells him the details about the brother's adoption. She also informs his mother about their conversation, after which his mother opens up and begins talking about Kuristo and her wish to go to America in order to be nearer to her lost son. She hopes that "someday your father will be gone and I can look for him [Kuristo]" (267). Insu also, finally, manages to ask this one burning question: "How could you marry someone who made you send your son away?" (267), to which his mother answers: "I used to think that every American was a millionaire and everyone owned his own house and had a car and drank Coca-Cola instead of water and had meat for every meal. I don't know where I got those ideas, but I had them" (267). His mother's answer offers only an indirect explanation that does not actually answer the moral outrage that Insu's question implies. Yet, it offers the honest answer for the hope of a better life – not only for herself, but for her second unborn child as well. And in a sense also for her firstborn son because sending him into an American family, for her, meant sending him into the land of the free and the rich.

This family story is one among many, as the novel shows. One of the other tragedies that frame the narrator's life is his friend James' death. The narrator realizes only in retrospect, that James was decidedly different from himself: although they were both sons of GIs, James' father was a black soldier. And when James' mother decided to start looking for a white American soldier as a future husband in order to improve her situation, she had to remove the lingering stain from her former engagements with a black soldier – her half-black son. The official story goes like this: James drowned in the sewer creek. Talking to his uncle, Insu voices his doubts because it is a very shallow creek. His uncle responds that "'[m]aybe she was trying to scrub the color off and she held his face down in the washbasin too long'" (229). For Insu, what remains from this story when he reflects upon it as an older narrator is the knowledge that "*women – even seemingly devoted mothers – will traffic in children for the mythic promise of America. And they would all look back in regret from the shores of the Westward Land*" (233). The way in which such examples simply belong to the narrator's life highlights the tragic history of U.S.-Korea relations in the proximity to the camptowns and the various 'hate splinters' that drove through these families' hearts.

The trafficking in children is in no way trivialized and the novel also exposes the complicity of the Korean side. As Grace M. Cho argues in *Haunting the Korean Diaspora* (2008), the Korean diaspora is constituted by transgenerational haunting. In Cho's analysis, the *yanggongju* – a term for Korean women who sleep with American soldiers – haunts the Korean diaspora. It refers to Korean war brides, who migrated to America with their husbands and were then shown as role models in America for happy interracial relations. Yet, their integration required a burial of any story that would run counter this myth. So, as participants of their own erasures, these families created the ghosts of their transgenerational hauntings (Cho 12–15). *Memories of My Ghost Brother* is, thus, one of the stories which finally expose the ghosts of this past. As Cho has it, Insu "remains haunted by both the white Korean brother sent to live in America and the black Korean brother left to die in Korea" (152–53). And yet, instead of blaming these mothers for their unbearable acts, Insu realizes that the complexity of the situation requires more nuanced readings, for

> "*[w]hat I felt in my heart then, and what I feel now, is a great blank emptiness. It is a profound sadness, a fatalism, a knowledge that the world is the way it is, and that the path of blame is not an arrow's flight, but the mad scatter of raindrops in the storm. I could have blamed James' mother, but that would have been too simple to do her justice. In the end there is no blame, only endurance.*" (Fenkl, *Memories of My Ghost Brother* 232)

The morally questionable acts that *Memories of My Ghost Brother* narrates are drawn together by the narrator to refrain from simplified blame. Even though blaming individuals would be easier to cope with, he wants to do justice to the situation at large, acknowledging that the world and life is unjust and unfair at times.

In *Ends of Empire* (2010), Jodi Kim reads cultural productions by Asian Americans from the 1990s in the framework of a 'protracted afterlife' of the Cold War. With this, she foregrounds the triangulation of the Cold War in Asia and views these works as critically reframing the imperial activities of the US in the area. With this argument, she intends to move away from identity politics as the basis of Asian American critique and attempts to show instead the multiple transnational layers of the field (Kim, *Ends of Empire* 3–32). Her inclusion of Fenkl's novel also supports her larger framework, arguing that it

> "shows how individual decisions that appear to be perverse or pathological are themselves symptomatic of a perversly imperialistic and militarized collective social architecture undergirded by racialized and gendered taxonomies of domination." (161)

In this sense, the imperial situation "upturns normative moral economies and preservation of life" (167). In Kim's reading, then, the morally questionable acts that *Memories of My Ghost Brother* centers on, highlight the wrongs of American imperial designs. While this reading tells, of course, part of the story that the novel narrates, it remains rather too one-sided.

What the novel emphasizes instead, as Grace Kyungwon Hong's states, is the "complexity of everyone's status; in the camptown, and indeed, in South Korea as both neocolony and subempire, it is not straightforward who is the victim and who is the perpetrator, who is an ally and who is an enemy" (Hong 64). In this sense, the novel remains ambiguous, certainly blaming the larger forces that shape the individual's lives, but stopping short of binary categorizations. Grace Kyungwon Hong adequately summarizes the point of the novel as follows:

> "Unwilling to forget the dead, *Memories of My Ghost Brother* finds a way to see ghosts.

In so doing, the memoir enacts a practice that is ethical while undermining universalized notions of ethics, and that is political while troubling the concept of a universalized politics. [...] In such a context, seeing ghosts is a way to reckon with violence without replicating its conditions, a way of mourning the deaths of others by acknowledging, rather than disavowing, the connection between those deaths and one's life." (64)

Hong foregrounds, thus, the intricate interconnections that the 'hate splinters' which Insu feels point to. Without directly referencing it, Hong refers to the concept of transgenerational haunting, arguing that the ghosts of the past continue to haunt the present. Having come to America, Insu is still haunted by these ghosts.

As Nicholas Rand has it in his introduction to Abrahm and Torok's volume,

"in the psychoanalytic realm, laying the dead to rest and cultivating our ancestors implies uncovering their shameful secrets, understanding their nameless and undisclosed suffering. We should engage in this unveiling and understanding of the former existence of the dead not because we may want to appease them or prevent them from perpetrating their nocturnal pranks, but because, unsuspected, the dead continue to lead a devastating psychic half-life in us." (Rand, "Secrets and Posterity" 167)

And although Rand is also referring here to the dead, staying within the framework of Abraham and Torok's phantom concept, a similar process is called for in *Memories of My Ghost Brother*. Instead of blaming his parents, Insu needs to understand the fear and suffering that they have experienced. Following his instincts, and finally even talking about his memories, Insu manages to address and name the phantom that haunts his family. Being able to claim this brother as his own and his memories as true, Insu begins to heal the devastating psychic half-life in himself. In order for this process to work, he needs to reduce the phantom. In Abraham's words, "reducing the 'phantom' entails reducing the sin attached to someone else's secret and stating it in acceptable terms so as to defy, circumvent, or domesticate the phantom's (and our) resistances, its (and our) refusals, gaining acceptance for a higher degree of 'truth'" (Abraham, "The Phantom of Hamlet" 189). Gabriele Schwab argues in *Haunting Legacies* (2010) that Abraham and Torok "focus on the possibility of reinstating meaning after its traumatic collapse" (Schwab 54). Literature offers a realm in which such encrypted secrets can begin to emerge because in Schwab's conception of literature as "transformational" it allows a "creative reworking and translation of experiences" (4). *Memories of My Ghost Brother* is such "an attempt to force the ghosts of violent histories into the open and work toward social recognition and reparation" (55).

For a Western reader with a Western approach, it seems obvious to focus on the ghost brother that appears in the title of Fenkl's novel. This ghost figure is an important one for the novel as a whole, it provides the frame for the narrator's maturation, for the family's relationships, for the haunted history of Korean-American relations. And yet, a chapter that focuses on the ghost figures that appear in *Memories of My Ghost Brother* should not be limited to this central figure. For this psychoanalytical/metaphorical figure is in good company with the many ones that fit into traditional Korean ghost beliefs. In their entirety, the novel's ghosts emphasize the existence of different traditions and theories of haunting. Thus, reading the ghosts simply with a Western psychoanalytic approach goes beside the point of the novel, which rather underlines the different traditions in their shared existence as haunting social figures, to take up Avery Gordon's term once more. All of the ghost figures exhibit a social force – and thus all of them call for recognition.

The novel's switches between its child perspective and the italicized adult passages invite a reflection of what the child's perspective offers that an adult narrator might not convey. Is this perspective – and its direct, unchanneled experience of the ghost figures – presented as the more realistic logic in the novel? Does it offer a perspective that allows a better understanding of the world? Or is the adult narrator's framing of these experiences as a psychological coping mechanism what the novel finally suggests? The answers to these questions cannot be conclusive – just like the ghost figures themselves. *Memories of My Ghost Brother* constructs the ghosts as independent and material existences that appear in both the child and the adult passages, undermining a clear-cut separation between these two perspectives. And yet, it also frames these figures as constructed and imagined, once again challenging the reality-status that it initially credits the ghosts with. The specific combination of such different haunting traditions makes the novel what it is: a Korean German American novel that borders on the autobiographical as well as the mythic.

4 Renegotiating a Global Asian America: The Ghost in Global Genre Fiction by Amitav Ghosh, Amy Tan, and Ed Lin

> "They saw themselves making History with their vast water-control experiments: they wanted to record every minute detail of what they had done, what they would do. Instead of having a historian sift through their dirt, looking for meanings, they wanted to do it themselves: they wanted to load their dirt with their own meanings." (Ghosh, *The Calcutta Chromosome* 7)

Amitav Ghosh begins *The Calcutta Chromosome* (1995) with disturbing descriptions of the narrator's computer "Ava"[1] and its employer, the International Water Council. The eerie atmosphere is created not only by the all-encompassing computerization or the existence of a seemingly endless cyberspace, but mostly by the globalization of such spheres. As the above passage suggests, the International Water Council, in the form of an anonymous 'they,' holds the knowledge and the power to 'make History.' Every little detail is sampled by Ava to store information about "the depletion of the world's water supplies" (6) and this information is sifted through by 'them' and only 'them' to construct an official version of 'their' history for the rest of the world. The International Water Council is seemingly in control. This organization functions as the umbrella of Amitav Ghosh's science fiction novel, which spans across various countries – the United States of America, Egypt, India – and across centuries – the nineteenth century to the immediate future.

While all of the chapters of *The Ghosts Within* deal with the notion of globalization – as, indeed, all works in postcolonial studies tend to do – this last chapter devotes itself in greater detail to this aspect. It discusses three novels –

1 The curious fact that this computer has a name and a gender will be discussed later.

Amitav Ghosh's *The Calcutta Chromosome* (1995), Amy Tan's *Saving Fish From Drowning* (2006), and Ed Lin's *Ghost Month* (2014) – which appear very different at first glance but share significant overlaps that demonstrate an ongoing trend in Asian American literature. A science fiction novel, a social comedy, and a mystery crime story all belong to the genre of the global novel and genre fiction in its diverse forms. This chapter focuses on the place of Asian American literature in a newly conceived global (Asian) American Studies. Although Yamanaka's *Behold the Many* and Fenkl's *Memories of My Ghost Brother* also use the ghost figures to critically rethink what it means to be Asian American, offering more heterogeneous, interconnected, and self-critical versions that also highlight the global reach of these narratives, the novels that this chapter focuses on address the aspect of Asian America from a more distinctly global perspective. What does it mean to establish oneself as both Asian American and a writer of world literature? How can authors participate in this trend even if they are associated with traditional Asian American writings? What are the risks and the chances of such participation? What is to win and what is to loose in its connection to genre fiction? Are these novels examples of a new global sensibility that promotes world peace via its liberal political orientation, or are they guilty of simply providing exoticized entertainment for the new global masses?

These questions curiously resonate with the questions that have driven Asian American Studies from its inception and they still dominate reviews of Asian American literature. So, this chapter asks, what happens to the ghost figures in these expanded yet similar surroundings? I argue that they exhibit a certain duality: they refer to concrete spiritual beliefs while they also become defamiliarized in this setting. This renegotiation moves in various directions: the figure is shown, on the one hand, as closely linked to the historically and culturally framed ghost beliefs with which the literature is connected. On the other hand, the figure is taken out of its original context and appears instead in larger conceptions of communities. This, then, is a move decidedly away from family, tradition, and nationality and into new territories of a postcolonial transnationality that also underwrites Asian America. The ghost motif simultaneously crosses over into scientific and biological discourses, into science fiction and mystery crime fiction, merging its spiritual roots with other strands of knowledge production. And the ghost moves within the form of the novel: from appearing as a character or a haunting presence to narrating the story itself, playing with the image of the ethnic author as tour guide. Overall, these changes highlight the visibility of the ghost figure and its complex and diverse appearances. This chapter argues that these new postcolonial adaptations of the ghost motif refer back to the old images – especially in the citations of specific spiritual figures –, engage and play with the critique of exoticization and selling out, and that they signal a move away from the identity politics that have dominated the field for a long time. In this, the ghosts function as figures that reflect upon the current position of Asian America as it re-imagines itself as a global configuration.

Beginning with Amitav Ghosh is fitting, therefore, for various reasons. He is one of the popular authors who begin to break away from easy identifications with a certain subfield of study and rather represent a global world literature. Born in India and having spent his life all over the world, including the United States, his writings reflect his transnational lifestyle. He is a highly acclaimed writer of both fiction and non-fiction. His non-fiction has appeared in book format, essay collections, as well as newspapers. His academic career also underlines his global lifestyle and reach: Ghosh has taught at many universities both in India and the United States. His novels,[2] originally written in English, were translated into more than twenty languages and won him numerous awards. In 2007, he was awarded the Padma Shri, one of India's highest honors, by the President of India.

His science fiction novel *The Calcutta Chromosome* won the Arthur C. Clarke award in 1997 (Ghosh, *Author's website* np). Its story line is not particularly suitable for a novel of Asian American literature because the classical themes of the field – in terms of identity politics or a rewriting of Asian American history – are only touched upon and the novel instead pronounces its transnational and postcolonial aspects. But it is exactly this global quality of his writings that this chapter wishes to emphasize. Although he identifies himself as Indian, his case is particularly interesting in terms of a self-fashioning of Asian America as global. For what makes Ghosh's case more striking than hair-splitting over his life and nationality is the very possibility of enlisting his work as 'Asian American,' as it reflects the field's changing self-conception. The field's growing diversity during the 1990s directly interlinks with a pronunciation of transnational and diasporic interconnections for Asian America. Christopher A. Shinn makes a similar point in his essay "On Machines and Mosquitoes" (2008), arguing that:

2 *The Circle of Reason* (1986), *The Shadow Lines* (1988), *The Calcutta Chromosome* (1995), *The Glass Palace* (2000), *The Hungry Tide* (2005), *Sea of Poppies* (2008), *River of Smoke* (2011), *Flood of Fire* (2015).

> "[a]lthough Ghosh's Indo-Anglian novels go beyond the borders of the Asian American literary canon, they also bring into greater disciplinary focus the important critical intersections of the Asian diaspora, transnational migration, post-national geographies and postcoloniality that […] contain direct relevance to the global study of Asian American literature." (Shinn 162)

It is in this sense that I begin this chapter on the changing figure of the ghost with Ghosh's *The Calcutta Chromosome*. As one of *the* early writers of what would now be termed 'global novels,' his case highlights a particular development of the discourses of haunting in Asian American literature. Since ghosts function as references to various interconnected – sometimes even contradictory – aspects, they are ideal figures for a reflection on recent global developments and their significance for Asian American literature. I argue that the use of such a classic and well-established motif of Asian American writing in this new context allows to keep a certain balance: to experiment with the new while referencing the ghosts' inherent traditionality, to use the ghosts as citations from different genres, to refer back to a concrete historical or cultural belief while engaging with new discourses, to critically reflect upon the current placelessness of contemporary literature, or, to put it differently, to imaginatively construct a new place for contemporary Asian American writing.

As already indicated above, the field of Asian American Studies has been driven by "phenomena of economic globalization, transnationalism, and diasporic dispersal" so that these ideas "are not as recent as it is often assumed," as Vanessa Künnemann and Ruth Mayer observe in the introduction to their edited volume *Trans-Pacific Interactions* (2009) focusing on relations between China and the United States from 1880–1950 (4). Lisa Lowe makes a similar point in her study "The Intimacies of Four Continents" (2006), where she focuses on the global market of the nineteenth century and its transnational routes of global exchange between Europe, Africa, Asia, and the Americas (192–212).

Indeed, Mita Banerjee claims,

> "[w]hile African American Studies can be regarded as a pioneering force that, since the 1960s, has infused the field of U.S. American literary and cultural studies with an awareness of difference and a spirit of resistance, Asian American Studies, with their more recent and growing focus on multiple identities and multiple migrations, can be credited with being a major force that has helped place American Studies within a global and transnational framework." (Banerjee and Carmen Birkle and Wilfried Raussert 311)

This recent concentration on 'multiple identities' and 'multiple migrations'[3] directly corresponds to Shelly Fisher Fishkin's wish for an American Studies that recognizes its "historical roots of multidirectional flows of people, ideas, and goods and the social, political, linguistic, cultural, and economic crossroads generated in the process" (Fishkin 22). Fishkin continues that

> "[t]he field of American studies toady is struggling to reach [...] a place where diasporic imaginations are valued for the dazzlingly hybrid synthesis they produce; a place where the term 'American' is understood in its broadest hemispheric sense." (26)

In recent years, publications in Asian American Studies have increasingly emphasized the inherent complexity of the field. Rocío Davis and Sämi Ludwig, for example, see Asian American literature in the introduction to their edited volume *Asian American Literature in the International Context* (2002) as a rich field of investigation because in it one needs to perceive and cross boundaries such as geography, nationality, ethnicity, and linguistic ones (Davis and Ludwig 9).[4] Positing Asian American Studies at the forefront of transnational approaches in American Studies surely increases the significance of the field in times where its relevance might be in danger of being questioned.[5]

---

3 Peter Jackson and others also emphasize, in the edited volume *Transnational Spaces,* the *contemporary* increase of transnational phenomena, for while "there are continuities with the past, transnationality is emerging as a phenomenon of ever-greater intensity and scope" (Jackson, Crang, and Dwyer 11).

4 Another example that recognizes the shift in the field of Asian American Studies is a review by Christopher Capozzola, which compares the perspectives of two edited volumes – Christian Collet and Pei-Te Lien's *The Transnational Politics of Asian Americans* (2009) and Setsu Shigematsu and Keith L. Camacho's *Militarized Currents: Toward a Decolonized Future in Asia and the Pacific* (2010). A generation ago these topics "would have fit uneasily on a bookshelf of Asian American Studies" whereas today, "scholars appreciate the need to confront power structures that span national boundaries by crossing our own national, disciplinary, and imaginary borders" (Capozzola 5).

5 Another answer for the relevance of subfields such as Asian American Studies is given by Transnational Studies themselves. For albeit the tendency to move beyond nation-states, a transnational approach always already depends on conceptions of nationality beyond which it might move. Furthermore, nationalism remains relevant even, and especially so, in transnational communities in that diasporic communities often reach back to their original homelands. Transnationalism, thus, sometimes even

Mita Banerjee's consideration of Asian American Studies as fundamentally concerned with 'multiple identities and multiple migrations' is linked to the success of authors such as Amitiav Ghosh or Salman Rushdie. Sarah Brouillette also positions Asian American writers at the forefront of global writings. She argues in *Postcolonial Writers in the Global Literary Marketplace* (2011) that

> "[t]here are a variety of reasons why English-language writers from South Asia, and in particular from India, seem to have produced an ideally cosmopolitan writing. Recent patterns of South Asian immigration have been characterized by the metropolitan movements of a relatively prosperous middle class of educated professionals who are thought to be fairly happily deterritorialized. Authors from this matrix are thought to combine social privilege with subversion: writing in English, they are available for consecration as embodying a national or supranational voice, unmoored from the more 'minor' perspectives identified with vernacular regional writing; they are willing to separate politics and aesthetics in the appropriate manner, to act as interpreters of the lands they have left behind, and to deploy a 'semantics of subalternity' attractive to Anglo-American readers." (Brouillette 87)

These writers combine privilege and dissent and Rushdie "normally stands as the paradigmatic figure of this privileged simultaneity" (87). To Brouillette, these postcolonial global authors' heritage fundamentally drives their success. Working with a 'strategic exoticism,' a term she borrows from Graham Huggan, these writers expose and trouble, reflect and negotiate their own self-consciousness as part of the field's marketability. While they are no longer bound to any one nationality or ethnicity in their status within a global world, their attachment to a 'Third World' country and the emphasized move beyond this location is necessary to establish them as part of this global world to begin with (61).

Brouillette summarizes the aspects of this writing that promise the greatest success in the current global market: "it is English-language fiction; it is relatively 'sophisticated' or 'complex' and often anti-realist; it is politically liberal and suspicious of nationalism; it uses a language of exile, hybridity, and 'mongrel' subjectivity" (61). According to David Damrosch, these global novels are "produced primarily for foreign consumption" (Damrosch 18). Thus, Tim Parks notices how the writing changes because of the author's and the reader's awareness of these novels as global products. He detects "a tendency to remove obstacles to international comprehension" such as a simple language that avoids

---

reinforces nationalist ideologies in both sending and receiving countries and the international communities that emerge out of these contexts (Khan 1–3).

word plays in order to make the translator's work easier or a tendency to use only character names that are easy for an English or international audience (Parks np). Parks also sees "a political sensibility that places the author [of a global novel] among those 'working for world peace'" within "a certain liberal position" (np). The negative consequences that Parks bemoans with regard to these tendencies reappear in this chapter's focus on Amy Tan's *Saving Fish From Drowning*. Tan's novel highlights the fine line that global literature walks: it risks meaninglessness because of its tendency to appeal to a broad readership with its emphasis on reviewing and scanning instead of developing a certain standpoint.

The unspecificity of this literature establishes a trend that is relatively new to Asian American writing. Instead of following a resistance narrative that is driven by a focus on agency and (Asian American) identity politics, these works establish themselves as significantly placeless. That they still take their marketability from an association with the author's 'Third World' origins makes the case even more puzzling. This combination of privilege and dissent invites criticism, but also, I believe, signals an unwillingness to stick to the narrow frames of a literature that is driven by a resistance/accommodation paradigm that focuses almost exclusively on identity politics. Although these novels are also driven by a rhetoric of resistance, this rhetoric now challenges larger systems; it confronts the problems of a globalized world, constructs global citizens and their touristic guilt, as in Amy Tan's *Saving Fish From Drowning* and Ed Lin's *Ghost Month*, or imagines an inhuman agency that takes over individuals, as in Amitav Ghosh's *The Calcutta Chromosome*.

Eleanor Ty also observes a shift away from the politics of recognition of the 1980s to a new globally conceptualized identity in Asian North American literature: she argues that these particular authors are 'global' because of a certain "sense of the cosmopolitan" in their novels. They feature "multiply-located and multiply-centered narratives" with often "more than one diasporic community involved" (Ty, "Representing 'Other' Diasporas" 101). Ty identifies three categories of "Asian global narratives": the first are works that directly address globalization, the second are works written by Asians in North America, Britain, or Australia, that do not feature any aspects related to the author's Western homeland, and the third are works by Asians in the diaspora but that do not have any Asian reference (Ty, "Rethinking the Hyphen" 240). The novels of this chapter fall either into the first or the second category, or both. According to Ty, these works "re-locate centres and redraw boundaries" (246). She argues that "[t]hese global narratives highlight movement, instability, and the importance of standpoint or location" (241). *The Calcutta Chromosome*, *Saving Fish From*

Drowning, and *Ghost Month* fit her descriptions, but the standpoint or location that these novels offer is always shifting and instable, revealing a current renegotiation of Asian American literature's place in a globalized world. And although these novels begin to diverge from earlier topics such as identity politics or diaspora, a recognition of these reference points provides a way to emphasize the importance of locality and historical specificity that these terms demand.

Ruth Mayer identifies in the essay "Postcolonial/ Transcultural/ Transnational" (2014) a "particular tonality in contemporary postcolonial writing" that "positions itself alternately by means of gestures against the mainstream and signals to the common reader, and it entails frequent assertions of the narrative's status as 'art' as opposed to the extremes of elitist experimental abstractions or popular mass-appeal and sensationalism." An analysis of these texts defies "the predominance of categories such as agency, identity, and authorial distinction," which currently stifles postcolonial theoretical discourse. She observes "new modes of expression and self-fashioning on a transnational scale" that call for a return to poststructuralist debates of authorship in their new formats of "collaborative authorship, ghostwriting, impersonation, and what could be called the aesthetic of the avatar." These novels, Mayer concludes, "seem to write themselves, rather than being attributable to one particular 'voice' or author" and "[a]s scholars of literature and culture we will have to deal with these changed conditions of access and reach, inclusion and exclusion, agency and mediation" (Mayer, "Postcolonial/Transcultural/Transnational" 139–155). Although none of the novels that this chapter addresses follows such a refrain of authorial distinction, Ruth Mayer's analysis helps to understand the novels' concern about ethnic authorship and the particularity of the narrator's voices in the current changing transnational conceptions of authorship.

I argue that Amitav Ghosh's *The Calcutta Chromosome* appears as an example of this particular 'tonality,' but in order to do so, I need to expand Mayer's argument. Although *The Calcutta Chromosome* does not participate in the new formats that Mayer observes, it still invites reflections on authorship as it becomes increasingly non-identitarian. In a way, Ghosh's example emphasizes the identity of the author – constructed and marketed as both global and Asian American –, but the move into the global ultimately undermines the importance of a certain locality. As such, Ghosh's is also a new mode of expression and self-fashioning that participates in the current re-fashioning of postcolonial approaches to literary texts. Agency and identity appear as categories in the novel, but both are deeply disturbed by forces that are inhuman and that reach far beyond the individual.

Amy Tan's *Saving Fish From Drowning* also engages aspects of authorship in its prominent shift away from Tan's previous themes of mother-daughter bonds complicated by ethnicity and (family) histories. After having established herself as an author of Asian American literature, Tan moves away from expected topics and tries to fashion herself as a global author. In addition, her novel plays with the persistent image of the ethnic author as a tour guide to a foreign culture. In using the classic ghost motif as the narrator of this story, and in making her a tour guide in spirit, *Saving Fish From Drowning* invites reflections about ethnic authorship in our globalized world. Ed Lin's *Ghost Month* does not address the aspect of authorship as directly as *Saving Fish From Drowning*, but it stages the conflicted status of ethnic, postcolonial writing in a globalized world. It plays with reader expectations, emphasizing the 'exotic' aspects of its Taiwanese setting – such as ghost beliefs or food –, building upon the appeal of an Asian mystery crime story, while also constantly referencing the problems and chances of such a way of 'selling out' an ethnic heritage.

Both Ghosh and Tan have been criticized in general and for these novels in particular. Critics accuse them of trivializing and of a cheap selling of their cultural backgrounds. Although the field of Asian American Studies has surely developed significantly over the last decades, these charges curiously refer back to the Chin-Kingston debate that I outline in the introduction of *The Ghosts Within*. Whereas Kingston has by now become a classical and respected figure of Asian American literature, Amy Tan, for example, has continuously been accused of purely entertaining the masses and of marketing her ethnic background in her novels. The debates about an author's representative function or her aesthetic freedom appear timeless: with the shift to global issues, the controversies have simply broadened the terrain.

Another central aspect of the Chin-Kingston controversy also reappears with new emphasis: the question of style. The old fears of entertainment and selling out are fuelled today by the broad appeal of Asian American genre fiction. In *Popular Fiction* (2004), Ken Gelder attempts a definition of the field of popular fiction, emphasizing the importance of certain terms such as "[p]roduction, output, deadlines, sequels, work" which "are some of the foregrounded logics and practices, then, that help to distinguish popular fiction from Literature" (Gelder 17). According to Gelder, 'Literature' with a capital 'L' is associated with the art world, and its authors are perceived as artists, whereas popular fiction is associated with work and industry and its authors are instead called writers (13–14). Gelder's attempt to establish such clear-cut distinctions between these two fields has been critically reviewed by Scott McCracken, for example, who calls for recognition of the vast field in-between the two opposites that

Gelder outlines.[6] Whether one follows Gelder's approach or not, such definitions clearly indicate the problematic interconnections between 'selling out,' easy readings and entertainment for the masses, and an acceptable position for ethnic writers who locate themselves in the field of popular fiction. Still, Christopher A. Shinn observes that "*The Calcutta Chromosome* appeared at a critical moment in the historic emergence of Asian American popular fiction in the early 1990s; Ghosh's science fiction thus resonates critically with new works in genre fiction by Asian American authors such as Cynthia Kadohata" (Shinn 162). Where Shinn recognizes a new trend, the wide popularity of authors of mystery crime fiction such as Ed Lin's *The Ghost Month* underlines the continuing relevance of globalized genre fiction.

Betsy Huang argues in *Contesting Genres in Contemporary Asian American Fiction* (2010) that genre fiction provides Asian American writers with a way out of the assumed 'autobiographic imperative:' "an interpretive disposition of readers who habitually read fiction by ethnic writers as autobiography, as testimonies to lived experiences, typically assumed to be those of immigrants" (Huang 11). She identifies three "highly structured types of genre fiction in particular" – immigrant fiction, crime fiction, and science fiction – as the places in which contemporary Asian American writers refute genre imperatives in order to re-write 'generic' narratives about Asian America (5). She argues that it "is precisely the reputed prescriptiveness of these genres that make them rich sites for assessing the regulatory power of genre conventions and the transformative power of genre experimentation" (5). In other words, Huang emphasizes the ways in which genre fiction – particularly because of its generic aspects – allows Asian American writers to diversify the assumed autobiographic and ethnographic content of their works. She draws on Wai Chi Dimock's conception of genre fiction as a reproductive process. In order to highlight this process, Dimock has coined the term 'regenreing' to "highlight the activity here as cumulative reuse, an alluvial process, sedimentary as well as migratory" (Dimock 1380).

I apply Huang's and Dimock's findings to the ghost figures, for I believe that the ghosts are even better suited to address such stereotypical narratives about Asian America. In a way, Dimock's process works similarly to the way in which ghost figures appear as referencing a certain tradition, background, and history while simultaneously offering new perspectives. The appeal of both lies in the productive tension between innovation and tradition, between expectations and

---

6 See Scott McCracken, "Review: The Field of Popular Fiction," *Twentieth Century Literature* 53.2 (Summer 2007): 218–223.

surprises. That genre literature is populated by ghost figures highlights their ambiguous function once again. These authors take a classic motif out of its usual context and integrate it into the new topics of globalization. Functioning at once as both promise and threat, these figures embody the possibilities and problems of the world as a global village: they address issues such as tourism, infections, cyberspace, and authorship. Even though they enter new, global terrain, they remain bound to their original reference points of culture, ethnicity, religion, and family belonging. It is exactly this twofold, contradictory drive that makes this motif so productive. The ghosts embody the paradoxical development of Asian American literature as it tries to position itself anew: they signal the placelessness of contemporary writings while they refer back to concrete places and beliefs.

HAUNTING POSTCOLONIAL ALTERNATIVES IN AMITAV GHOSH'S *THE CALCUTTA CHROMOSOME*

"He felt a cool soft touch upon his shoulder and his hand flew up to take off the SimVis headgear. But now there was a restraining hand upon his wrist, and a voice in his ear, Tara's voice, whispering. 'Keep watching; we're here; we're all with you.'

There were voices everywhere now, in his room, in his head, in his ears, it was as though a crowd of people was in the room with him. They were saying: 'We're with you; you're not alone; we'll help you across.'

He sat back and sighed like he hadn't sighed in years." (Ghosh, *The Calcutta Chromosome* 306)

This scene is from the very ending of Amitav Ghosh's *The Calcutta Chromosome*. In its final chapter and these final moments, the protagonist Antar is finally exposed as part of the few chosen people who can transfer – move from one body into another. The way in which Antar experiences this transference of his soul exemplifies the central points of the novel. It mirrors its gloomy, ghostly atmosphere. In this sense, Antar's crossing is both promise and threat. Like all other characters – and as well as the reader –, he remains in the dark as to what exactly this crossing entails: it connects him to a larger web of recurring characters and opens new possibilities, yet it also turns him into a shadowy and uncertain existence, even more so since Antar was chosen for this and did not choose this existence for himself. The figure and atmosphere of the ghostly appears as a suitable narrative technique. Taken out of its original context of family hauntings and cultural traditions, the ghost emerges in all its ambiguity:

as a figure of possibility and a figure of uncertainty and inexplicability. The ghostly transference only works on people who suffer from malaria, so that this disease becomes the point of interconnection across class, gender, ethnicity, nationality, and time. Thus, haunted and precarious post-human postcolonial subjectivities are constructed on a transnational level.

The secrecy of such transference possibilities drives this science fiction story and is rendered ghostly throughout. The emerging postcolonial subjectivities appear as haunted themselves: they are driven not only by powerful figures such as Mangala – who appears in her reincarnation as Tara in the above quote and seemingly is in charge of the transference process – but all of them, including Mangala, are being directed by non-human forces beyond their control. For even Mangala seems limited and controlled by the non-human agency of the malaria pathogens. Such non-human agency might not be particularly interesting in science fiction novels per se, but its appearance in Asian American global fiction highlights the field's expanded topics. Even though the novel narrates its characters' involvement with the research of the disease of malaria and addresses the conflicts of (post)colonial research and the global dimension of today's world, it refrains from giving its protagonists the expected power and agency that one would ascribe to people who can transfer from one body into another. The novel rather highlights the curious way in which these subjects no longer matter as individuals: they have vanished into puppets of a global non-human agency, becoming ghost-like themselves.

That Antar experiences his crossing via cyberspace takes the ghostly, de-individualized aspect even to another level. Although earlier transference ceremonies appear as similarly troublesome and its participants as clueless, this last transference even disconnects the process from any direct human interaction. With this, the world has become even smaller: the characters are not only globally interconnected via the obvious routes, but also via cyberspace. The way in which the novel combines this new technologized and de-individualized ghostly realm with classical Indian ghost stories once again reveals the various functions of this motif. The ghost figures remain bound to earlier conceptions, to family and cultural traditions, to folk belief and storytelling, but they can also merge with new discourses of globalization, interconnection, de-humanization, computerization, and de-individualization. As such, these ghosts showcase a contemporary renegotiation of a place for Asian American literature in its globalized conception.

Amitav Ghosh's novel *The Calcutta Chromosome* offers a multilayered story line whose interconnections are only revealed towards the end. It is hard to classify, but has been labeled science fiction, detective story, postcolonial thriller, ghost story, medical mystery, and historical novel; in other words, it is considered genre fiction.[7] The overarching story line is set in the near future in New York, where Antar, an Egypt-born immigrant, works for the corporation International Water Council. Antar's transference at the end of the novel is triggered at its beginning when his computer stumbles upon an ID card of L. Murugan. He is a former colleague of Antar's who has disappeared. This opens the second story line of the novel, which is set in the 1990s and follows Murugan's trip to Calcutta to research Ronald Ross's discovery of the conveyance of malaria via mosquitoes. Murugan believes that Ross's findings were driven by a secret counter-science working on a way to transfer into other bodies. Reappearances of characters in new bodies connect all three story lines, as the reader learns by the end of the novel. The third story line is set in the 1890s and tells about Ronald Ross's discoveries, but in opposition to official history, the novel highlights the role of his assistants Lutchman/Laakhan and Mangala. The two are secretly working on the process of transference in its connection to malaria.

The novel presents the confusions of transnational postcolonial identities by way of a surreal world, in which a disease spans not only radically different places and continents but also different times. The "interconnectedness between people, unbeknownst to them" (Wassef 92) is given in their connection to malaria and the possibility of transference. As such, *The Calcutta Chromosome* "explodes the idea of cultural, religious, national or other definitions of identity" (76). In taking this observation, many critics read the novel as a postcolonial subversive resistance narrative. In their readings of Ghosh's novel, Claire Chambers, Diane M. Nelson or Barbara Romanik, for example, highlight the agency of the colonized people and celebrate a critical rewriting of postcolonial history.[8] They foreground the story line in which Ronald Ross's research is exposed to be channeled by the indigenous group around Mangala. Ross's

7 See, for example: Christopher Shinn, "On Machines and Mosquitoes," p. 145.

8 See: Chambers, Claire. "Postcolonial Science Fiction: Amitav Ghosh's *The Calcutta Chromosome.*" *Journal of Commonwealth Literature* 3.1 (2003): 57–72; Nelson, Diane M. "A Social Science of Fevers, Delirium and Discovery: 'The Calcutta Chromosome,' the Colonial Laboratory, and the Postcolonial New Human." *Science Fiction Studies* 30.2 (2003): 246–66; Romanik, Barbara. "Transforming the Colonial City: Science and the Practice of Dwelling in *The Calcutta Chromosome.*" *Mosaic (Winnipeg)* 38.3 (2005): np. Web.http://go.galegroup.com/ps/i.do?id=GALE%7CA137077505&v=2.1&u=fub&it=r&p=LitRC&sw=w&asid=7bab2800f147090806db63e00eb15f17.

blindness to this research behind his back is seen as ironic commentary on the ignorance of colonial and postcolonial history to indigenous influences. According to Chambers, "[t]his allows Ghosh to make the important point that science, technology and medicine were not conveyed to India by the British in a one-way process of transfer, but were in fact involved in a complex series of cross-cultural exchanges, translations and mutations" (Chambers 58).

In a similar vein, Andrew Hock Soon Ng – one of the few critics working on ghost figures in the novel – reads Mangala as "the 'ghost,' or surplus, that haunts the limits of Western medical history and consistently troubles its carefully guarded boundaries" (Ng, *Interrogating Interstices* 224), arguing that specters like her expose the gaps in Western knowledge and allow agency for the subaltern people. With this reading he supports his claim that Eastern ghost stories – in contrast to Western ones – "often function as important existential alternatives to otherwise repressive and marginalising socio-ideological systems" (223). And yet, while the ghost figures represent this subversive resistance paradigm, they also highlight its inherent haunted status. Not only is Ross's science haunted by Mangala's counter-science but also by Western religious explanations, and Mangala's scientific advances, in turn, work towards the literal reincarnation that structures Hindu believes. Mangala's work is, thus, haunted by the ideas of reincarnation and the caste system in which the multiple transferences first appear before they become transnational manifestations. There is, then, a layering of discourses of haunting that structures the novel's engagement with knowledge construction and history writing. And while the resistance paradigm is certainly correct and forms part of the narrative that *The Calcutta Chromosome* tells, a singular focus on this aspect obscures new and fascinating possibilities that the novel offers in its move into global interconnections and away from identity politics: the placelessness of its characters, the inhuman agency of the malaria pathogens, the uncertainty of transference and the precariousness of its ghosted subjects, who no longer seem to matter as individuals.

While the novel does construct a malarial agency – one that strikingly moves beyond the powers of any individual, it refrains from further explanations. And this unknowability of both the process itself and also its outcome seem to be the main point that the novel makes. This unknowability is carried by the figure and the atmosphere of the ghostly – for it is typically via the figure of the ghost that gaps and silences are being conveyed, those of the past but also those of the present as well as the future. Thus, the novel presents the colonial history as a haunted one – haunted by neglected indigenous knowledge and by the uncertainty of its own premises. But in my opinion, it presents future possibilities for social co-existence as similarly haunted. The novel does not depict a celebratory non-critical picture of a subversive postcolonial transnational subjectivity as a result of exposing the gaps of colonial history. Instead, it shows the dark underside that any subversive counter-science always already embodies, rendering this realm ghostly as well. Strikingly, the novel undermines any sense of postcolonial agency.

With its focus on disease, *The Calcutta Chromosome* portrays what Peter Jackson, et. al., envision in their edited volume *Transnational Spaces* (2004) to "extend the study of transnationality beyond the confines of still-bounded-but-displaced 'ethnic communities' to encompass a more multidimensional, materially heterogeneous social field, characterized by multiple inhabitations and disjunctions" (Jackson, Crang, and Dwyer 15). For the novel no longer depicts a community bound by ethnic belonging, but rather a community that is thread together – involuntarily and often without its members' knowledge – by research surrounding a disease and the possibility of transference. These individuals are bound to each other in their search for secrets and their exposure to malaria and decidedly not in their search for coherent ethnic identities.

The strong emphasis on the disease as a connection point across ethnic, gender, national, and class boundaries highlights the global status of the novel and its characters. It also links the novel to what Priscilla Wald calls 'contagion fiction.' In *Contagious: Cultures, Carriers, and the Outbreak Narrative* (2008), Wald focuses on the development of what she terms 'the outbreak narrative.' This narrative

> "follows a formulaic plot that begins with the identification of an emerging infection, includes discussion of the global networks throughout which it travels, and chronicles the epidemiological work that ends with its containment. As epidemiologists trace the routes of the microbes, they catalog the spaces and interactions of global modernity. Microbes, spaces, and interactions blend together as they animate the landscape and motivate the plot of the outbreak narrative: a contradictory but compelling story of the perils of human interdependence and the triumph of human connection and cooperation, scientific authority and the evolutionary advantages of the microbe, ecological balance and impending disaster." (Wald 2)

The human interdependence that Wald notices is also part of early 'Gothic' contagion fiction, such as Charles Brockden Brown's *Arthur Mervyn* (1799), which chronicles the "collapse of social relations, rituals, and institutions" (11) in the face of disease. But contagion also simultaneously provides a space for social and biological belonging. Humanity is exposed as deeply susceptible, with no protection of either rich or poor. The plague is, therefore, often perceived as a great equalizer in this literature (12). Just as in *The Calcutta Chromosome*, disease functions both as a challenge to community or nation, but it also creates new possibilities of connections across the usual divides.

The outbreak narrative is tightly bound to ideas of globalization. Wald argues that globalization was even the source of the spread – as the microbes began to travel via the new routes of air travel and commerce. Not surprisingly, the exposure of these global disease channels produced contact anxieties (25). These anxieties centered on strangers, foreigners, travelers, and particularly immigrants (42–43). Whereas these fears remain connected to certain groups that are then packaged as scapegoats or threats to national safety, mid-twentieth century created a new type of fiction: science fiction horror (160). Its classic threats are those of viral agency and invasion, surely linked to the logics of the Cold War. In contrast to bacteria, "viral microbes existed on – and seemed to define – the border between the living and the nonliving" (158). These microbes "did not simply gain nutrients from host cells, but actually harnessed the cell's apparatus to duplicate themselves" (162), striving simply for their own reproduction. They were immediately anthropomorphized as "penetrating, forceful, and predatory" (169), but remained uncontrollable ghostly, non-human forces. Signaling both the fear of hybridity and of viral agency, the "monstrous hybrids in the contemporary epidemiological horror stories are not strangers, but transformed familiars [...]. They embody the dangerously transformative nature of global networks that undergirds the vocabulary of disease emergence" (261).

Wald's conception of these figures is close to Freud's descriptions of the uncanny and to Bhabha's conception of the unhomely where the home becomes estranged as it is shown in its contacts with the world. They are not foreign, but transformed familiars. The 'monstrous hybrid,' thus, signals the fears of changes that occur as the result of contacts – enhanced in this case by the global interconnections. While *The Calcutta Chromosome* is not a typical 'contagion narrative' that reproduces the outbreak narrative, it does address several of the issues that Priscilla Wald connects to this narrative. As already stated above, the novel stages its narrative as a global one. It is populated by such 'monstrous hybrids' and 'transformed familiars,' that form a new globally interlinked group of chosen ones. It reproduces the anxieties about viral infections – even though, strictly speaking, malaria is neither a virus nor a bacterial infection – especially in its depictions of the non-human agency of the malaria pathogen. The disease is, after all, the precondition for transference. Keeping Wald's findings in mind helps to conceive *The Calcutta Chromosome* as a story about the global reach of disease and the inability of human beings to either contain it or control it in the form of transference.

Mangala – the one who gets closest to control the disease and its workings – is first introduced to the reader when Murugan tells Antar about a young doctor, Elijah Farley, who was looking for the parasite that Laveran claimed to have discovered. In this search he met Mangala at a laboratory. She is introduced to Farley as the sweeper woman. Farley notices her unusual knowledge about the laboratory's slides and assumes that she knows far more than anyone would guess. When Farley begins his research at the laboratory the next day, he sees a group of syphilitics in the last stages of the disease. They are sitting close to Mangala and are engaged in some kind of group chant. Farley sees the hope in their eyes, when they look at Mangala and thinks about their fatal condition that does not allow for such hope (Ghosh, *The Calcutta Chromosome* 148–50). Farley begins his work of detecting the Laveran parasite, but does not make any progress. Finally, the assistant who brings him the slides seems to change his mind about which slides he wants to show to him. Driven by his curiosity, Farley

> "made his way silently across the laboratory. Flattening himself against the wall, he crept toward the door until he had maneuvered himself into a position where he could look into the anteroom without himself being detected.
> Farley had steeled himself for anything, or so he thought, but he was unprepared for what he saw next. First the assistant went up to the woman, Mangala, still regally ensconced on her divan, and touched his forehead to her feet. Then in the manner of a courtier or acolyte he whispered some word of advice into her ear. She nodded in agreement and took the clean slides from him. Reaching for the birdcages [with dying pigeons] she allowed her hand to rest upon each of the birds in turn, as though she were trying to ascertain something. Then she seemed to come to a decision; she reached into a cage, and took one of the shivering birds into her lap. She folded her hands over it and her mouth began to move as though muttering a prayer. Then suddenly a scalpel appeared in her right hand; she held the bird away from her and with a single flick of her wrist beheaded the dying pigeon. Once the flow of blood had lessened, she picked up the clean slides, smeared them across the severed neck, and handed them to the assistant." (151)

This scene establishes the atmosphere in which Farley will make his discovery. Mangala is introduced as a driving force, she seems to be in control of the whole group and the process, the people regard her as their last chance of healing or survival, her assistant even bows to her. The whole scene is rendered in a ghostly atmosphere: there is a secret to be kept, there are dying people and birds, and there is a force perceptible that lights the hopes of these sick people and keeps Farley bound to his seat in his research.

Next, the assistant brings Farley the slides and invites him to take a look at this new material through the microscope.

"Farley turned the slides over in his hand. 'But,' he said, 'these are not properly stained: the blood on them is still fresh.'
'Yes, sir,' said the assistant, offhandedly. 'Perhaps that which you are looking for can only be seen in freshly drawn blood.'
Farley placed the slide under the microscope and looked into the instrument. At first he saw nothing unusual; nothing that would have indicated to him, had he not known, that this exhibit came from a pigeon. He noticed the familiar granules of malarial pigment. But then suddenly he saw movement; under his eyes amoeboid forms began to squirm and move, undulating slowly across the glassy surface. Then all at once there was a flurry of movement and they began to disintegrate: it was then that he saw Laveran's rods appear, hundreds of them, tiny cylindrical things, with their pointed, penetrating heads piercing the bloody miasma.
The sweat began to drip off Farley's forehead now, as he watched the horned creatures burrowing, writhing, wriggling in frantic search. His breath grew labored; his head began to spin. He sat up, gasping, the sight of these willful, struggling creatures still vivid in his eyes." (152)

In this scene, then, Farley finally detects what he was looking for. But he does not find it by himself; instead, it is presented to him, when Mangala shares this knowledge with him. She even explains to the puzzled Farley that the creatures are coupling. While the whole encounter again underlines the idea of a Western approach as undermined and haunted by indigenous knowledge, it also establishes the ghostly agency of the malaria pathogen that ultimately enables Mangala to try her process of transference. As in Priscilla Wald's contagion narrative, the malaria pathogen is anthropomorphized: Farley not only calls them 'creatures,' but even assumes that they are 'willful.' Just like Wald's viral agents, these malaria pathogens appear as a mass – 'hundreds of them' – and they 'wriggle' in order to reproduce even further, engaging in an act of 'willful' agency. As they form the basis of the whole process of transference, their significance for the story cannot be overstated. Their ghostly status as neither dead nor fully alive references the state of the syphilitics who hope to be selected for transference and it foreshadows the ghostly status of the new subjects that they will bring about. The necessary power seems to lie in the existence of these creatures and the transformations that they create in people who suffer from malaria.

This is as close as the reader gets to understanding the mysterious, biological forces that enable the process of transference. The story surrounding Mangala and her rituals is conveyed only in bits and pieces. The few things that characters such as Farley or, in a scene just 10 pages later in the novel, Sonali, see when they secretly observe one of her rituals are scary and confusing. Sonali Das, a Bollywood film star, is friends with both Mrs Aratounian and Urmila – both women are incarnations of Mangala. Sonali enters a seemingly empty mansion on Robinson Street at night, looking for her boyfriend Romen Haldar. She finds the construction gang and other strangers preoccupied in some kind of ceremony, but a lot of smoke and her fear of what might be done to her if she were to be detected keep her from going too close to the scene. She witnesses Romen's passing into a new body, without fully grasping what is happening. This whole scene – with the haunted mansion, the smoke, the broken staircase in which Sonali becomes trapped, the chanting and rhythmic drumming – is rendered in ghostly fashion (160–66). Sonali observes what is happening

"She [Mangala, in the body of Mrs Aratounian] arranged the plates and the scalpel in front of her. […] Then she reached out, placed her hands on whatever it was that was lying before the fire and smiled – a look of extraordinary sweetness came over her face.
Raising her voice, the woman said to the crowd, in archaic rustic Bengali: 'The time is here, pray that all goes well for our Laakhan, once again.'
Suddenly Sonali was struck by a terrible sense of foreboding. Raising her head as high as she dared she looked again into the space by the fire. She caught a glimpse of a body, lying on the floor.
The drumming rose to a crescendo: there was a flash of bright metal and a necklace of blood flew up and fell sizzling on the fire.
Sonali's head crashed to the floor and everything went dark." (166)

When Sonali loses consciousness and is only woken the next day when Urmila and Murugan find her, this scene is not explained away with rational explanations. Its mystic atmosphere remains, leaving both the reader and the characters puzzled. Although we learn by the end of the novel that Romen passed into a new incarnation during this ceremony, the actual passing and its consequences remain obscure, and thus unknowable. In a ghostly repetition of the earlier scene – Farley's witnessing of the beheading of the pigeons – this process of transference appears as particularly gruesome in its association with a beheaded human being whose uncanny existence is far from certain. Observing this scene through Sonali's eyes, the reader shares her confusion and fear. An optimistic reading of this scene would focus on the positive outcome of this ceremony and ascribe the haunting atmosphere to Sonali's cluelessness and her entering into restricted territory. And yet, although the woman with the scalpel looks at her victim with 'extraordinary sweetness,' she still raises the scalpel to create a 'necklace of blood.' And it even seems that the woman herself is not entirely sure that her sacrifice will work, when she encourages her followers to 'pray that all goes well.' This prayer not only uncannily reminds the reader of the prayer that Mangala spoke before beheading the pigeon, it also emphasizes her own limits and establishes an aura of helplessness. Although she appears as the one in charge of these transference processes, she is still bound to larger forces, inhuman, beyond her influence, and strikingly connected to the ghostly agency of the malaria pathogens. Taken together, Mangala's own uncertainty and Sonali's confusion and fear become the reader's. We, as readers, are left with a 'terrible sense of foreboding,' when the novel also moves into its second part, returning to this scene only towards the very end of the novel. Instead of joyful considerations of alternative lives, Sonali and the reader remain subjected to an all-encompassing unknowability.

In spite of this threatening prospect, Murugan wishes to become part of the transference process, like many others. They are driven by a human longing, which readers can certainly relate to. Murugan expresses this hope, when he asks Antar: "Just think, a fresh start: when your body fails you, you leave it, you migrate – you or at least a matching symptomology of yourself. You begin all over again, another body, another being. Just think: no mistakes, a fresh start. What would you give for that Ant […]?"(107). This idea of a 'fresh start' when your body fails you or when you are disappointed about life in general, creates a seductive pull towards the process of transference. Transference becomes a 'pharmakon,' to use one of Derrida's concepts.

In his essay "Plato's Pharmacy" Derrida reflects upon the positive and negative aspects of writing in contrast to speaking. Although writing helps to remember, it always already undermines memory because it offers a way to remember without actually keeping something in mind. Derrida reflects that writing is a 'pharmakon' in that it is a

> "'medicine,' this philter, which acts as both remedy and poison, already introduces itself into the body of the discourse with all its ambivalence. This charm, this spellbinding virtue, this power of fascination, can be – alternatively or simultaneously – beneficent or maleficent." (Derrida, *Dissemination* 70)

He continues that "[o]perating through seduction, the *pharmakon* makes one stray from one's general, natural, habitual paths and laws" (70). Thinking about transference as a pharmakon allows to reflect about its seductive power and its inherent ambivalence. While it represents a remedy for the sick person – in leaving the sick body behind, it does not offer a cure of the sickness itself. For the process of transference is inherently linked to malaria. Instead of presenting the 'fresh start' that Murugan dreams of, transference offers immortality, yet always already overshadowed by the continuing sickness that is then, once again, necessary for the next transference.

Derrida's reflections about the pharmakon also include a passage on repetition. He writes that "[w]hat is is not what it is, identical and identical to itself, unique, unless it adds to itself the possibility of being repeated as such. And its identity is hollowed out by that addition, withdraws itself in the supplement that presents it" so that "there is no repetition possible without the graphics of supplementarity, which supplies, for the lack of a full unity, another unit that comes to relieve it, being enough the same and enough other so that it can replace by addition" (168). If – as in *The Calcutta Chromosome* – human beings become part of such supplementarity and repetition, their identities appear to be deeply shaken, something to which Murugan already hints in his reflections when he stumbles upon the phrase 'you or at least a matching symptomology of yourself.' It remains unclear, which parts of a person will continue to exist after transference. The transference from one incarnation to the next is therefore both remedy and poison. And it embodies the problematics of writing: instead of memory and identity, the process creates something else – something alike, yet othered.

This ambivalence is also reproduced in the figure of Mangala: in her power and her uncertainty. Robbie Goh and Christopher Shinn discuss the negative aspects that surround the development of this counter-scientific realm. They foreground Mangala's "unethical ways" her involvement in murder, sabotage, and human and animal sacrifice, simply using humans for her own advance – without initiating them to her plans. Thus, Mangala's own role and legitimization remain unclear, especially because her goals remain obscure (Shinn 151–52). What becomes clear, however, is the rigorous and violent way in which these plans are being pushed forward. Goh adds that even if

> "the deliberately fragmentary and often obscurist narrative conceals the full extent of the native gang's sinister plans and pseudo-scientific methods, it cannot quite conceal their transformation into an exploitative power elite that bears more than a passing resemblance to colonialists and corporations." (Goh, Robbie B. H. 58)

Although the novel seemingly empowers the colonized, it constructs these 'new humans' as complicit and morally dubious (58). Goh and Shinn not only unravel the paradoxical status that Mangala's empowerment entails, but also unveil the uncertain future of the products of her experimentations. The characters of Mangala's transmigatory possibility may partake in her schemes, however, they remain clueless about both the process itself and their future selves so that Goh concludes that one "of the most unsettling things about this novel is the way in which the reader's experience of the main characters is ultimately overshadowed by the uncertain fate that awaits them, in the face of the technology of identity-transference" (56).

Even Urmila, whom Mangala has chosen to be one of her own reincarnations, remains clueless a few moments before her transition. Murugan seems to have made the connection, asking her

"'Don't you see?' he said. 'You're the one she's chosen.'
Urmila gasped. 'For what?'
'For herself.'
Suddenly, taking Urmila by surprise, Murugan fell to his knees, squeezing himself into the narrow leg space of the back seat. Bending low he touched his forehead to her feet. 'Don't forget me,' he begged her. 'If you have it in your power to change the script, write me in. Don't leave me behind. Please.'
Urmila laughed. She put a hand on his head and an arm around Sonali's shoulders. 'Don't worry,' she said. 'I'll take you both with me, wherever I go.'" (Ghosh, *The Calcutta Chromosome* 304)

The passion with which Murugan begs Urmila underlines his desperation. He seems to be the person with the most concrete understanding of Mangala's counter-science and the possibilities this offers. But he fears that exactly this kind of knowledge might be his only contribution to the overall master plan. And although he finally enters into Antar's body at the end of the novel, he appears as caught in the power webs of different systems from beginning to end. His appearance at the end – as a naked man with a "blanket of matted, ropy hair hung halfway down a swollen, distended belly; his upper body was encrusted with dead leaves and straw, and his thighs were caked with mud and excrement" and in steel hand-cuffs (291) – implies his imprisonment and suffering before his wish was finally granted. And before his quest to Calcutta and his search of and surrender to transference's life-and-death power, he was spiritually imprisoned by his unsatisfactory work for LifeWatch, their attempts to keep him from going to India, and his friends' and colleagues' misrecognition of his rewritings of Ronald Ross's famous findings. Rather than exposing a carefree passage from one happy reincarnation into the next, Murugan's story particularly highlights the unpredictable and uncertain status that all of the characters face. The transnational power structures which underline Murugan's life story – of international corporations, of religious cults, of secret subversive strategies – also shape the whole process of transference. Far from being a celebratory story of powerful counter-existences, the possibility of transference remains bound to transnational power structures and is haunted by its own complicity in these systems. Goh similarly concludes, that

> "the doubleness of this narrative project thus consists in the fact that it is both a reminder of the abiding differentiations of race and development even within globalization and technological futures, as well as a discursive perpetuation of – and arguably a complicity in – that differentiation." (Goh, Robbie B. H. 68)

For, as Hugh Charles O'Connell writes, while

> "the novel begins from a particularly Indian postcolonial locale and thus could perhaps be said to institute a particularly postcolonial Indian vision of the future, it ultimately wishes to break with the tyranny of nationalities and bounded nation-states altogether in favor of a postnational supra-global domain of 'genuine discovery' and interconnectedness. *The Calcutta Chromosome*'s globality is really the transcendence of the globe itself and is thus without nationality, without nations or bodies. Rather, it is pure information in a 'postcolonial cyberspace' as the arrival of an event beyond current concepts of humanity or even current governing notions of reality." (O'Connell 791)

The way in which globality is reconfigured in the novel mirrors the way in which individuals become part of a larger system of interconnections. There is no longer an emphasis on either nation or body, as O'Connell has it. Although in the earlier processes of transference the bodies as bodies become highly important, the transference from one body into another exposes the de-humanized status of these ghostly shells. What comes under erasure throughout is not only the body itself but the individual it embodies. The individualized concepts of nation or identity have been replaced by larger webs of disease and of global interconnection.

The final attempt at transference has even changed the process dramatically. When Murugan finally tries to cross over into Antar, this transference is brought about not by personal contact, but simply via cyberspace. In the scene that also begins this part of the chapter, Murugan "reappears to Antar in his New York apartment as a startling holographic projection, informing Antar that [...] [he] will need to enter into virtual reality" "to join Mangala and her followers [...] [who] eventually will be united in cyberspace" (Shinn 146). When the characters were before bound to a sick body, they now appear as particularly body-less in this new space, which signals the ultimate erasure of the body as referencing an individual.

As the advanced technologies of the computer highlight the de-individualization that the process of transference always already embodies, the anthropomorphized state of Antar's computer, Ava, invites reflections about this reversal. Ava is introduced as female and she tries to self-improve her knowledge endlessly. For example, once she would have all necessary and unnecessary data about an object, "she'd give the object on her screen a final spin, with a bizarrely human smugness, before propelling it into the horizonless limbo of her memory" (Ghosh, *The Calcutta Chromosome* 4). Christopher A. Shinn argues that Ava performs a similar function to the earlier mosquito or pigeon in becoming a primary carrier:

"Much as the mosquito has recombinatory powers, Ava has the ability to transpose information and data, merging with Antar and other subaltern subjects. Like the mosquito that merely channels and redistributes the malaria virus, the computer unleashes a potent biological force that it aims to control while maintaining its autonomy." (Shinn 156)

Although Ava does not appear as a technologized force working on the destruction of humanity, the comparison with the other carriers and hosts connects her to ideas of viral agency and non-human forces that ultimately drive the whole process. Her humanized state further underlines the de-humanized state of the other characters. As the ultimate goal of transference seems to be its own reproduction and betterment, Ava appears as a highly productive carrier due to her limitless knowledge. As a computer, she stores masses of information and can reproduce anything at any time: she, thus, represents the possibility of endless repetition. Taking Derrida's reflections of writing as a pharmakon even one step further, the computer is both threat as well as possibility. In providing a way of engaging in endless repetition, simulation, and transformation, Ava's entering into the formula of transference might finally resolve the problem of using sickened bodies for the process. But *The Calcutta Chromosome* only hints at this solution by way of its conclusion. In any case, the undecidablity of transference as a pharmakon is highly pronounced in this crossover into cyberspace so that it foregrounds the inherent logic of de-individualization and globalization that drives the process from its very beginning.

Whereas Murugan embodies the destruction of agency for Mangala's followers and exposes the dark side of her counter-science, Laakhan becomes the ultimate protector of Mangala's secret research; albeit a similarly de-individualized subject. Laakhan is the figure who connects various points of the novel. He protects the secret, yet also highlights the precarious position of those seemingly empowered. Moreover, he also allows further reflections about the ghost motif within the realm of global Asian American writings as he references widely different traditions. Not coincidentally, it is Laakhan who appears as the most fully realized ghost character of Ghosh's novel. It is this ghost figure who combines revenants of mythological Indian figures, vernacular Indian ghost stories, the colonial ghost stories of Rudyard Kipling, and the genre of science fiction. The process of transference is organized around the idea of migration of souls. The whole novel, thus, literalizes Hindu beliefs. And it is via the figure of Laakhan that this connection is most explicitly played out. This ghost therefore signals the historical and cultural specificity that the rest of the novel's ghostly references rather neglect. It brings back the traditional frames of Asian American ghost figures, but also relates these to Laakhan's new position as a global, ghostly, 'new human.' Laakhan's ghost functions as such a dual reference.

Laakhan haunts the novel, appearing and reappearing in various forms, bearing the names Lutchman, Laakhan, Romen, and Lucky. He materializes at every important step, connecting to most characters in person. In this interconnected world of reincarnated characters this seems of no particular relevance. Yet, Laakhan seems to actively shape the course of the characters' lives, for example when he directs Ronald Ross in his research and becomes his assistant. It is, interestingly, not Mangala herself who seems to reach out to her followers, but rather Laakhan. Most significantly, he is the one in charge of protecting the secret research, so that he takes even violent measures if necessary. Fittingly, his name refers to a mythological figure: Lakshman, the brother of the god Ram. When Ram needs to leave for a fourteen year exile, Lakshman leaves his wife and everything else behind to accompany his brother. This act is one of pure love and loyalty so that the name is associated with these characteristics. But it also refers to someone who comes second, who follows. Significantly, Lakshman also protects his brother throughout (Ghosh, "On Grafting the Vernacular" 216–17). With this referent, Laakhan's role as Mangala's loyal protector and follower becomes particularly highlighted and connects him to traditional Indian mythology.

The novel tells three different yet connected 'ghost stories' that feature Laakhan. All of them underline his willingness to fulfill his role of protector for he appears as a haunting character to all those who come dangerously close to revealing the secrets around Mangala's research. Elijah Farley, for example, suddenly disappears after he begins to understand the workings of the 'creatures' he observed in the laboratory. The reader later learns that he was run over by a train and accompanied by a boy whose description fits Laakhan, so that we can assume that he was killed for what he knew. This assumption is based on the longest ghost story that precedes the information about Farley's death.

This ghost story includes the writer Phulboni and serves as the explanation for his madness and retreat, and as inspiration for his 'Laakhan stories.' It is in this story that Laakhan is depicted most recognizably as a ghost figure. When Phulboni is invited to the town Renupur, he is greeted by the stationmaster. Because of the bad weather conditions, he spends the night alone at the signal-room against the station-master's advice. He lights the lantern and it mysteriously goes out, this happens repeatedly. After he has fallen asleep, he wakes up and notices that the door is open and the lantern missing. He assumes that the stationmaster came back and goes outside, following the lantern's light. Just as in the earlier stories, a train mysteriously appears and almost kills Phulboni. After its passage, Phulboni realizes that the rails are absolutely still and that there is no sound of a train anywhere to be heard. Moreover, he discovers "that the undergrowth that he had seen earlier that day, growing over the tracks, showed no signs of having been disturbed by the passage of a train" (Ghosh, *The Calcutta Chromosome* 272). Phulboni's fear grows, and he runs back to the signal room, when "the lantern appeared in the doorway. It stepped in and began to approach him; a hand appeared, bathed in the red light of the lantern. The face was still in darkness but suddenly that inhuman voice rang through the room again. It said just that one word, 'Laakhan'" (273). In his fear, Phulboni fires his gun at the signal lantern. When Phulboni wakes up the next morning, the lantern is in its place, unbroken and clean as always, as the stationmaster informs Phulboni. Suddenly, while talking to the stationmaster, Phulboni reaches out his arm and touches a rail, which causes him to open his eyes. Just in time to escape from the tracks before an approaching train hits him. This train is real and when Phulboni gets on board, the chief engineer tells him that there has not been a stationmaster for over thirty years. This last stationmaster had driven away a young orphan called Laakhan and was then run over by a train (276–80).

The recurring image of the railway and the train that connects all of the three Laakhan stories serves as an emblem of colonial modernization. With this in mind, the stories reference the ghost stories by Rudyard Kipling. His ghost stories, such as "The Phantom Rickshaw," do not follow a logic of European colonizer versus monstrous, Eastern 'Other.' Instead, following a psychoanalytical approach, they deal with the internal conflicts of the European colonizers themselves: the haunting refers to the burden of the white man's own conscience (Goodwin 239; 242; 245). Following a similar depiction of troubled colonial identities, Bishnupriya Ghosh links these ghost stories to a tradition of

Indian/Bengali vernacular ghost writing. She identifies the writers Phanishwarnath Renu and Rabindranath Tagore as main inspirations for the Laakhan stories, citing a number of internal references. Their stories are "tales of betrayal, and both writers use ghosts as literary devices for raising those ethical questions of exclusion and coercion that trouble the (native) colonial and postcolonial bureaucrat," Renu focusing on rural subjects and Tagore on the colonial metropolitan milieu (Ghosh, "On Grafting the Vernacular" 201). Bishnupriya Ghosh draws on Amitav Ghosh's own interpretation of Renu's and Tagore's writings, where he states that it "tropes the divided colonial subject [...] in the protagonist's obsessive changing of clothes and switching of identities" which "comprise the colonial subject's glimpse into his own alienation" (200). And, in Bishnupriya Ghosh's view, *The Calcutta Chromosome* drives this trope to its ultimate end: the switching of bodies.

Bishnupriya Ghosh focuses on the aspect of haunting that shapes *The Calcutta Chromosome.* She calls Amitav Ghosh's work a "hauntological literary oeuvre" in the sense that his historiographic projects are haunted by an 'other' archive of vernaculars – in particular, in this novel, the "stalking of the novel in English by vernacular Indian fiction" (197). She argues that the novel "dramatizes the danger of forgetting" for we "encounter multiple levels of lost epistemologies (counterscientific discourse, folk medicine practices, Spiritualism and Hindu popular religion, such as *tantra*) owned by the phantom presences in the novel (Mangala, Lakhaan [sic], European Spiritualists [...])"(202). These phantom presences become the bearers of the 'other' archive.

She sees the Laakhan stories as tales of revenge, for he

> "becomes the recursive ghost of the postcolonial state [...] who reminds the liberal urban postcolonial bureaucrat of an ethical failure; the rural or tribal other *is* that figure of excess for whom 'free' India cannot account and for whom there are no rights and no redress." (216)

For her, ghosts are "the literary devices that return us to those ethical questions of historical cultural and economic violence that trouble Tagore and Renu – a violence replayed only a little differently at our current phase of 'empire'" (217).[9]

9 Pramod Nayar offers a similar reading of the specters that populate Amitav Ghosh's *The Hungry Tide* when she concludes that he "proposes a deeply humanist critique of the postcolonial condition here. The refugees are what come after (like ghosts, who come *after*) such emancipatory moves, the creation of welfare states and social

Laakhan's original appearance as an orphan who was driven away as part of the region's modernization actually supports these critic's claims. When this aspect of the character is taken center stage, the ghosts appear once again as corrective figures, as reminders of past and present wrongs, demanding recognition. Most importantly, they are social figures, as in Avery Gordon's conception. These figures are seen as raising important ethical concerns that continue to haunt a postcolonial society. They challenge the official Western history and they also trouble the self-conceptions of a postcolonial identity in its complicity with Western power structures.

Although I agree with such a reading, I propose that the ghosts – and especially the ghostly figure of Laakhan – go even further in their troubling haunting. Laakhan appears as a character who is not only chosen by Mangala for transference, but who seems to be the only one initiated into Mangala's secrets. In this position, Laakhan emerges as powerful in his role of protector of ultimate powers. It is actually Laakhan – not Mangala herself –, who does not shy away from murder, when he sees the secret in danger of being detected. In this role, Laakhan becomes the ghost that haunts Western conceptions of knowledge construction, the ghost that reminds the postcolonial state of its 'ethical failure' to include everyone. But although he represents the powerful agency of a subversive resistance gang which offers an alternative future, he also embodies the haunted state of this alternative form. While he embodies the possibilities of a different future, he also undermines an imagination of this future as trouble-free utopia. *The Calcutta Chromosome* thus envisions a future, but this future is similarly haunted by its own basis in violence. As such, Laakhan challenges not only the power structures that shape the colonial system or its postcolonial bureaucrats, but also those that appear as the bearers of a resistance narrative. It is ultimately his shape-shifting ghostly appearance that represents the newly imagined transnational postcolonial identity. Like a pharmakon, he is both threat and possibility.

It is Laakhan as ghost who refers to the different layers of the novel and the ghost motif for he brings together the classical references of Indian ghost figures but also opens the ground for new, global transformations of this motif. His figure references tradition and folk belief, vernacular ghost stories, and colonial ghost stories, but it also links these to the possibilities of new identities that cut across national, ethnic, and even bodily boundaries. Taken together, all of these references show the ways in which the ghost motif works in contemporary Asian

mechanisms of charity and development. The spectral refugee is a comment on the inadequacy of the postcolonial state" (Nayar 105).

American literature: as signaling an ethnic reference but also a new trend of moving beyond this framework within the same text. Instead of shedding earlier references to the classical ghost motif, the globalized figures rather highlight the interconnections of the global village that is haunted by various ghosts.

Suitably, Amitav Ghosh recombines literary genres and traditions. As Bishnupriya Ghosh has it: "this is a medical thriller, a ghost story, a murder mystery, a philosophical rumination, and a historiographic project" (Ghosh, "On Grafting the Vernacular" 199). She continues by stating that

> "if we take seriously Ghosh's postcolonial unraveling of an established colonial truth, then the very *genre* of truth-telling must suffer. Indeed, a great deal of 'resourcefulness' is required to graft onto the body of a mystery a manner of telling more capable of visionary praxis; hence the traffic in ghosts." (199)

This reading takes the ghosts from a thematic level onto a generic level, arguing that they not only haunt the characters, the setting, or the imagined postcolonial subjectivities, but also the idea of a clear-cut genre. In other words, Gosh's historiographic project also crosses over into genre fiction. His combination of science fiction with classical vernacular ghost stories presents a new 'tonality,' new formats, new modes of expression – to come back to Ruth Mayer's terms. His novel is neither elitist sophistication nor is it mass entertainment: it positions itself somewhere in between and this positioning is driven particularly by its conceptions of ghostliness.

In his reflections about what one means when referring to 'global science fiction,' Istvan Csicsery-Ronay argues that

> "[w]ith the availability of sf by more non-European – and especially second-generation, emigré and multilingual – writers on the rise, we can expect to see the interflow of fantastic elements, – oneiric, visionary, hallucinatory, folkloric, mythological, supernatural, surrealistic – to increase, not just as entertainment augmentors or artistic experiments, but as naturalized alternative rationalities, aspects of a larger commitment to breaking down technoscientism and its plausability norms from within the myth itself, simultaneously reflecting the blending of alternative ontologies and prefiguring the inevitable spectralization of material science as it encounters spookier and spookier phenomena in the folds of matter." (Csicsery-Ronay, Istvan, Jr. 481)

Such an 'interflow of fantastic elements' is precisely what makes *The Calcutta Chromosome* so hard to categorize. It also highlights the current uncertainty of Asian American literature in its relation to broader fields of study. In combining its classical motifs and ways of narrating with science fiction elements, works such as Gosh's stage the contemporary search for a new place for Asian American writing.

Hugh Charles O'Connell also concentrates on possibilities which the novel offers other than the common focus on a rewriting of history from a postcolonial perspective. He foregrounds the science fiction status of the novel and focuses

> "on the compliment of SF characteristics that provide the utopian inflationary surplus to the novel. This shifts the emphasis of this postcolonial critique, centered on the concept of what the novel refers to as a 'counter-science,' from narrative recovery and restoration to its more SF-oriented *novum* of interpersonal transference understood as the literal transference of one's personality and voice, one's essence as such, into another's body. Doing so highlights the text's function not only as a postcolonial reclamation of lost or marginalized voices within the dominant colonial discourse as a form of scholarly detective work, but also as a utopian vision of futurity that lies beyond the confines of present conceptions of knowledge or being." (O'Connell 779–80)

O'Connell explains how

> "the unknowable mutations caused by the gaps in the narrative, the silences and secrets [...] slowly mutate into radical possibility. [...] [T]here is no political or social program really to speak of, no blueprint for the better society, only a belief that something other could potentially reside in the silences of modernity." (778)

Science Fiction here appears as a rewriting of postcolonial identities, without a given political or moral goal in mind. Such generic mixing suits the need or wish to distance oneself from the original stories that Asian America told about itself while maintaining a strange and strong connection nevertheless to these origins. This is the effect that science fiction writing offers Asian American Studies – and the ghost might be just the right figure to combine such new conceptualizations of global identities.

O'Connel highlights the genre of science fiction and its focus on the future rather than the past. And although he does not discuss the presence of ghosts or haunting, his choice of words nevertheless already lends itself to the ghost's imagery. For ghosts reference similarly the past as well as the future, and this second aspect is often neglected. The scholar who prominently calls for recognition of the ghost's connection to futurity is Jacques Derrida. In *Specters of Marx* (1994), he emphasizes the ghost's connection to temporality: he describes the specter as a "question of repetition: a specter is always a *revenant.* One cannot control its comings and goings because it *begins by coming back*" (Derrida, *Specters of Marx* 11). And again, he claims that "[a]t bottom, the specter is the future, it is always to come, it presents itself only as that which could come or come back" (39). As such, Derrida argues that the ghost shatters conceptions of a temporality that is "made up of the *successive* linking of presents identical to themselves and contemporary with themselves" (70). The ghost is, therefore, pregnant with possibilities: it allows a reconfiguration of the past as well as a glimpse into the future. Derrida also combines this consideration of spectrality and hauntology with a certain ethical obligation. Derrida's idea of justice in politics decidedly includes the past, the present, and the future. In this conception of justice, Derrida refers to a "*politics* of memory, of inheritance, and of generations" (xix). Only via recognition of an inheritance that is taken on responsibly – an inheritance that is a given in the figure of the ghost, and only then, can a just society emerge, as Derrida has it.

The ghost figures in *The Calcutta Chromosome* offer such a triple vision: they challenge the past and its reconstructions, they present a challenge to the present situation, and they also embody a possible future – albeit a haunted one. The ghost figures in this novel attempt a shift into the future via transference. Reading them with Derrida's ethical demands in mind, exposes the neglect of the figure's specific histories. Instead of a rightful engagement with the past – and in the hope of a better future – they appear as puppets in the larger frames of global transference. This lack of a clear moral or political goal creates a sense of uncanny vagueness.

Diane M. Nelson also focuses on the problems and possibilities included in the genre of social science fiction, to which she counts Amitav Ghosh's novel. Social science fiction adequately transports the dual message of possibility and threat that the ghost also inherently carries. For, according to her, in social science fiction "[w]e are always already both mechanist and shaper. Indeed, social science fiction is itself a pharmakon, a poison and a cure, a threat and a promise, a warning sign and a how-to guide for postcolonial new humans" (Nelson 262). In her view, this genre "may be the most adequate way to think about the delirious products and unlikely networks of these colonial laboratories" (246). Nelson here applies the Derridean concept of the pharmakon to the level of genre, in trying to answer the question of who the new postcolonial Indians might be, highlighting the need to allow for ambiguity and paradoxes. While the ghost figures appear mostly as references to the precarious situation of the new humans, they also at the same time offer reflections on their traditional associations with Indian ghost beliefs.

James H. Thrall also calls attention to the inconsistencies that drive this science fiction novel, underlining the generic mixing that Amitav Ghosh presents:

"Someone more inured to even the broadest traditions of the trade might not have embedded an old-fashioned ghost story in the midst of his science fiction [...]. At the same time, since the ghostly presence that haunts the station house, and nearly costs Phulboni his life, is the same Lakhaan who figures in Mangala's reincarnation narrative, Ghosh manages to play with a common fluidity in fantastic conceptions of the human self. Ghost stories, religious narratives of reincarnation, scientific imaginings of DNA-borne identities, and cyber-constellations of uploaded personalities all draw on overlapping conceptions of the self as a transferrable entity. Critical complaints about the novel have pointed, in fact, to what is perceived to be Ghosh's inattention to maintaining a logically comprehensible narrative thread, in part because of confusion generated by his characters' shifting natures. [...] And yet, in a novel that ultimately addresses the confusion of contemporary postcolonial identity, the blurring and crossing of conceptions of 'self' may best express the multitudinous and often contradictory self-representations defining inhabitants of a postcolonial world." (Thrall 300)

In addition to Thrall's convincing observation, the ghost figures are highly suitable to fulfill the contradictory and paradoxical narrative that Ghosh spins: in their inherent ambiguity they carry the positive associations of a postcolonial rewriting of history, of an ethical construction of future subjectivities, but also the negative consequences and violence that any structure of power necessarily generates and includes. The ghost figure, thus, moves from its original context of family, tradition, and ethnicity into a broader conception of transnational interconnections via time and place. Its original function as reminder of the past and carrier of radical possibilities remains the same, but it now branches its ghostly hand along transnational locations, contexts, and subjectivities while it introduces a new version of haunting; one that is biologically induced and also crosses into cyberspace. As such, the ghost motif highlights the contemporary ambiguous status of Asian American writing in general. It retains the classical references, yet embodies the placelessness that drives many contemporary works of fiction in a newly globalized, interconnected world.

A VISIT TO POLITICALLY CHARGED TERRITORIES IN SPIRIT: AMY TAN'S GHOST NARRATOR

"When I died, I thought that was the end. But it was not. When my friends were found, I thought that would be the end. [...] But here I am. That is the nature of endings, it seems. They never end." (Tan, *Saving Fish From Drowning* 472)

Amy Tan's novel *Saving Fish From Drowning* takes the well-established figure of the ghost in Asian American literature into new territory once again. Instead of frequent appearances in the form of a ghost character or a character haunted by her family's past, the novel is told by a ghost. Its narrator struggles with her existence as a ghost – puzzled by new skills and emotions –, with her unresolved tragic death – which might have been a murder –, and with her disobedient friends whom she joins in spirit during their planned trip to China and Burma[10] – driven mad by their constant changes of her original plans and her inability to interfere to avoid disaster. And yet, at the same time, Tan uses the ghost figure as reference to Burmese spirit worships. The tourists' bad luck during their trip is ascribed to their stupidity for changing Bibi's original plans, but it is also – in a kind of second layer – associated with their ignorance of local beliefs. The novel suggests that they might be cursed by enraged Nats. Several times throughout the story, Nats appear as possible explanations for what is happening. These two layers – of rational and supernatural reasoning – remain side by side as possibilities. This use of the ghosts, then, links *Saving Fish From Drowning* to cultural approaches of these figures. These ghosts are clearly marked as Burmese. And although Fenkl's *Memories of My Ghost Brother* also employs such distinctive Asian – in his case Korean – ghost figures, his novel rather offers a reflection on the different, yet, for the narrator interconnected, perceptions and explanations of these figures. While Fenkl's novel plays with the various interlinked traditions of haunting, Tan's novel uses the differing ghost figures – the Burmese spirits and the disconnected ghost narrator – to negotiate a global space for Asian American literature. The interlinking of the ghost as both reference to specific national spirit beliefs and the significant move away from these classic reference points in the figure of the ghost narrator, emphasize the current duality of this motif. While it remains linked to its ethnic,

10 In calling Myanmar by its former name, Burma, I use the name that is used in the novel. There is a part, where the narrator explains her reasons for this choice: she is too old to change with the times and is used to the old names (see Tan 151).

spiritualist origins in Asian American literature, it also stages other numerous reference points.

What exactly, then, does the ghost narrator add to the novel? Why must she join her friends only as a spirit? What does this striking choice reveal about the figure of the ghost in recent global Asian American literature? In the form of Bibi Chen's ghost, Tan moves out of the original context in which the figure appears most at home: haunting family members or certain locations in order to remind someone of an almost forgotten past. Bibi Chen, the ghost narrator of *Saving Fish From Drowning*, instead, joins her friends after her death on their trip, observing critically what she sees from a certain distance, with the omniscient knowledge of a ghost but with its limited capacity to intervene. Thus removed from the setting, the ghost narrator can voice morally ugly questions without being obliged to find answers or actions: her position in-between life and death allows her to say what the living might not dare say and it gives her an opportunity to visit politically and morally charged territories – in both its concrete and its metaphorical sense – without the risk of getting too close. Her inevitable disconnection due to her ghost status paradoxically creates an engagement of a new kind: nothing is spared from her ironic commentary which borders on cynicism, except her readers. The bond that she constructs with her readers – via her ironic distance to the rest of the novel – and her status as a ghost demands reflections about the concept of authorship that this novel employs. How distanced or engaged is this narrator? Why does she appear as a tour guide to foreign Asian countries, yet, as a tour guide in spirit only? While this narrator ironically plays with classic conceptions of ethnic authorship, it also positions itself as viewing everything from above, literally. This dual use of the ghost figure pinpoints the problems of an Asian America that positions itself anew. Read this way, the ghost narrator functions as a meta-critical figure. Her ironic distancing provides commentary about the distanced global novel itself: just like her, instead of direct engagement, the (Asian American) global novel is always threatened of becoming position-less, meaningless.

Saving Fish From Drowning revolves around questions of (good) intentions and their sometimes negative outcomes, especially when it comes to intercultural activities and travelling. From its beginning, the narrator establishes the trip to China and Burma as a morally charged subject. After their tour leader's death at the beginning of the novel, the various characters voice their differing opinions of how to treat tourism to a politically instable country like Burma: should one go in order to strengthen the people who depend on tourism or should one boycott a country led by the military junta? Both decisions would have consequences – the outcome remains unclear, however. Both could hurt innocent people. Since they neglected to buy trip insurance and would not get a refund for cancelling the trip, they decide to go anyway. The group consists of 12 members: the new tour leader Bennie, the oldest of the group being in her sixties, Vera, the lovers Wyatt and Wendy, the latter working as an activist and journalist for Free to Speak International, the married couple Dwight and Roxanne, Roxanne's half-sister Heidi, Moff with his teenage son Rupert, Marlena and her twelve year old daughter Esme, and dog behaviorist and TV star Harry. The group is supposed to visit southern China first and then move into Burma along the famed Burma Road. Had she been there, the narrator informs us, none of the tragic incidents would have happened: "It was not my fault. If only the group had followed my original itinerary without changing it hither, thither, and yon, this debacle would never have happened. But such was not the case, and there you have it, I regret to say" (1).

Following from a series of such changes of the original plan and some misunderstandings, the group leaves China early so that they include extra activities during their time in Burma. One of these is an early boat trip with a special Christmas surprise, during which the group is kidnapped without realizing it. A subgroup of the indigenous Karen, which identifies itself as the Lord's Army, believes Rupert to be their reincarnated Younger White Brother, who – according to their myths – will make them invisible and thereby rescue them from the military. Most of the Karen have already been killed by military soldiers and the survivors now live in the jungle in hiding. Thinking that the bridge they had crossed to get to this 'authentic jungle village surprise' has fallen down, the group stays involuntarily with the Karen for about three weeks. During this time, some suffer from a malaria outbreak, which is contained due to the Karen's herbal medicine. Slowly, the group learns to depend on the Karen's knowledge and on each other. However, their interaction with the Karen is mostly driven by misunderstandings. In a parallel story line, Harry, the dog behaviorist and TV star, stays behind at the hotel and so is not part of the abduction. He wishes to help find his friends and becomes part of a TV series that features him in on-the-spot searches with two rescue dogs. Always led to search in the most scenic tourist spots, he does not realize that he is simply being used by the Burmese military to boost the image of the country. Although the international media attention finally leads to the rescue of the eleven missing tourists, the long-term negative consequences for the nature and the Karen are clear by the end of the novel. The ghost narrator observes the action, comments on the stupidity of her tour group, highlights the cultural and linguistic misunderstandings between the Karen and her friends, constantly voices her concern about media representations of any kind, and reflects on moral questions that do not offer easy answers.

The novel begins with a paratext: a note to the reader, and a newspaper report about the missing tourists. In the note to the reader, Amy Tan informs her readers about her inspiration for the novel: when she escaped from a thunderstorm in New York, she entered the American Society for Psychical Research and was fascinated by a story she found in the archive: the writing of Karen Lundegaard, a medium who recorded the story of the spirit Bibi Chen. Tan claims to have known Bibi Chen in passing and after getting the medium's approval, she decides to write Bibi's story. She apologizes for mistakes that might be part of this story, but argues that she meant to stick to Bibi's original narrative. This, then, takes the story out of its author's hands, and puts it into those of the narrator/ghost, highlighting the significance of this distinction. Tan ends this note by thanking the people and organizations who have supported her in writing this novel. Before Bibi's story begins, the readers are presented a newspaper report about a group of missing tourists, written for the *San Francisco Chronicle*. It lists the problematic situation of the region: drug trade, the human rights violations of the Burmese military regime, the arrest of the opposition leader Aung San Suu Kyi, and the positive and negative consequences of the increasing tourism to this area, and in referencing these aspects indicates the possibility that the tour group has been kidnapped because of illegal investigations by the journalist of the group. Taken together, these short introductory passages create the illusion of truthfulness. The story that the reader is about to engage in seems to be grounded in everyday reality, even though it is being told by a ghost.

And yet, Amy Tan informs her readers in an interview that both pieces are inventions, completely made up (NPR News Weekend Edition n.p.). She explains that "I started to see that people's acceptance of what is true and not true has a lot to do with their assumptions, their existing beliefs. […] What is true in anything we see and read and hear? […] I wanted to play around with that notion of truth in the book" (Tan, "A Conversation With Amy Tan" 4). In other words, the paratext lends credibility to the larger story, but is finally exposed as completely fictional. Aliki Varvogli argues that "Tan must have felt the need to emphasize the outlandish 'made-upness' of her story as a way of silencing those critics who crave authenticity and corrective representation in the work of the ethnic author" (Varvogli 56). According to Florian Sedlmeier, paratexts are often those spaces in literature that are the border zones where a text "coincides but also collides with its surrounding modes of production and reception" (Sedlmeier 223). Sedlmeier's conception of contemporary ethnic literature as 'postethnic' is grounded in this literature's self-reflective positioning "from within and against the marked and marketed versions" of their respective ethnic traditions (215). One way to engage in such self-reflective positioning is the paratext, for it tends to highlight the tensions "between cultural and literary value" (223) – in other words, the negotiation of a text's representative or aesthetic function. Although this chapter does not engage with the concept of the postethnic – this aspect is addressed in the conclusion of *The Ghosts Within* –, Sedlmeier's reading of the paratext focuses on the importance of the framing of ethnic novels. This, then, invites reflections about reader expectations, about the impossibility of a fact/fiction divide, about the truth of any report or story, as well as about the narrator/author of novels. This paratext establishes the ironic framing of the novel: the reader never knows what or whom to believe.

Throughout the novel, the media coverage of the abduction of the tourists in Burma emphasizes the manipulative and partial presentation of 'facts,' even more so in a globalized world. Not only does Harry fail to perceive that his TV covered search for his friends is simply a way to improve the image of the country, but he also engages in a most favorable representation of his 'dear friends,' particularly his 'fiancé,' Marlena, who at that point is not his fiancé at all. The media also tries to cover every bad aspect about the missing tourists, for these are the 'hot news.' And finally, supporting the ghost narrator in her cynic stand, the media coverage results in negative consequences for the Karen and the country: along with international support rises also the critique of the military government so that their already problematic relations with other Asian countries are even further complicated. The unreliability of information, news, and media is established from the beginning so that the unreliability of a ghost narrator does not appear as particularly relevant.

These two pieces introduce two of the main themes of the novel: the problems of any kind of representation, especially in its global reach, and the curious ways in which people are led by their beliefs and assumptions. The novel exposes these issues on all levels: the Karen, the travelers, the readers, and its ghost narrator. The ghost is introduced via an American medium. But the newspaper report already establishes links to 'mischievous spirits in Burmese superstitions,' engaging in assumptions about Asian spiritualist beliefs and Orientalist representations thereof. The ghost narrator is therefore already framed in various ways before it begins its own story. It is exposed as grounded in various cultural and religious beliefs, is shown to raise different associations and expectations, in short, it is presented as a motif that references various traditions and that cannot be controlled by any one of them.

The ghost's inability to lead her tourist group – and in close connection to this, the readers tour through this story – is another irony that is directed at the novel's audience. The narrator is simply not in a position to guide them through this confusing terrain without them thinking for themselves. She provides different ways of approaching her story; the way in which the ghost narrator is already framed at the very beginning already invites a thorough reflection of the readers expectations. That Bibi herself might be a Nat – a Burmeses spirit – is another ironic exoticizing move. With this, one can see the close interconnections between the irony on the meta-level as it is reflected in the story line.

The idea of 'mischievous spirits' as the reason for the tourist's disappearance is also taken up in Bibi's story. For Bibi credits a Nat for the turn to the worse, for "this began when their [her friends'] backs were turned to the TV, when they felt they no longer needed to watch out or worry. They did not realize that in the jungle a TV is not just a TV. It is a Nat. You must watch it continually, or it will get angry and change the story" (Tan, *Saving Fish From Drowning* 420). As they were not attentive to Chinese and Burmese religious beliefs, they were cursed due to their misbehavior at a holy place in China. And when they are already in Burma, this inattention continues. Their local tour guide, Walter, explains the belief in Nats to the group when they are looking at a shrine for one:

> "Nats were believed to be the spirits of nature – the lake, the trees, the mountains, the snakes and birds. They were numberless. But thirty-seven had been designated official Nats, most of them historical people associated with myths or real tales of heroism. [...] Regardless of their origins, they were easily disturbed, given to making a fuss when not treated with respect. [...]
>
> There were also local Nats in villages, and household Nats that lived in shrines in family homes. People gave them gifts, food and drink. They were everywhere, as were bad luck and the need to find reasons for it." (186)

Only some of the tourists give offerings to this Nat, and the "rest of them offered nothing. The rest of them didn't think you had to show respect to something that obviously did not exist" (170). According to this second line of explanation, the angry Nats punish the tourists for their disrespect of other cultures and religions. Even before the abduction, Harry is left behind by the group after a bus stop and is found by two military police men, who might also be Nats. Bibi explains that the tourists disturbed two Nats on a nearby field after which Harry is found by two police men who fit the description of the Nats perfectly (181). As with the other cases, the existence of Nats is never finally admitted nor neglected. It remains a possibility. This possibility is directly linked to Asia, or more precisely to Burmese spirit worship. The novel depicts these beliefs as foreign to the tourists, but it also shows how they can become entangled in them because of their visit to China and Burma. It thus emphasizes the ways in which people, cultures, and beliefs begin to interact in our globalized world and lives.

When Walter notices that he has left Harry behind, he blames Bibi for it:

> "What had led him to make such a mistake? As soon as the question formed in his mind, he knew. Miss Chen, the Nat. Trouble was starting already. [...] Don't be ridiculous, I shouted, but to no avail. I wasn't a Nat. Or was I? Insane people often don't know they are insane. Did I not know I was a Nat? I would have to find a way to prove I was not." (186)

With this utterance, Bibi's status as ghost narrator is once again highlighted. And because she does not find a way to prove that she is not a Nat, it is left open what exactly she is. Following a cultural approach to these figures, this inclusion of the Nat-explanations emphasizes the different ghost beliefs in different countries. But it also ultimately connects them: for it underlines the wish to explain consequences. And Bibi's status as possibly being a Nat herself further highlights the similarities. As a Nat, Bibi might have caused all the trouble – without even realizing this herself. This storyline challenges Bibi's straightforward conception of herself: as a ghost who cannot interfere. This problem is not resolved. The novel here briefly touches upon Asian ghost beliefs, but does not engage further in them. Whether this story line is read as Orientalist depictions of Asian traditions or humorous references to different ghost beliefs and Western misunderstandings of Asian traditions, the novel engages in various discourses around ghosts and ghost beliefs and it establishes a kind of ironic distance on every level. Like the other novels that *The Ghosts Within* refers to, in general, instead of crediting one explanation, the novel allows for different stories to emerge and exist side by side.

Coming full circle, this line of explanation, in its connection to Burmese ghost beliefs, resurfaces at the end of the novel. Bibi Chen's death is finally shown to have been an accident after all. Yet, an accident that might have been brought about by ghosts as a curse for steeling jewelry. The narrator's mother died when she was a baby and so she was raised by her father's second wife: Sweet Ma. Their relationship was terrible and Bibi began to hide her feelings "so well I forgot where I had placed them" (30). Her stepmother puts a curse on her so that she "would never know the full depth and breadth of love, beauty, or happiness" (29). This curse is broken by the end of the novel, when Bibi receives her family's stolen jewelry back. Among these is her mother's haircomb, a gift her mother got from her father when she had given birth to Bibi. When Bibi allows herself to feel her mother's love for the first time, – "I let you and love and sorrow wash over me" (472) – she falls off the stool that she stands on and is stabbed by the haircomb. Her death is related to her stepmother's curse, as the story implies. Moreover, the letter that comes with the jewelry tells Bibi about the cursed jewelry: whoever stole it and kept it, would die. The end, thus, implicitly takes up this cultural ghost story line of the novel: however, once again, explanations are never complete. The reader leaves the novel without being told whether Bibi's death was simply a tragic accident or the result of her curses. In offering various possible solutions and referencing different traditions, the novel here also remains at a certain distance: it does not favor one over the other. It simply collects, presents, reviews, sights.

With this plot and its characters, Amy Tan challenges her "loyal following of readers fascinated by her exploration of familial relationships steeped in the culture and folklore of China" (NPR News Weekend Edition n.p.). This is probably one of the reasons for the abundance of frustrated reviews of *Saving Fish From Drowning*. Reviewer Andrew Solomon summarizes the tone of her critics adequately, when he ends his review by stating that "Amy Tan is wonderful at old fictions of ancient lands; let us hope she will return to that territory in the future" (Solomon, *Review* n.p.). The territory that Solomon hopes Tan will return to, are her close-knit historical family stories which usually revolve around either mothers and daughters or sisters – which, by the way, she did in her novel *The Valley of Amazement* (2013).

Born in 1952 as the daughter of Chinese immigrants in Oakland, California, Chinese American writer Amy Tan published her first novel *The Joy Luck Club* in 1989 and obviously hit the nerve of the time, with the book instantly becoming a sensational bestseller. All of her following novels – *The Kitchen God's Wife* (1991), *The Hundred Secret Senses* (1995), *The Bonesetter's Daughter* (2000), *Saving Fish From Drowning* (2005), *The Valley of Amazement* (2013), and *Where the Past Begins: A Writer's Memoir* (2017) – have been *New York Times* bestsellers as well as recipients of many awards. Amy Tan has also published children's books as well as non-fiction (Academy of Achievement n.p.). That her work has been translated into thirty-five languages further supports the claim that Amy Tan has struck a chord not only at home but also internationally (Tan, *Amy Tan website* n.p.). It is interesting that Amy Tan – such an established Asian American writer – participates in the recent boom of the global novel. Diverging from her earlier, classic themes of family, tradition, history, and culture, *Saving Fish From Drowning* attempts a broadening: it tells a story of diverse characters, focuses on the problems of media representations, of intercultural communication, of travelling to unstable countries, of the tourist as a morally charged subject, and of global interconnections between diverse places.

The popularity of Amy Tan's writings has, however, not increased her standing among scholars of Asian American Studies. In a review of *The Bonesetter's Daughter* Sharan Gibson laments that "[t]oo often she doesn't get the critical respect she deserves because her books are such tremendous best sellers. If her writing is that popular, some critics conclude, it must be less serious than that of lesser-known artists like Maxine Hong Kingston, whose *Woman Warrior* is taught at many universities" (Gibson n.p.). Sau-ling Cynthia Wong focuses on the reasons for Tan's popularity, what she calls 'the Amy Tan phenomenon.' She summarizes Tan's position nicely, stating that she has "a little bit of something for everyone" because she is playing into the multicultural attitudes that began to emerge in the early 1990s while not challenging the neoconservative rhetoric (Wong, "'Sugar Sisterhood'" 191). Wong argues that in her focus on mother/daughter relations and the strong bond of sisterhood, Amy Tan caters to a discourse around matrilineage that serves feminist ideals of middle-class American readers. In Wong's words, "for the feminist audience, the Chinese American mother/daughter dyad [...] allegorizes a Third World/First World encounter that allows mainstream American feminism to construct itself in a flattering, because depoliticized manner" (181). Her texts establish a sisterhood beyond race differences that allows a shift from the political fights around civil rights at home to the much more demanding situation in other areas and cultures.

Wong argues that it is not only Amy Tan's choice of such a topical theme, but also her choice of style. While her prose remains an easy read, Sau-ling Cynthia Wong detects an ideological ambiguity. She states that Amy Tan

> "manages to balance on a knife edge of ambiguity, producing texts in which Orientalist and counter-Orientalist interpretive possibilities jostle each other, sometimes within the same speech or scene. The complex, unstable interplay of these possibilities makes for a larger readership than that enjoyed by a text with a consistently articulated, readily identifiable ideological perspective. The nonintellectual consumer of Orientalism can find much in *The Joy Luck Club* and *The Kitchen God's Wife* to satisfy her curiosity about China and Chinatown; at the same time, subversions of naive voyeurism can be detected by the reader attuned to questions of cultural production." (191)

Such an approach also shapes *Saving Fish From Drowning*. The novel once again offers 'a little bit of something for everyone' in its engagement with a recent global reorientation of Asian American literature. It features Oriental images – Nat beliefs, curses – and places them side by side with Western spiritualist beliefs. It offers a tour through China and Burma, it sights the losses and chances of tourism, it stages intercultural misunderstandings. But it refrains from offering solutions, from giving advice, from direct engagement. *Saving Fish From Drowning* remains at a distance; and it does so with the help of its ironic ghost narrator.

The irony that underlines the novel's play with conceptions of truthfulness, media representations, and Orientalist versions of traditional ghost beliefs appears at times too clearly stated and at other times understated. This shifting creates a style that diverges significantly from her previous works. As a result, it seems hard to place this novel in terms of genre. Andrew Solomon's scathing review, for example, reads:

> "The deliberately absurd plot, not moving enough for the kind of elegiac fiction that has made Tan famous and not meaningful enough to pass for allegory, appears to be satire. It aspires to the mordant social burlesque […], but it lacks […] lightness and wit, so the caricatures seem hackneyed instead of clever, the dialogue dim instead of playful, and the sorties into political incorrectness obnoxious and even colonialist rather than daringly honest and self-assured." (Solomon, *Review* n.p.)

Solomon struggles to place the novel in a humorous genre, opting for 'satire' and finding flaws in the way the humor is being used. He argues that the characters are clichéd with "the persistent vulgarity, rudeness and genial solipsism of the Americans, and the primitivism and inanity of the Burmese" so that he concludes that the "book is patronizing to the Karen people, and it is patronizing of its readers, too, and though Tan would like to pass this off as Bibi's attitude, it feels like the work of the author" (n.p.). Whether one follows Solomon's charged criticism or not, the novel's set-up certainly calls for further reflection. Another review in *Entertainment Weekly*, characterizes the novel in a similarly negative frame a "frothy social comedy" (Entertainment Weekly n.p.). Whether the ironic distancing of the novel is perceived as successfully funny or not, it nevertheless is a new tone of Tan's that emerges in *Saving Fish From Drowning*.

This tonality is then re-connected to classical genre fiction. In an interview with the author that is part of the Harper Perennial edition of *Saving Fish From Drowning,* Amy Tan categorizes her text as "not completely a political novel, but whenever you're talking about a situation in the world like the one in Burma, you traipse into what is political" (Tan, "A Conversation With Amy Tan" 7). She lists "twelve or more genres" in which the novel participates: "murder mystery, romance, picaresque, comic novel, magical realism, fable, myth, police detective, political farce, and so forth" (6), all of which are genre fiction. This combination of genre writing and ironic distancing produces a puzzling reading experience, even more so, if one approaches her novel with the author's previous works in mind. *Saving Fish From Drowning* follows the easy flow of genre writing, but it disconnects the readers from their comfortable position of simply being entertained because it creates an ironic distance to its subject matter. Moving out of her usual historically framed family narratives, Tan places this novel in a contemporary, politically unstable setting. And yet, this setting is one that the narrator, the characters, and the reader significantly only visit temporarily. The novel as a whole, just like its ghost narrator, remains at a distance: it sights and scans, but it does not develop its own standpoint.

This distance is also kept in terms of generic classification. While the novel participates in various genres, it is hard to categorize. This move out of Tan's classical historical family romance, then, further underlines the placelessness of much contemporary writing. It showcases an ethnic author's attempt to position herself anew. Curiously, the figure which provides orientation in this generic and thematic mix-up is the ghost narrator: the ghost as spiritual tour guide through this new, rough terrain. Yet, it only gives a certain structure and balance, for a ghost – in its inherent (non)being – can only provide a momentary, distanced, and ultimately placeless space.

The figure of the ghost is not alien to readers of Amy Tan's works. However, so far, ghosts have appeared in a different framework, serving as motifs that appear within the familial setting of the novels. These figures have been read as ethnic ornamentation – one of the many Orientalist details that Sau-ling Cynthia Wong lists – or as part of a stabilizing effect of traditional Chinese beliefs in the immigrants' changing worlds (Hamilton 126–27). Following a cultural reading of these figures, Ken-fang Lee argues that in Tan's novels "ghosts represent the haunting past and the cultural memory of the immigrant sisters and mothers, waiting to be remembered and then exorcised" (Lee, "Cultural Translation and the Exorcist" 116). He states that ghosts "exemplify [the characters'] 'in-between' situation" (106). Kathleen Brogan argues in a similar vein that ghosts in contemporary American ethnic literature function to re-create ethnic identity in referencing a neglected cultural past that is then fitted to support the image of the present (Brogan 4).

The ghost in *Saving Fish From Drowning* deviates significantly from this original context of cultural memory and identity construction. Bibi Chen is a single woman with no children, decidedly a very rich businesswoman, a patron of the arts, and a socialite. In comparison to previous ghost figures, Bibi Chen offers no connection either to family hauntings or to ethnic religious beliefs. Its main goal is not to represent a haunting past or a cultural memory that shapes immigrants' lives. It does not exemplify the in-between status of immigrants as caught between past and present, between cultures and beliefs. Bibi Chen does not struggle with her status as a Chinese American. Neither her state as a ghost nor her depictions of her friends nor her reminiscences of her own life are shaped by questions of ethnic identity. She is not preoccupied with fears of losing a cultural past or ideas about assimilation. Instead of wishing to right wrongs, Bibi simply remains as a presence after her death to observe what is happening at her funeral, during the trip she was supposed to lead as tour guide, to finally learn about the mystery surrounding her own death, and the changes that the trip brought for her friends after their return home. What, then, does this deviation entail? What is this ghost preoccupied with?

Read against the background of the critical debates around Amy Tan's previous novels – the charges of 'selling out,' of constructing Orientalist images to cater to white middleclass readers –, *Saving Fish From Drowning* appears as a conscious move into new territory thematically. The female characters bound by blood and/or fate of the earlier novels are replaced by a loose set of characters who happen to belong to the same tourist group. While the earlier characters invite identification in their struggles between cultures, the characters of *Saving Fish From Drowning* represent a motley group of American tourists abroad. Just like the ghost narrator, the characters have moved out of a usual frame of familial connections and traditions. The ghost narrator is, thus, preoccupied with their behavior in a foreign land and culture, focusing on their misbehavior, their misunderstandings, their naïve approach to almost everything, their misguided wish for an authentic experience, and their stupidity during their abduction. Although the group includes an African American as well as a Chinese American lady and her daughter, these do not fare better in terms of intercultural competency and none of the characters are concerned with their own place within the American society: instead, they are exposed as global citizens, confused by what that might mean for each of them. As Aliki Varvogli summarizes, their status as "American tourist" provides a "temporary suspension of ethnicity" (Varvogli 58): they are preoccupied with their identity as rich Americans abroad, challenged to position themselves as Americans in a global setting.

Bibi Chen also sketches their relationships with each other, the romances that develop and break apart, the friendships, and the complications of patch-work families. Through these various encounters, the guiding principles of the ghost narrator emerge: she is preoccupied with the topic of intentions and consequences, especially in their global reach. After her death – in a state where she does not fear consequences – the narrator moves to those large moral questions which it is human nature not to address too directly: via the characters' interactions and Bibi Chen's ironic commentary, such moral standpoints shape the novel without ever being finally resolved. Thus, this novel moves away from concerns of ethnic identity politics, and instead enters a broader global arena: this includes the ironic and skeptical depictions of media coverage as well as the moral question of tourism to countries led by military dictatorships. This move to global ethical topics is to a large extent carried out by the ghost narrator and her distanced state. Whereas the characters often remain misinformed, the ghost narrator's enlarged consciousness allows her to also enlarge the topics being addressed. But because her state also produces a distance and a disconnection, her reviewing of these larger topics is threatened to become meaningless. Although Bibi's opinionated character and her sarcastic commentary create a special bond with her readers, this also distances her readers from the story that is being told.

As Tan herself states in an interview, ghost narrators "have instant credentials for at least partial omniscience. [...] The fact of the matter is, ghost narrators are the ticket when you need a first-person voice with personality and an ability to comment on the thoughts and motivations of others" (Penguiun Randomhouse n.p.). Bibi describes her partial omniscience and her initial puzzlement about it as follows:

> "How I knew all this, I had no notion at first, didn't even wonder how I knew it. But I sensed others as clearly as I sensed myself; their feelings became mine. I was privy to their secret thoughts: their motives and desires, guilt feelings and regrets, joys and fears, as well as the shades of truth within what they said, and what they refrained from saying. The thoughts swam about me like schools of colorful fish, and as people spoke, their true feelings drove through me in a flash. It was shocking and effortless. The Mind of Others – that's what the Buddha would have called it." (Tan, *Saving Fish From Drowning* 34)

She also explains that she begins to notice how she can enter into dreams and even how this is much easier with "those who were predisposed to magic" (335), referring once again to the way in which assumptions shape our understanding of reality.

In opposition to all other characters, Bibi Chen is the only fully realized character of the novel. Bibi is what Seymour Chatman has termed an 'overt narrator.' She is clearly telling her story, framing it, and articulating her own views. She makes her presence felt, very much so, commenting on the character's appearance and behavior (Chatman 196–214). She is drawn in considerable detail.[11] And suitably for such an overt presence, her attitude and tone are already established within the first chapter of the novel. The narrator begins her story by addressing her current state: "I died. There. I've finally said it, as unbelievable as it sounds" (Tan, *Saving Fish From Drowning* 2). She is still in shock about her death and her existence as a ghost. She continues to lament that she does not remember how she died. "In those last moments, what was I doing? Whom did I see wielding the instrument of death? Was it painful? Perhaps it was so awful that I blocked it from my memory. It's human nature to do that. And am I not still human, even if I'm dead?" (3). The narrator struggles both with her status as a ghost – is she human or not? – and with her enlarged consciousness that obviously does not include everything. And yet, instead of becoming acutely depressed, this ghost begins to take out her frustration on others, blaming them for making obvious mistakes.

> "The autopsy concluded that I was not strangled but had drowned in my own blood. It was ghastly to hear. So far none of this information has been of any use whatsoever. A little rake in my throat, a rope around my neck – this was an accident? You'd have to be brainless to think so, as more than a few evidently were." (3–4)

While the police seems sure about this being an accident, the narrator voices her doubts vehemently. One would expect that this ghost remains because of her unfinished business of sorting out her own murder. And while she does learn by the end of the novel that her death was indeed an accident – or a curse, as stated above –, this ghost is not preoccupied with her own story. Instead, she soon moves on to listen to her friends during her funeral.

And yet, again, Bibi is not pleased with what she sees. She is shocked to learn that she only got one wing named after her for her donation of twenty million dollars to the Asian Art Museum.

11 She could also be called an 'embodied I,' to use Franz K. Stanzel's terminology. However, for this discussion a distinction is not needed in detail because the focus on the strong presence of the narrator figure is given in both Stanzel and Chatman. I use Chatman here as his terminology is probably more familiar to readers of American Studies.

> "One wing! I knew I should have specified the degree of recognition I should receive for my twenty million. What's more, the plaque was a modest square, brushed stainless steel, and my name was engraved in letters so small that even the people in the front row had to lean forward and squint." (18)

Even in death, Bibi cannot let others take charge. She laments that she 'should have specified' her expectations. As art was her only true love in life, she clings to what is left of herself in this sphere, memories sustained by a donation and a plaque. Where other ghosts might stay close to their family members, Bibi – as a single with no offspring – sticks to her life's devotion: art and her recognition within this community. This main character of Amy Tan's novel is, then, obviously and explicitly not concerned with her ethnic background. Her thoughts function as ironic comment upon such expectations: her lack of any meaningful connections to other human beings as well as her wish for self-representation even after her death serve as reminders of what she is *not* worrying about.

As a ghost, she is on the verge of leaving everything behind. She is already in a state where she almost cannot interfere anymore. When her friends discuss the possibility of cancelling the trip and begin to blame Bibi for not having booked trip insurance, Bibi is outraged, but impotent:

> "Why was Vera *apologizing* for my sake? As everyone murmured varying degrees of shock, dismay, and disgust, I shouted and pounded my fist into my palm to make my point. But no one could hear me, of course, except Poochini [her dog], who perked his ears, raised his nose, and yelped as he tried to sniff me out." (38)

As a ghost, Bibi can only observe what is happening. She is in an "acutely nostalgic state, and on the verge of ceasing to exist altogether" (Yurkovsky n.p.). For it seems that "only those who have lost their lives can appreciate their preciousness, whether painful, pleasurable or boring" (n.p.). And since a ghost narrator has already passed away, and is on the verge of leaving, the reader is more forgiving of her envy. Bibi realizes only after her death, what she could have done differently. She summarizes her life at one point, saying that "I felt like a rich vagabond who had passed through the world, paving my way with gold fairy dust, then realizing too late that the path disintegrated as soon as I passed over it" (Tan, *Saving Fish From Drowning* 7). Such sad reflections pull the reader into the narrator's story and create a bond in which the reader quickly develops a level of understanding and compassion, even if the narrator voices strong opinions or dubious moral attitudes. Readers are probably more forgiving of mean comments by this narrator, exactly because of her status as ghost. Just like one could imagine oneself to react in her situation, Bibi constantly shifts between envy and elation.

In her elated state and with her 'Mind of Others,' Bibi sticks close to her friends during their journey. As Bibi shares this partial omniscience with her readers, she invites them to tag along so that she becomes a tour guide to her readers instead of the actual tour group. And so it is the reader with whom Bibi shares her experience as a ghost and her current placelessness. She does not appear as a ghost to the other characters, except in one dream. This bond between readers and ghost narrator not only distances the reader from the other characters – for they are all perceived through the eyes and via the ironic commentary of the ghost narrator –, it also binds her to the ghost narrator as they share from such a distanced perspective the funny and stupid behavior of the tourist group. This bond of shared knowledge by reader and ghost narrator – knowledge that the other characters lack –, creates the irony that is most central to *Saving Fish From Drowning*.

This irony serves to tighten the bond between reader and ghost narrator in their shared elevation above the rest of the characters. The misinterpretations of the characters' behavior towards one another is one of the funny aspects which the ghost narrator foregrounds. Harry Bailey and Marlena Chu, for example, become a couple in the course of the novel. Their awkward behavior with one another during their early romance is told via the narrator's ironic commentary. One misunderstanding, for example, revolves around Marlena's glances at Harry, while he explains to the tourist group that fish can drown even though this sounds counter-intuitive. Harry enjoys sharing his knowledge with the rest of the group, focusing on Marlena's reaction. "He saw that Marlena was staring at him, mesmerized, a look that said to him: You are so incredibly powerful and sexy. If there were a bed right here, I'd jump your bones. Actually, Marlena was wondering why he took so much pleasure in describing how fish die" (164). In this case, it is not ironic commentary by the ghost narrator but her ability of reading others' minds that creates a funny situation. This fun, however, is only shared by ghost narrator and reader – to the characters, the situation is neither funny nor particularly interesting. This technique of leaving the characters in the dark about each others' feelings, each others' needs, or each others' thoughts and wishes, runs through the novel. It once again distances the reader from the characters and their plight. But it also creates a closeness, the wish on the side of the reader to somehow interfere and help them understand each other. And then, again, this feeling of impotence binds the reader to the ghost narrator, mirroring her state of invisibility and her frustration.

And while the narrator can admit to previous mistakes in the past, she is free from the need to correct them in the future. This freedom from consequences drives the ghost's story as well. Bibi narrates again and again how moral questions remain without satisfying answers. One example is related to the title of the book. When the tour group visits a market, they see fish flopping around on the tables, gasping for oxygen, still alive. They are being told that these fishers think they are saving the fish from drowning by taking them out of the water and a discussion evolves among the tourists:

"'It's horrible,' she [Heidi] said at last. 'It's worse than if they just killed them outright rather than justifying it as an act of kindness.'
'No worse than what we do in other countries,' Dwight said.
'What are you talking about?' Moff said.
'Saving people for their own good,' he replied. 'Invading countries, having them suffer collateral damage, as we call it. Killing them as an unfortunate consequence of helping them. You know, like Vietnam, Bosnia.'
'Those aren't the same thing,' Bennie said. 'And what are you suggesting, that we just stand around and do nothing when ethnic cleansing goes on?'
'Just saying we should be aware of consequences. You can't have intentions without consequences. The question is, who pays for the consequences? Saving fish from drowning. Same thing. Who's saved? Who's not?'
'I'm sorry,' Bennie huffed, 'but that is *not* the same thing at all.'
The others were quiet. It wasn't that they agreed with Dwight, whom they hated to agree with, no matter what he said. But they could not entirely disagree. It was like a brain twister, one of those silhouettes that was a beautiful girl with a hat, then a crone with a crooked nose. It depended on how you viewed it." (162–63)

Often, when the novel deals with such moral issues, it shifts to such a scenic presentation, which depicts the characters' conversation without the otherwise frequent comments by the narrator. This technique constructs a nearness to what is being told and it reduces the presence of the narrator (Fludernik 35). The characters take on the different approaches and views of a certain moral dilemma. The novel never arrives at satisfying answers to these problems. While the novel revolves around such moral questions, it does not resolve them in any way: it seems to circle around these topics from a distance. Just like the ghost narrator, who can – from her distanced perspective –, depict these morally uncomfortable situations without the need to interfere or take a position herself. Although she is usually a person with strong opinions, in these situations, she becomes unusually quiet. This is also because Bibi's status as ghost frees her from obligations to have an opinion.

The narrator is similarly reduced when the tragic history of the Karen is being narrated. This story is told by the grandmother of the twins during a trance-like session. She explains how the twins were spared from the massacre of the Karen by disappearing from the soldiers who raped and killed all other members (Tan, *Saving Fish From Drowning* 278–83). This sudden break with the usual format of the narration underlines the importance of this brutal history. Although Bibi is usually very outspoken and makes ironic comments about almost everything, in this case, she is reduced to a minimum. This is not the ghost's story or history, and therefore it should be told by the grandmother herself. This grandmother's voice, her presence as a survivor of this massacre, creates a closeness and immediacy between reader and story. Without the ghost narrator as filter, this story can stand on its own, which again highlights the significance of this violated history: it is the reason for their hiding in the jungle, it is the reason for their fear of the Myanmar soldiers, and it is the reason for their desperate belief in a mythic helper which results in their kidnapping of the tourists. Furthermore, this story reveals the tragedies that should be considered when thinking about the other moral conflicts of the novel: who is suffering the consequences of others' intentions? And how are we, as human beings – in contrast to the ghost narrator – to react to such injustice? In a way, Bibi functions as a mirror for the readers: while Bibi *as ghost* is in a position to simply narrate, scan, and review, she poses a challenge to the reader's own lack of initiative. Her distanced irony is understandable and maybe even excusable, but what about ours?

In contrast to the reader, Bibi occupies a position that is "inaccessible to ordinary human beings" (Heinze 288), so that she fulfills the criteria for Rüdiger Heinze's typology of paraleptic narrators in first person fiction. According to his definition, paralepsis occurs when the narrator assumes competence and knowledge she cannot have as a first-person narrator.[12] *Saving Fish From Drowning*

12 Heinze distinguishes illusory paralepsis (where the paralepsis is only pretense), humorous paralepsis (which self-reflexively acknowledges its own impossibility), mnemonic paralepsis (a now lucid self turning back to confused younger self), global paralepsis (situated within a non-natural impossible frame), and local paralepsis (situated in a natural frame in which narrator assumes knowledge). The last two types are what he calls 'non-natural:' "because their paralepsis cannot be rationalized in a natural world" and are therefore "true *violations of mimetic epistemology*" (Heinze 285–86).

works with what Heinze calls 'global paralepsis:' these narratives are situated within a non-natural impossible frame. The narrator, for example, is dead and speaks from the grave or has not yet been born. By transporting a narrator beyond the realm of the living, and

> "thus into a narrative position of alleged otherworldly serenity and peace and of privileged observation, her narrative is, paradoxically, rendered reliable, although she does voice opinions, emotions, and resentments. This is paradoxical because the entire premise is necessarily preposterous, and because that violation of mimetic epistemology, once accepted, actually enforces the mimetic and the anthropomorphic." (289)

This paradoxical reliability of the ghost narrator is useful for Bibi's story. She can voice her own opinions, rave about mistakes and misunderstandings, make ironic and mean-spirited comments about her friends, share her hidden truths, exactly because of her unusual position as a ghost. In her position as ghost, she is, paradoxically, rendered more human.

Next to this paradoxical humanity of the ghost narrator, however, Heinze observes another, interrelated function of this narrative perspective. He summarizes that

> "paralepsis in first-person narrators can then be read as a satiric comment not only on the alleged panopticism of authorial narratives but also on those critiques of these fictions that read them as panoptic [...]. These narrators are the legitimate heirs of the postmodern language games and indeterminable cognitive parameters [...]: they break out of Bentham's panopticon of even assumed epistemic control and coherence. If epistemic unity – or its pretense – is a form of assuming discursive control, then these narratives assume an impossible control, emphasizing that it has always been illusory anyway." (292)

Emphasizing the impossibility of discursive control, these ghost narrators are themselves a satiric comment on authorial depictions in general. The ghost narrator of *Saving Fish From Drowning* appears therefore as an ironic reference to such conceptions of ethnic authorship.

One of its classic images is that of a tour guide: Sau-ling Cynthia Wong, for example, argues about Chinese American writers that they

> "may still capitalize on white curiosity by conducting the literary equivalent of a guided Chinatown tour: by providing explanations on the manners and mores of the Chinese-American community from the vantage point of a 'native.' This stance has indeed been

adopted by some, and, in a sort of involuntary intertextuality, even those works that do not share it will most likely be read as anthropological guidebooks." (Wong, "Autobiography as Guided Chinatown Tour" 262)

The ghost narrator of *Saving Fish From Drowning* appears therefore as an ironic reference to such authorial depictions. In a slight variation of this original, she is the reader's tour guide through the rough terrain of Asian countries. Her status as ghost plays with reader expectations of exotic Asian mysteries and emphasizes the impossibility of any authentic representation. Thinking back to the ironic rendition of media coverage, the ghost narrator herself embodies the impossibility of coherence and truthfulness. Just as the media can only relate partial truths, the ghost narrator remains an illusory narrator despite her supposed humanity. And yet, the novel is framed by a paratext that interacts paradoxically with the ghost narrator's reliability. Read with this knowledge, the paratext not only supports the general mistrust of 'truths' but it also enhances the ghost narrator's credibility: her status as ghost has been clear from the very beginning. She is always already in the grey zones, neither dead nor alive, neither fully present nor fully absent.

A ghost narrator is always already distanced from the story she tells as well as from the debates that might surround certain topics. She occupies an elated sphere – somewhere beyond human interaction. And still, Bibi lingers to observe and reflect upon one of the most human aspects: questions of morality in a newly globalized world. Maybe her elated state is the most suitable arena to do this, for – as a ghost – she is bound to observation without intervention. Since most of the problems she dwells on have no easy solution, this distanced position is surely fitting. The ghost – as well as the novel as a whole – scans and reviews, but refrains from providing any answers. And then again, her envy of the living creates strong ties with which a reader might identify easily. This combination of elation and envy, of distanced reflection, marks the ghost status, into which the ghost narrator takes the reader as her tour guide in spirit. And yet, Bibi's ongoing sarcastic commentary only underlines the novel's ultimate lack of commentary upon the problems it addresses. As such, it fits into the realm of the new global novel that appears on the verge of becoming meaningless, random, arbitrary, to refer back to Tim Parks' negative observation of the field. Parks calls these novels "dull" and as lacking the depth of more specified examples (Parks np). Although Parks certainly has a valid point, the ghost's – and by extension the novel's – distanced state provides a way of thematizing the changing place of Asian American writing as part of global literature. And this place might be one just like the ghost's in their dual function: shifting, unstable, disembodied.

GLOBAL GENRE FICTION AND GHOST BELIEFS IN ED LIN'S *GHOST MONTH*

> "'I'm here for the ghost celebrations,' [...] [Megan] said.
> I glanced at the other people in her group. They stood nearby, anxious to get their food and pleased they could buy it from someone fluent in English. Otherwise, they wouldn't trust that the food was safe for eating.
> 'Be careful!' I warned the woman. 'You can't say the word "ghost." It's bad luck. Call them "good brothers."'
> 'Oh, no! I've been saying it all day!'
> 'It's all right,' I said. She was safe. No gluttonous spirits would try to possess an American body. Too many food allergies." (Lin, *Ghost Month* 36)

The narrator of Ed Lin's *Ghost Month* (2014), 25-year-old Jing-nan, owner of a food stall at the Shilin Night Market in Taipei, explains Taiwanese ghost beliefs to a tourist. Just like Bibi Chen in *Saving Fish From Drowning*, he acts as a tour guide through Asia, in this case through Taiwan. Although he is not an actual tour guide like Bibi, he is often in contact with tourists at his workplace, where he likes to give advice about Taiwanese customs and beliefs. Jing-nan's personal struggle with Taiwanese customs and ghost beliefs is embedded in an overall tour through Taiwan's history and culture into which he directly invites his readers. He openly addresses this reader as a potential tourist to Taipei and imagines this tourist/reader as inherently Western as he constantly provides comparisons with the United States. The novel can therefore be seen as a global novel in various ways: it is clearly written for a broader Western audience, it acts as an interpreter of Taiwan for this audience, and its story line is also driven by interconnections between America and Taiwan.

And although this crime mystery moves into a global setting, its ghost figures continue to reference classical Taiwanese tradition in a similar way as Tan's novel employs the Burmese spirit beliefs. As the title already indicates, the ghost motif dominates the novel. According to Taiwanese beliefs, during Ghost Month, the seventh lunar month at the end of July, the gates to the underworld open and the ghosts come out to haunt the living. In contrast to more various uses – even in early literature such as Maxine Hong Kingston's *The Woman Warrior* – its cultural references are pronounced and explained in detail. *Ghost*

Month, thus, participates in the generic form of a crime story, but it adds 'exotic' elements via its setting in Taipei. Taiwanese food and Taiwanese ghost beliefs function for a Western audience as references to an unknown culture. In exploring the mysteries of Taiwan – its culture in general and the mysterious murder case of the narrator's fiancé in particular –, *Ghost Month* interlinks its plot and its generic choices: it works with expectations and norms, raises familiar stereotypes, and stages the possibilities and risks of a certain way of 'selling' Taiwan to a global readership.

Whether this use of ghost figures is perceived as a kind of 'selling out' of traditional Taiwanese culture or as an education of the masses, they exemplify what the novel as a whole stages openly: the conflicted state of a young Taiwanese man catering to tourists' wishes in taking on his 'Johnny' persona, acting as a young Taiwanese man, happy to serve great authentic food and advice to tourists, capitalizing on his fluency in English. Just like Tan's novel, *Ghost Month* plays with the theoretical and ethical problems of postcolonial global literature. But whereas Tan's novel emphasizes the current placelessness of Asian American literature via its use of ghost figures, Lin's stages the possible gains and problems of this new positionality in its story line. It asks how to position oneself in a field that is inherently self-conscious about its participation in the Anglo-American market place. Sarah Brouillette's *Postcolonial Writers in the Global Literary Marketplace* (2011) focuses primarily on the function and (self-)representation of specific authors in the marketing and positioning of postcolonial global literature, emphasizing their "defensive self-criticism" (Brouillette viii). This chapter does not engage in reflections about the author Ed Lin, but highlights instead how the novel as a whole functions as a self-reflection of its postcolonial position in giving a tourist tour through Taiwanese culture in the contested form of a mystery crime story.

Ed Lin was born in New York as the son of Taiwanese and Chinese parents. He is the first author to win three Asian American Literary Awards for his novels *Waylaid* (2002), *Snakes Can't Run* (2010), and *This Is a Bust* (2007). Lin is famous for his crime series set in New York Chinatown in the 1970s, which revolve around Chinese American police detective Robert Chow (Lin, *Ed Lin For President* np). In *Contesting Genres* (2010), Betsy Huang argues that Ed Lin "uses the conventions of detective and noir fiction only to abandon them deliberately through a critical thematic shift in the story, a significant, radical narrative act that declares the old formulas of the genre a failure, a 'bust' for Asian American writers" (Huang 65). Although Robert Chow first appears to be the typical hero of hard-boiled crime fiction – male, veteran, heterosexual, alcohol-consuming –, he ultimately undermines these supposed pillars of manhood: he is not only an Asian American instead of a white detective, he is also depicted as a man who is emotionally crippled by his war experience and an alcoholic, as Calvin McMillin observes (McMillin 229–30). As such, Robert Chow begins to rewrite the script of American crime fiction that is dominated by images of the Asian criminal – think of the serialized Dr. Fu Manchu[13] – and of the Asian model minority detective – think of Charlie Chan. Betsy Huang shows how these images have influenced the cultural formation of Asian America (Huang 49–51). Asian American writers have only entered crime fiction in the past two decades, for example, Leonard Chang's Allen Choice series or Naomi Hirahara's Mas Arai mysteries. According to Huang, for

> "these authors, the process of detection and the unraveling of the plot are useful devices for their role as 'cultural informants,' allowing them to depict aspects of Asian American culture and history that may be unfamiliar to the genre's predominantly white, middle-class fanbase." (56)

She concludes that they introduce new content, but remain very much bound to the norms of the genre whereas Ed Lin begins to question these very norms from within. Huang reads detective Robert Chow's

> "transformation from a minority subject who mimics institutional power to one who learns to negotiate and manipulate its imperatives [...] [as] a metaphor for Lin's own negotiations with the imperatives of the crime fiction genre. Lin suggests that the Law – in both social and narrative senses of the word – is coercive but malleable, and thus able to serve the interests of the disciplined subject who sees through and learns to manipulate its regulatory functions." (80)

She emphasizes that the series presents Chinatown – in contrast to the reductionist representations in American crime fiction – as "a real place with a rich and complex history that defies boilerplate portraits" (80).

Ed Lin engages in a similar strategy in his new novel, *Ghost Month*, which moves its detective figure out of the conventional police and Chinatown setting, replacing him with an 'ordinary' guy in a quite different setting. Instead of offering insights into the Chinatown community and thus presenting it as diverse and rich, Lin now invites his readers to a tour through Taipei, but the strategy remains the same: to exemplify the variety that Taiwan has to offer as a 'real

13 See, for example, Ruth Mayer, *Serial Fu Manchu: The Chinese Super-villain and the Spread of Yellow Peril Ideology*, Temple University Press, 2013.

place.' Just like the author's earlier Robert Chow series, *Ghost Month* addresses existing stereotypes straightforwardly, playing with the images of an exotic country and culture – most significantly in terms of food and ghost beliefs – and the idea of selling these to foreign tourists/readers. In an interview with TaiwaneseAmerican.org, Lin even reveals that he hopes *Ghost Month* will be the first volume of a mystery series featuring Jing-nan, arguing that he likes to develop characters over a long time span (Anna np). Significantly, Lin refers to his hoped-for Jing-nan series as a 'mystery series' instead of a crime series, thus emphasizing once again the way in which he playfully constructs and undermines stereotypes of Taiwan and its culture as 'exotic' and 'mysterious.'

In *Ghost Month,* Jing-nan tries to solve the murder of his highschool sweetheart and fiancé Julia. Seven years earlier, they both left Taiwan to study at an American university and promised not to contact each other until they were settled in America and could get married. They kept their promise, which is why Jing-nan learns about her murder from a local newspaper. He had to return to Taiwan without having finished his degree because his parents died and he took over their food stall and the family debt, yet still vaguely hoping that he would at some point continue his studies. After he learns that Julia has been shot while working as a "betel nut beauty" also back in Taipei, he meets Julia's family, who begs him to investigate her murder because the police seem reluctant. Bit by bit, with the help of his new girlfriend Nancy, Jing-nan discovers that Julia worked as an undercover agent for the CIA at the betel nut stand, and that she was given the task to chase rich Taiwanese men, who worked as spies for China.

In contrast to the book's title, the novel's plot is not driven by ghost figures. Although the setting and atmosphere raise expectations, even Julia does not appear as a fully fleshed-out ghost character such as Aki in *Behold the Many*. On one level, Julia is the metaphorical ghost from Jing-nan's past, haunting him because he did not keep his promise to come for her. Towards the end of the novel, Jing-nan states that "Now I was using Nancy to chase a ghost from the past. In all honesty, that's what Julia was. By the time she was murdered, I hadn't seen or spoken to her in years. I didn't know the person she had become" (Lin, *Ghost Month* 278). Yet, on another level, Julia appears in Jing-nan's dreams and although he tries to dismiss her appearances, she develops within the course of the novel into a ghost figure that follows her own agenda.

The first dreams are just short references – "I had a dream that Julia was trying to tell me something using only her right eyebrow. I wasn't sad when I woke up. Just confused" (159) – but her appearances become more frequent and longer as the novel progresses. In all of them, Julia tries to get her message across, but the reader only realizes this after she was successful. Reading the novel for the first time, it is easy to follow Jing-nan's rational explanation for these appearances. He openly rejects her wishes:

"I dreamed I was in a shadowy hall in a temple, standing before a fiery brazier. I heard Julia tell me to do something, but I didn't want to do it. I looked down at my hands. They were full of reams of bamboo joss paper with small patches of gold foil in the center that were traditionally burned to send money to deceased loved ones. A Western Union to the dead.
I peeled off a sheet of paper and a friendly flame caught in the middle, below the gold mark. I saw letters in the soft light, but I couldn't read them. What did they say?
Julia was now standing above me, pointing at the paper in my hands and indicating that I needed to feed it into the brazier. A breeze began to blow, and her full-length, translucent dress flowed back like a jellyfish in a current.
No, I won't. That would be playing into the whole myth of the underworld I refused to believe in." (193)

Without knowing about Julia's secret message, these dreams seem to highlight Jing-nan's struggle with Taiwanese beliefs in an afterlife. He is torn between his own rational take on death and the culture that surrounds him. Jing-nan appears stuck in time with his unfulfilled promise. Since he did not have a chance to grow up with Julia in real life – she has become a ghost to him –, it seems as if he needs to do so belatedly in his dreams. In these dreams, he develops from a teenage boy with a naïve, almost childish, binary black and white conception of the world – with America as the rational and Taiwan as the backward irrational country – into a young man who becomes capable of allowing different shades of grey.

These dreams become more pressing and frightening in the course of the novel. Jing-nan's confusion is shared by the reader because the barrier between dreaming and waking is no longer clearly marked at the beginning of a dream. One of them begins as follows:

"I stepped into an elevator to find that the air-conditioning unit was broken. I immediately broke out into a light sweat. I had expected more from a high-class building like Nancy's. I was about to step out when a white-gloved hand reached out and gently blocked my exit, also obscuring my view of the man's face.
'Sir, this elevator was called for you,' he said. […]
The doors closed and the walls became transparent. Stars surrounded us. Why was I having such strange experiences with elevators?
[…]

We were drawing closer to the light, and I felt the car heating up.
'Can't we do something about the temperature?'
'Sir, only the lady can.'
'You mean Julia, of course. Let me ask her for help.' I saw her in the distance, asleep on the floor of her own elevator car, also bound for the sun.
[…]
I pressed the button and watched Julia stir in her car and then answer the intercom.
'Jing-nan, is that you?' She didn't bother to cover up a huge yawn.
'Yes! Julia, I need your help!'
'Where are you? Have you been out here the whole time?'
'I'm behind you. Listen, can you do something about the air conditioning? It's broken.'
'I could, but I don't have the money to send a repairman there.'
'I have money. How do I get it to you?'
'Just burn it and I'll get it.'
'Do you mean burn notes as if you were a dead person?'
'It's similar to that. You and I don't believe in such things, but this is how it works out here. There's no other way.'" (260–61)

Jing-nan begins to burn money and Julia insists on more. When he complains about the heat in the elevator, Julia corrects him:

"'You're not on an elevator, […] [y]ou're in a coffin, Jing-nan.'
I tried to stand up, but the elevator had shrunk to the size of a coffin. I didn't have enough room to even turn my head. Where had the man who was with me gone?
'I don't want to die!' I bleated.
'We all have to die, Jing-nan. I'm just ahead of you. Now burn some money so I can help you!'
'It's just making it hotter in here, Julia.'
'If you're not going to send me money, then I'll have to go to work for it.' The intercom clicked off.
I looked at Julia. She shed her clothes and then began to swivel her hips around. She was completely naked. '*Binlang, binlang!*' I could hear her cry though space." (261–62)

While Jing-nan fought with Julia and his own beliefs in the first few dreams, they are now both in distress. As a more dominant force and capable of speaking to Jing-nan, Julia finally convinces him to burn money for her, to 'play into the whole myth of the underworld,' to use Jing-nan's earlier phrase. In the course of their conversation, Jing-nan's discomfort continuously increases and he burns the money only to safe himself. When Julia in the end needs to take charge after all, selling herself as a betel nut beauty, it exposes Jing-nan's bad conscience. Jing-nan is haunted by what he neglected to do in the past. That Julia appears in his dreams and in very direct relation to his bad conscience implies a psychoanalytical reading that follows Freud's approach of dreams: Jing-nan's repressed guilt becomes expressed in his dreams. So far, Julia's ghost appears as a psychological reference only. And it is this rational take that initially dominates other possible versions.

Yet, their conversation of 'how it works out here' already foreshadows the next and last dream, the one in which Julia finally gets her message across. In it, Julia and Jing-nan are lying on a beach in Taiwan, reflecting upon their childhood dream.

"'[Y]ou and I made a big mistake.'
'What?'
'We had no right to put down other people's beliefs. If people want to go to temples or *tang-kis* for comfort or consolation, it's none of our business. We didn't have to call them stupid or backward.'
'But there are no such things as gods!' I blurted out.
'Maybe for you there aren't.'
The sun was now setting behind our backs.
'You know now whether they exist, don't you, Julia?'
She smiled and tilted her head away from me. I had forgotten that she used to do that when she was reluctant to say something.
'It's not for me to tell you, Jing-nan. In any case, only you and I are here right now.'
[…]
'What's going to happen now, Julia?'
'I have a letter for you.'
'A letter?'
'A goodbye letter, Jing-nan.' Her hands seemed to be empty.
I sighed and pulled my legs up. 'Well, let's have it, then.'
'You have to do something for me, first. Burn my diploma at Longshan Temple.'
'Why?'
'Because I want to have it.' She stood up.
'If I burn the diploma for you, you'll give me a letter?'
'Yes.'
[…] I sensed that she was walking away.
'Wait,' I said.
I woke up with the late-morning sun in my eyes and the dream vividly etched on my mind." (282–83)

This dream is different from the previous ones in that Julia and Jing-nan are not threatened but have a peaceful conversation in which Julia explains to him that they were wrong. She invites him to open his mind to other beliefs. Without actually saying that she now shares these beliefs, her appearance implies exactly that. But more importantly, their conversation allows Jing-nan to finally grow up: he can let go of his black and white world view because he reconnected to the woman that Julia had grown up to be instead of sticking to his teenage promise and former self.

The dream is also different in that Julia finally says straightforwardly what she wants Jing-nan to do. Most importantly, it is this dream that establishes Julia as a ghost, a presence that is able to actually accomplish something in this world. She can no longer be seen as simply a reference to Jing-nan's psyche because she now begins to follow her own agenda. With the dream still so vivid on his mind after waking up, Jing-nan goes to the temple to burn Julia's diploma to find her secret message, which explains that she never felt at home in America and intended to help improve what she did not like about Taiwan by taking her job with the CIA. She also says goodbye and hopes that he will have had a happy and fulfilled life with a wife and children. As Julia certainly becomes a haunting and pressing presence as the novel progresses, her status as a ghost develops from a psychoanalytical to a spiritual presence. However, her status is always already tied in with Jing-nan's own doubts about ghost beliefs, his teenage self and worldview, and it always references his bad conscience. Nevertheless, she appears as a presence that is now separated from Jing-nan's conscience and that invites other, cultural readings.

For, instead of Jing-nan, it is his new girlfriend Nancy, who once feels Julia's spirit when she is awake. She tells Jing-nan about what happened when she went to a temple with Julia's mother.

"'Anyway, when we entered Guandu Temple, something weird happened.' She rubbed her hands and arms as if spreading lotion.
I put the knife down [Jing-nan is trying to open a box with Julia's things in it]. 'What happened?' I asked. 'Did Mrs. Huang start freaking out?'
'Not yet,' Nancy said. She was now rubbing her knees. 'I felt something walk right through me. From my back to my front. It felt like a cool breeze, only it went through my body, not just over my skin. It was definitely a spirit.'
'There's no such thing as ghosts.' I put a hand on her back. 'You were just nervous.'
She sat down and turned away. 'It was definitely something. It is Ghost Month, right?'
I went back to the box. 'Nancy, Santa Claus isn't real, either. It's just stuff for a holiday.' I severed the other end of the tape band. Now I just had to slit the tape along the flap edge.

'*I* don't believe in ghosts, Jing-nan. Honestly. But it was really something. Anyway, Mrs. Huang was walking in front of me and all of a sudden froze, as if that thing had just walked through her, too. She began to shake, and then she screamed that Julia was there.' I put the knife down again. 'Are you serious, Nancy?'" (218–19)

Even though Jing-nan does not initially take her experience seriously and is preoccupied with his own task at hand, Nancy's story finally catches his full attention. Just like Jing-nan, the reader oscillates between disbelief and puzzlement. This earlier account – although only narrated by Nancy and not experienced first-hand – lends Julia's ghost status credibility as the story progresses. Nancy's spiritual connection to Julia is once more revealed when Jing-nan has his final dream about Julia. Interestingly, Nancy also dreams about Julia in the same night. When Jing-nan kisses her in the morning, she wakes up and says that she had a dream: "'I saw Julia!' 'What did she say?' 'I don't remember, but she was smiling'" (283). It seems as if Julia gives Jing-nan and Nancy her blessing. It is also Nancy who tells Jing-nan at the very end of the novel that "'[s]ome people say that the dead can talk to us in our dreams.'" She continues saying that she hears him talk to Julia every night: "'You usually laugh. Like a little boy. […] A few nights ago, though, you told her you've found someone new, and you sounded happy'" (309). Although Nancy's observation further emphasizes Jing-nan's psychological need to reconnect with Julia in order to finally let her go, it also highlights the possibility of having contact to the deceased. Thus, the novel once again plays with different explanations: the psychological one in which both Nancy and Jing-nan need to appease their guilt about having a relationship after Julia has passed away and the spiritual one in which Julia becomes a material presence on her own. The reader is left with this uncertainty at the novel's end.

Yet, except for Julia, there are no ghost figures in the novel. Still, the ghost motif remains a central part of *Ghost Month* and its representations of spirits also frame the way in which the reader perceives Julia's ghost. Right at the beginning of the novel, Jing-nan watches other people setting up their offering tables for human spirits:

"The makeshift offering tables were meant to appease not only the spirits of one's ancestors, but also those of people who died with no heirs. Supposedly if no one was around to pray for you and offer money and food throughout the year, you really suffered in the afterlife. You might be pierced with hooks, hung upside down and set on fire, depending on what your specific beliefs were. After eleven months of pain and hunger, these ghosts were looking to take out their wrath on anybody alive." (2)

Jing-nan introduces the ghost beliefs skeptically and even ironically, for instance when using the word 'supposedly' or the phrase 'depending on what your specific beliefs were.' The reader does not encounter one of these ghosts in the novel – except maybe Julia –, but is kept in a constant anticipation of a ghostly appearance. As such, the ghost motif runs through the novel without ever being fully realized. The motif does not carry the plot of the novel, but it does influence its tone and atmosphere. These theoretical ghost beliefs not only highlight Jing-nan's personal struggle, they are also tightly intertwined with the reader's perception of Taiwan.

Just like the tourist, Megan, who was discussed earlier in this chapter, the reader is also offered a glimpse into Taiwanese life and history. Their conversation about not saying 'ghost' continues with Megan asking: "'The whole thing is a Taoist holiday, right? […] Some other people were calling it Buddhist, and I was correcting them.' 'All of you are right. In the seventh lunar month both Buddhists and Taoists celebrate their ancestors, so it's all mixed'" (36). There are many asides in *Ghost Month* that explain something about Taiwanese history or culture. For example, Jing-nan reflects upon Longshan Temple when he passes by:

> "A gigantic open-air complex built in 1738, probably the top foreign-tourist destination in Wanhua [a district of Taipei]. […] The temple stood here when the British invaded Taiwan in 1840 during the Opium War. It was here when the French invaded in 1844 during the Sino-French War. Longshan Temple was already one of Taipei's oldest temples in 1885, when Qing Dynasty China finally decided that Taiwan was indeed a Chinese province and not merely a 'ball of mud.' When the Japanese took over Taiwan in 1895, they wisely decided to leave Longshan be, although they destroyed other temples that featured Chinese folk deities in a quest to desinicize the island. The temple survived World War II, when the US bombed the shit out of it, convinced that Japan was hiding armaments among the idols of the immortals. […] Lit up by the moon, lanterns and streetlights, Longshan, literally 'Dragon Mountain,' looks just like a temple should. Even a nonbeliever could agree to that. Dragon sculptures in full color prowl around the tiled roofs and columns while phoenixes and other supernatural-creature pals do their best to keep up. The walls and ceilings are covered with painted, carved wood and stone. Angry guardians painted on open doors warn evil spirits not to enter." (102)

These parts of the novel read almost like passages from a tour guide to Taiwan, as they both educate the reader about Taiwan's troubled history and paint a picture of this 'top foreign-tourist destination' that gives insights into the cultural meanings of the temple's decors. Passages such as these have triggered highly diverse responses from reviewers of the novel. Some celebrate the "teeming Taipei setting" (Kirkus Review, *Review of Ghost Month* np), others find "the various digressions overwhelming" (Lelia T np). Whether reviewed favorably or negatively, this 'exotic' setting is mentioned in almost all reviews of *Ghost Month* as it appears as a central element of the novel's overall atmosphere.

At one point, Jing-nan compares the ethnic set-up of Taiwan to a traditional Taiwanese dish, called 'zongzi,' which is a "glutinous rice dumpling packed with a bunch of different fillings and wrapped in dark green bamboo leaves in a tetrahedral shape (think of a soft, three-sided pyramid)" (Lin, *Ghost Month* 58). As he does in other scenes, Jing-nan continues to describe the food in detail before he begins to unravel how the fillings of the dumplings reflect the different ethnic groups living in Taiwan. He distinguishes the 'benshengren,' "descendents of people who came to Taiwan from China before the Japanese colonization in 1895," the 'waishengren,' "people who came to Taiwan after the Chinese Civil War ended in 1949," the 'Hakka,' "probably the only distinct ethnic group of Han Chinese that hasn't been assimilated into the larger population," and the 'native Taiwanese,' "the various tribes who lived here centuries before any Chinese arrived" (59). Although Jing-nan continues to identify his family and his friends according to these distinctions, this background information does not add anything to the plot of the story. These statements refer, instead, to the torn identity of the island, as Jing-nan ends this paragraph by asking, "[b]ut what are we, really? Do we have a broader identity that covers us all?". He answers himself that "[w]e are people who work hard and disagree about a lot of things. Luckily for me, everybody loves to eat, and no one ever says the food in Taiwan sucks" (61). His detailed descriptions of Taiwanese food, of how flavors explode in his mouth so that his eyes begin to water, and of where to get such food certainly support the layer of the exotic that the larger story veils itself in. These asides are clearly directed at a Western audience that is unfamiliar with but curious about Taiwan's history and culture.

This combination of education about 'exotic' food and customs, interlinked with questions of identity, are not new to readers of Asian American literature. In a way, these passages refer back to one of the early novels in the tradition: Jade Snow Wong's *Fifth Chinese Daughter* (1945). The autobiographical novel narrates Wong's growing up as an Asian American during the 1920s to 1940s and it caters to the idea of the model minority myth: it depicts Asian Americans as educated and hard-working, easily assimilated into larger American society. *Fifth Chinese Daughter* is also rich in detailed descriptions of Chinese customs, for example the Chinese New Year celebrations, or traditional Chinese food. The novel offers these 'exotic' highlights as colorful and flavorful additions to the

American way of life. Frank Chin accused writers such as Jade Snow Wong of 'selling out' to white racist readers. His term 'food pornography,' as developed in his play *The Year of the Dragon* (1974), problematizes this sort of catering to the wishes of the white mainstream. Cynthia Sau-ling Wong summarizes 'food pornography' as the intended self-promotion of a certain ethnic background in a larger exploitative capitalist framework (Wong, *Reading Asian American Literature* 58–62). Anita Mannur pointedly states how writing about food can "exoticize[…] Asian cultures for an American audience eager to consume the palatable elements of multiculturalist differences" (Mannur 95).

In other words, the emphasis on food that *Ghost Month* offers to its readers refers back to a long struggle in Asian American literature. Food and ghost beliefs function very similarly in this crime mystery: both cater to the wishes of readers who look for encounters with the 'exotic' while being entertained, yet both are presented as lived traditions of a different country and culture. The novel spotlights these Orientalizing motifs, offering an easy read and a tour through exotic Taiwan, but it also critically reflects upon the very idea of 'selling out.' *Ghost Month* stages the possibilities, necessities, and risks of a certain form of selling out in Jing-nan's business personality: his 'Johnny mode.' Early on in the novel, he introduces the persona that he assumes when he is at work: "As the Shilin Night Market came into view, I thankfully felt myself shifting into work mode, Johnny mode. Fake mode. Uncaring mode. Just like I was to those Australian tourists. Put on a smile and show" (Lin, *Ghost Month* 20). As Johnny, Jing-nan happily sells 'Taiwan' to tourists: as with Megan above, he sells his Taiwanese food along with advice and 'insider information.'

And although Jing-nan obviously informs the reader about his character switches and outs Johnny as 'fake,' some passages in the novel seem to be written by Johnny, when he directly addresses the reader as a potential tourist: "Don't think of my food stall as a restaurant. I don't" (21) and continues saying that

> "[a]ll the tourist brochures tell people how to get here in general, but I'll tell you how to get to my specific flavor emporium, Unknown Pleasures.
> Here's what you do. Take the red line of the Taipei Metro – the MRT – to Jiantan Station. The stench of stinky tofu should swaddle you even before you leave the elevated station. I suggest bearing east up Dadong Road, away from Bailing High School, unless you want to see mischievous boys trying to swat each other in the nuts and devious girls egging them on.
> Yes, continue walking past the large indoor market – sure, there's great food in there, but there's amazing food throughout. Be adventurous! […]

> The crowds talk loudly, eat loudly and belch loudly, but they aren't ever pushy. If you're not Asian, people will probably stare openly at you. [...]
> Please come by and get some skewers to go, or step inside and order a spicy stew from Dwayne [...]. Point to the pictures of what you want and you're good. Order more than you think you can eat. Come early during your stay in Taipei so you can come back and eventually try everything on the menu. I need the money." (22–24)

Johnny not only invites the reader to his little food stall, but very directly to Taiwan and Taipei in general, giving instructions how to get there and even what to expect and how to negotiate this particular setting. He intends to sell his own food, but along with it the whole 'authentic' experience of the Shilin Night Market. At the end of this passage, Jing-nan resurfaces with the addition – 'I need the money.' In this instant, both persona become visible at once. This addition changes the so-far carefree tone of Johnny's explanations. It highlights not only the necessity for Jing-nan to constantly perform for his business to work, but also shows the material reasons for Jing-nan's performance. Johnny's use of the second person address is "a convention of the travel guide" that presents the narrator as "a trusty tour guide helping [...] [a] predominantly white readership navigate this unfamiliar and potentially dangerous space" (Huang 60).[14] Just as in the earlier crime series with Robert Chow as a tour guide through Chinatown, Johnny appears as a tour guide through another country and culture. Yet, in integrating the issue of 'selling out' so openly within the plot of the novel, *Ghost Month* indicates the necessity of working with and alongside these accusations.

As the novel imagines its readers not only as tourists, but also as Westerners unfamiliar with Taiwan, it features a glossary of terms that provides information about the historical background, the use of certain words, the political parties of Taiwan, or the different ethnic groups and their respective histories. Whenever a Taiwanese term is used, it is immediately explained. The novel is targeted at an international audience that is interested in learning something about this foreign country, but it also emphasizes the intricate connections between the West and the East. Although the story is set throughout in Taipei, it presents this city and its inhabitants as deeply attached to America and affected by global affairs.

Julia's murder case is finally closed when Jing-nan learns about her work for the CIA. Their original plan to migrate to America has been transformed into a

---

14 In the original quote, Huang refers to Dashiell Hammett's use of the second person address in "Dead Yellow Women" (1947), but the comparison with the use of this narrative device in *Ghost Month* works well.

project 'back home,' but it indicates the interconnections between the two countries. Julia provides the direct link. Another one is her Taiwanese American colleague who threatens and protects Jing-nan in the course of the novel, trying to keep him away from the dangerous work Julia has done. Another feature of the image of a global village that the novel constructs, are the tourists to Taiwan and the music that they all listen to. Jing-nan's food stall, for example, is called Unknown Pleasures, the title of an album of the English post-punk band Joy Division. He is a big fan and veils himself in their music, beginning his days with a certain record and ending them with another, and he also connects immediately with other fans from all over the world. For Jing-nan, music and tourism bring the world to Taipei and the other way around as well. So, despite its seemingly traditional use of exoticizing motifs, *Ghost Month* constructs Taipei and its specific culture as significantly part of the postcolonial transnationality of recent Asian American writing. Instead of struggling for a place as an accepted Asian American, Jing-nan and the novel as a whole attempt to position themselves in a globalized world.

Although the crime mystery is set in Taipei, Jing-nan reflects upon the time he spent in the United States, when working towards a college degree. It is this experience that enables him to sell 'Taiwan' even more successfully: he can not only address the tourists and readers in fluent English, he can also explain Taiwanese history and culture by providing comparisons. His knowledge of both cultures allows him to act as a sensitive tour guide, intuiting what his Western readers might find curious or interesting. He explains, for example, how there are no public garbage cans in Taipei so that he needs to take his trash with him wherever he goes:

"In Los Angeles and probably all over America, you can leave your trash by the side of the road to be picked up. That wouldn't work in Taiwan. The heat, humidity and relentless vermin would reduce each block to a swampland. We have to buy blue garbage bags from shops approved by the Taipei City Government. It's not cheap, either. A twenty-pack of twenty-five-liter bags (half the size of the American standard thirteen-gallon kitchen bag) runs 225 NT – almost eight US dollars! […]
We keep the bagged garbage in our home until the trucks come in at night. The yellow truck in the lead flashes lights and blares cheesy versions of 'Für Elise' or 'A Maiden's Prayer' like a smelly music box. When the music plays, we have about a minute to run down to the street and personally throw our garbage into the truck's compactor. […]
I grew up carrying around my garbage, a habit that was suppressed while I was at UCLA. Someone said I looked like I was homeless, walking with a bag of trash." (Lin, *Ghost Month* 131–32)

Jing-nan explains the reasons for odd habits like carrying trash around. Examples like these serve the dual purpose of educating the readers about Taiwanese customs and of making these readers feel welcome and safe with the narrator. He knows his way around, he provides comparisons and even takes the trouble of converting liter to gallon sizes and NT to dollar prices upon himself so that we simply have to listen and trust him. In the final part, he also shares his own experience of acting in a strange way in a different country with the reader. All of this adds to the feeling that he is a trustworthy tour guide, helping the reader to understand the customs and culture of this exotic setting. In this context, Jing-nan's initial rejection of Taiwanese ghost beliefs and his slow development of a more nuanced and positive reflection of these customs invites the readers to follow his example and progress in the same way. Although the customs initially appear exotic and superfluous, the reader is urged to join her tour guide in his growing appreciation of Taiwanese ghost beliefs.

Taken together, Jing-nan's excursions into Taiwanese customs or history and the pointedly artificial Johnny-mode that he allows his readers to observe stage what Sarah Brouillette calls the 'strategic exoticism' of an ethnic author in the global marketplace. Following Graham Huggan's observations, she finds it

> "more fruitful to understand strategic exoticism, [...], as comprised of a set of literary strategies that operate through assumptions shared between the author and the reader, as both producer and consumer work to negotiate with, if not absolve themselves of, postcoloniality's touristic guilt. Like the business of tourism, any postcoloniality industry depends upon the very marketability of self-consciousness about the production and consumption of what circulates within it." (Brouillette 7)

Instead of ignoring the 'touristic guilt' that might impede a global mystery crime story, *Ghost Month* takes these conflicts center-stage. The novel stages them within the plot – in the narrator's Johnny mode, in the various descriptions of Taiwanese food, and in the looming motif of the ghost – and on the level of narration – in the various asides obviously directed at a Western/global readership and its use of the genre of mystery crime fiction. It becomes in this sense a meta-critical reference to the current place of Asian American literature in its global re-framing.

Genre fiction is driven by factors such as structure, repetition, and clarity and it provides a certain sense of reassurance to its readers for they know what to expect (Holland 217–18). To use Jacques Derrida's words, from his essay "The Law of Genre," "[a]s soon as the word *genre* is sounded, as soon as it is heard, as soon as one attempts to conceive it, a limit is drawn. And when a limit is established, norms and interdictions are not far behind" (Derrida, "The Law of Genre" 224). Derrida continues by demonstrating the inherent impurity of genre as "a principle of contamination, a law of impurity, a parasitical economy" and a "sort of participation without belonging" (227). Even though genre implies rules, regulations, and norms, according to Derrida, it is always already undermined in its use of repetition: there is at heart a divergence inherent to the laws of genre. In its shuttling between tradition and innovation, it always belongs uneasily.

In his Robert Chow series, Ed Lin already experimented with this productive tension of genre fiction for his American crime story. In *Ghost Month*, this tension takes on the added dimension of a mystery being set in Asia. The use of the ghost motif in this mystery crime story exemplifies the aspect of 'selling out:' while the novel raises expectations of a fully fleshed-out ghost appearance, it does not meet them in the end. Instead of engaging in concrete depictions of ghost figures, the novel provides general information about ghost beliefs in Taiwan. The figure who invites representation as a ghost – the murdered Julia – appears as a ghost only in Jing-nan's dreams. Throughout the novel, her appearances become increasingly more ghost-like: she slowly develops from a simple psychological reference that weighs on Jing-nan's bad conscience to a separate existence grounded in spiritualist beliefs. Julia's ghost, thus, haunts the novel. However, her appearances and the reader's explanations of them are deeply interlinked with the general presentation of Taiwanese customs that the novel provides much more dominantly. The narration and the plot of *Ghost Month* mutually reinforce each other in order to convey a portrait of Taiwan, but to simultaneously challenge the raised expectations, and to address the problems of such a 'selling' of Taiwanese culture to a global audience. In contrast to *The Calcutta Chromosome* and *Saving Fish From Drowning*, *Ghost Month* does not defamiliarize the ghost motif in terms of new non-familial, non-traditional conceptions, but instead re-emphasizes the exotic flavor that this motif adds to a crime story – only to then constantly play with this expectation of the mysterious. As such, *Ghost Month* at once builds upon exotic details and undermines a straight-forward judgment of this strategy.

GLOBAL ASIAN AMERICA: THE GHOST BETWEEN TRADITION AND INNOVATION

Although *The Calcutta Chromosome*, *Saving Fish From Drowning*, and *Ghost Month* are novels that differ significantly in terms of style, narration, theme, and location, they all share an engagement with ghosts that takes the motif out of its traditional frame and into a new globally conceived terrain. This move highlights the contradictory drive of ghost figures, their shuttling between tradition and innovation. All of the novels play with this productive tension: Ghosh's combination of a biological haunting in science fiction with vernacular Indian ghost stories, Tan's inclusion of traditional Burmese ghost beliefs and curses as they haunt her intriguing ghost narrator, or Lin's explicit introduction of the ghost motif as exoticized Taiwanese addition to his crime mystery. With the help of the ghost figures, these novels enter not only the global terrain, but also that of genre fiction. In all cases, the ghost motif supports a re-drawing of generic boundaries, especially in its function of referencing highly diverse traditions.

The ghosts that appear as Asian in these novels invite cultural explanations, but not in the sense of Kathleen Brogan's search for an ethnic identity that is both part of America and its respective Asian background, but rather as a reference back to the origins of the ghost beliefs in Asia itself. These novels' use of the explicit Asian spirit beliefs function to emphasize the specificity that the idea of the global stifles. But they also employ the ghost as a figure that crosses these cultural aspects, as a figure that begins to haunt the new places that Asian America imagines for itself.

The ghost, thus, emerges again in this new place that Asian American literature currently seeks for itself. Its productive tension of tradition and innovation embodies the contemporary struggle of conceiving oneself as a global player without losing one's original reference points. Instead of addressing aspects of identity politics – instead of dealing with how to fit into America, how to become recognized as Asian American, and of how to picture this hyphenated status in the form of ghosts –, these novels foreground the ways in which Asian America might seek out a place for itself in the globalized world. And they rely on the well-known shape-shifting, uncertain, and ambiguous ghost motif to begin to imagine what this place might be.

Conclusion

The Ghosts Within: Literary Imaginations of Asian America observes ghost figures as they appear in and shape contemporary Asian American literature. It argues that these figures at the same time function as references to traditional Asian ghost beliefs or ghost stories and serve to move beyond this narrow framework in order to express the field's changing position. In this, the ghost figures highlight the reference poles within which Asian America places itself. Following the multiple explanations for these figures – spiritual, psychoanalytical, sociological, allegorical –, I read the ghosts as self-reflexive figures: they stage the ambiguous, paradoxical, and shifting positionality of what it means to be Asian American.

Starting from the assumption that the ghost figures express such positionality, the chapters of *The Ghosts Within* reflect upon the changing contexts: Yamanaka reframes the category 'Asian America' from within, Fenkl approaches the ghost figures from the specific South Korean German American setting in which his narrator grows up, and the last chapter repositions these figures as expressions of the new global position of the field. These reflections are linked to the changes within the field of Asian American Studies. One such reframing of the field is the current engagement with the term 'postethnic,' and it is via an excursion into this recent trend that I wish to conclude *The Ghosts Within*. The conception of a postrace society and postethnic writings has become prominent in the last decade as part of the changing discourses within Asian American Studies and its border fields. By way of a conclusion, I highlight the continuities and differences between this recent trend and my project's specific focus on ghost figures in contemporary Asian American literature.

From the mid 1990s onward, one can detect a growing insistence on 'postethnic' aspects in North American scholarship, for instance in David A. Hollinger's *Postethnic America: Beyond Multiculturalism* (1995). This text establishes a celebratory reading of liberal American attitudes, hoping for a healing of American ethnic divisions through postethnicity. Hollinger thus moves beyond the multiculturalist paradigm of the time in order to create voluntary connections between different ethnic groups and to invigorate cosmopolitanism with a new sensitivity to the importance of roots (Hollinger 1–18). Whereas Hollinger's approach couches this concept in a liberal progressive narrative, right-wing political activists have readily taken on this narrative to veil persisting racist attitudes. It is in this context that social scientists refer to today's color-blind racism, post-civil rights color apathy, or racism without racists.[1] Ideas of the postracial have been employed in order to end the ethnic groups' struggle for recognition by arguing that it signals the end of racial oppression.

However, theories by scholars such as Kenneth Warren or Ramon Saldívar, that discuss the postracial, are far more complex than right-wing political activists make them out to be. Kenneth Warren argues in his seminal *What Was African American Literature* (2011) that with the success of the Civil Rights movements, African American literature has lost its unifying theme of fighting racial segregation. He argues that with this shift, African American literature became retrospective instead of prospective and proposes that today's criticism should also focus on the economic problems and inequalities instead of only dicussing race (Warren W. 9; 18). Ramon Saldivar builds on this logic by stating that a new generation of ethnic writers has come to prominence in America. This generation has not been part of the political struggles of the 1960s and therefore demands a new way of writing. For him, the term 'postracial' signifies a new stage of race relations in the United States. This does not imply, however, an end of thinking about race, but rather offers the chance to think about it differently (Saldivar, "The Second Elevation" 15). Therefore, Saldivar argues for the existence of a new aesthetic in these authors' writings, one that is not done with race as a theme, but instead approaches it differently.

Saldivar outlined four features of this new aesthetic in his lecture "Historical Fantasy, Speculative Realism, and Postrace Aesthetics in Contemporary American Culture:" it engages in a critical dialogue with postmodern aesthetics, it mixes generic forms of realism and lowbrow genre writing, it is invested in the real while working in the mode of historical fantasy, and it seeks a new racial imaginary (Saldivar, "Historical Fantasy" n.p.). He used Susshu Foster's *Atomik Aztex* (2005) as an example to illustrate this new aesthetic, focusing on the various genre traditions in which the novel participates, namely, science fiction,

---

1 See, for example, Eduardo Bonilla-Silva, *Racism Without Racists: Color-Blind Racism and the Persistence of Racial Inequality in the United States*. Lanham, MD: Rowman & Littlefield, 2003.

alternative history, historical fiction, and surrealism. Saldivar highlights the new mode of 'historical fantasy,' which is essentially a mixing of genres, specifically history and fantasy writing, that disturbs ethno-centric readings and instead offers a multitude of possible identifications (n.p.). Saldivar's concept of historical fantasy indicates his indebtedness to Winfried Fluck's reception theory. Drawing on Fluck's 'cultural imaginary' and highlighting its 'articulation effect,' Saldivar observes a special connection between fantasy and history: it constantly negotiates between these two poles and in this Saldivar sees 'postrace' fictions' political potential.

Even though Saldivar's attempt at establishing a new postethnic genre calls for critical revisions – what exactly is his definition of postethnic authors, who is included and who is excluded and on which basis, and what is the 'something more' of postethnic literature more explicitly? – his connections between postethnic literature and fantasy are interesting observations. *The Ghosts Within* also engages with the combination of genre fiction and global novels, but Saldivar continues to place this trend in both a transnational and a postethnic frame. Significantly, the fantasy that Saldivar refers to does not include classical ghost figures, but appears as a haunting presence of shifting realities. All of the examples that Saldivar gives from within the Asian American tradition – Karen Tei Yamashita's *Tropic of Orange* (1997), Larissa Lai's *Salt Fish Girl* (2002), and Sesshu Foster's *Atomik Aztex* (2005) – include such a layering of realities, yet without concrete ghost figures.

By connecting history and fantasy, the novels that *The Ghosts Within* focuses on could be read as such postethnic historical fantasies. However, that they are not included in Saldivar's list has various reasons. Even though they do follow the general conception of his outlined genre, they also diverge from these ideas. Saldivar conceives of fantasy as a special questioning of reality – as in the multiple realities of *Atomik Aztex*. The ghost figures that shape the novels which *The Ghosts Within* has centered upon, however, play with the ghosts' reality status by oscillating between or rather allowing allegorical, spiritual, and psychoanalytical explanations. Instead of offering alternative, layered realities, the ghosts embody various reference points. Thus, although I do not engage in a reading of ghosts as such postethnic figures, this concept allows me to relate my project to current trends in ethnic literature and to address the issue of its political potential and expectations once again. The concept explicitly raises a renewed awareness of how the themes around which Asian American literature circles today rather focus on global aspects and interconnections within postcolonial histories.

The phases of Asian American Studies that I outline in my introduction already highlight that Asian American discourses appear to move into this direction. While the first phase was particularly concerned with finding a place and a voice for Asian Americans in America, the recent phase of Asian American Studies has shifted its focus. After they secured their place within the North American context, the critical self-fashioning of the field now begins to find a new place within the global, transnational sphere that has come to dominate American Studies as a whole. The concept of the postethnic can be understood in relation to such re-positioning: it finds new ways of expressing the concerns of Asian America. In a similar vein, Florian Sedlmeier conceives of the postethnic as contemporary literature's self-reflective positioning within and against preconceived notions of what ethnic writing is and should be (Sedlmeier 215). *The Ghosts Within* is indebted to such critical rethinking in its focus on ghost figures.

The Ghosts Within argues that the ghost figures in these novels serve as haunting presences that expose the ambiguity, paradoxes, complicity, interconnections, and the various reference points of Asian American postcolonial narratives. The unplaceable figure of Seth's ghost in Lois-Ann Yamanaka's *Behold the Many* functions as a reference to the paradoxical interconnections between seemingly opposed systems – of colonizer/colonized or Christian/indigenous – in Hawaii's colonial world. The ghostly self that appears as the narrator of Heinz Insu Fenkl's *Memories of My Ghost Brother* also nicely embodies such ambiguous constructions of identity and history in the context of its Americanized Korea. The ghost figures, therefore, possess a similarly 'abstract political aspect' as Saldivar's postrace aesthetic, but their politics are less clear and rather foreground ambiguity. If one approaches these texts and these ghosts with a pre-given political expectation of what ethnic or postcolonial literature should criticize, then these figures are bound to frustrate the readers. But if one approaches these figures anew, their hauntings are imbued with political issues, albeit in a more fundamentally shadowy and inconclusive way.

In a way, both Yamanaka's and Fenkl's novels in general and their ghost figures in particular are centrally shaped by questions of ethnic tradition and by the narrator's quest for finding a place and a voice. But these novels already begin to establish themselves in new contexts: Yamanaka questions the picture of Hawaii as an interethnic paradise and Fenkl narrates the problems and privileges of growing up as a Korean German American boy in South Korea, thus already referring to America's transnational reach. In its discussion of Amitav Ghosh's *The Calcutta Chromosome*, Amy Tan's *Saving Fish From Drowning*, and Ed Lin's *Ghost Month*, *The Ghosts Within* comes closest to

Saldivar's concept of a postracial aesthetic. It argues that these novels reflect the current placelessness of Asian American writing: they renegotiate the boundaries of Asian America in its global reach and by doing so diverge from the identity politics that originally dominated the field. They stage these new self-fashionings as explicitly bound to global reconfigurations of Asian America. Ghosh's science fiction novel provides a vision of postcolonial posthuman transference that reaches across ethnic groups and across countries, observing the uncanny process of transference and the ghostly state of its re-born subjects. Tan's ghost narrator also diverges from the original reference points of family and tradition: this ghost is not preoccupied with its Asian American identity, but rather accompanies its friends on a trip to China and Burma which results in the constant negotiations of Americans' place abroad. Lin's mystery crime fiction plays with the conception of an ethnic author as tour guide: he takes his readers along to a tour through Taiwan, diverging from the original framework of taking them through the various Chinatowns in the United States.

Although these ghost figures begin to tentatively move beyond their classical reference points of tradition and family, the discussed narratives still provide links to traditional ghost beliefs: these become apparent in the specific mixture of Christian and Asian traditions in Yamanaka's postcolonial melodrama, the Korean folklore that shapes Fenkl's autobiographical narrative, the Indian ghost tales that haunt Ghosh's science fiction novel, the Burmese spiritualist beliefs that serve as a second story line to Tan's travel comedy, and the presentation of Taiwanese ghost beliefs and rituals that frame Lin's mystery crime fiction. My project's specific focus on the ghost figures not only frees from pre-given political approaches to Asian American literature, but also offers a way to reflect upon formal aspects. As the ghosts serve as reminders and references to various traditions, they also appear as part of highly diverse genre traditions. *The Ghosts Within* thus observes how these ghost figures interact with each novel's genre, arguing that they take on an important role in reframing these to fit the imaginations of Asian America. This is one of the central points that *The Ghosts Within* makes in its selection of novels and the set-up of its chapters: the ghost figures of contemporary Asian America use the productive tension between tradition and innovation on the formal as well as the story level.

It is also where my project most clearly diverges from Saldivar's conception of a new genre. That Saldivar's examples of his postracial aesthetic build upon fantasy traditions, yet refrain from depicting classical ghost figures, underlines the necessity for his aesthetic to move beyond the ghost's implied reference to ethnic ghost beliefs. The figure of the ghost is probably too much part of a narrative of identity politics, too intertwined with ethnic traditions, and plays too heavily into the readers' expectations in terms of what is marked and marketed as ethnic literature to move into such a postethnic direction. Yet, in a way, the ghost figures have crossed into this genre by way of a transformation from their classical appearances as referencing ethnic ghost beliefs into ghostly haunting presences that emerge out of multilayered realities. The literary works that *The Ghosts Within* focuses on can be seen as marking this shift: upon close inspection, the ghosts always already unfold their multiple reference points and their ambiguity.

Works Cited

Abraham, Nicolas. "Notes on the Phantom: A Complement to Freud's Metapsychology." 1975. *The Shell and the Kernel: Renewals of Psychoanalysis*. Ed. Nicolas Abraham, Maria Torok, and Nicholas T. Rand. Chicago and London: Univ. of Chicago Press, 1994. 171–76.

---. "The Phantom of Hamlet or The Sixth Act Preceded by the Intermission of 'Truth.'" *The Shell and the Kernel: Renewals of Psychoanalysis*. Ed. Nicolas Abraham, Maria Torok, and Nicholas T. Rand. Chicago and London: Univ. of Chicago Press, 1994. 187–205.

Academy of Achievement, ed. *Amy Tan Biography: Academy of Achievement*, 2013. Web. http://www.achievement.org/autodoc/page/tan0bio-1.

Ahmad, Aijaz. "Reconciling Derrida: 'Specters of Marx' and Deconstructive Politics." *Ghostly Demarcations: A Symposium on Jacques Derrida's Spectres of Marx*. 1999. Ed. Michael Sprinker. London, New York: Verso, 2008. 88–109.

Ancuta, Katarzyna. "Asian Gothic." *A New Companion to the Gothic*. Ed. David Punter. Chichester, UK: Blackwell Publishing Ltd, 2012. 428–41. https://doi.org/10.1002/9781444354959.ch29

Anderson, Linda. *Autobiography*. 2001. 2nd edition. London and New York: Routledge, 2011.

Anna: *An Interview With Ed Lin*, 3rd 2014. Web. http://www.taiwaneseamerican.org/2014/09/ed-lin-interview/.

Armitt, Lucie. *Theorising the Fantastic*. London, New York: Arnold; Distributed exclusively in the USA by St. Martin's Press, 1996.

Assmann, Jan. "Kollektives Gedächtnis und kulturelle Identität." *Kultur und Gedächtnis*. Ed. Jan Assmann and Tonio Hölscher. Frankfurt am Main: Suhrkamp, 1988. 9–19.

---. *Das kulturelle Gedächtnis: Schrift, Erinnerung und politische Identität in frühen Hochkulturen*. 2nd ed. München: Beck, 1999.

Attridge, Derek. "Derrida and the Questioning of Literature." *Acts of Literature*. Ed. Derek Attridge. New York and London: Routledge, 1992. 1–29.

Bacchilega, Cristina. *Legendary Hawai'i and the Politics of Place: Tradition, Translation, and Tourism*. Philadelphia: University of Pennsylvania Press, 2007.

Banerjee, Mita, and Carmen Birkle and Wilfried Raussert. "Introduction." *Amerikastudien/American Studies* 51.3 (2006): 311–21.

Baßler, Moritz, Bettina Gruber, and Martina Wagner-Egelhaaf. "Einleitung." *Gespenster: Erscheinungen – Medien – Theorien*. Ed. Moritz Baßler, Bettina Gruber, and Martina Wagner-Egelhaaf. Würzburg: Königshausen & Neumann, 2005. 9–21.

Benesch, Klaus. "Transnational Studies: Looking Backward to the Future." *Transnational American Studies*. Ed. Udo J. Hebel. Heidelberg: Winter, 2012. 615–18.

Bergland, Betty A. "Representing Ethnicity in Autobiography: Narratives of Opposition." *The Yearbook of English Studies* 24 (1994): 67–93. https://doi.org/10.2307/3507883

Bergland, Renée. *The National Uncanny: Indian Ghosts and American Subjects*. Hanover and London: University Press of New England, 2000.

Bhabha, Homi K. *The Location of Culture*. London and New York: Routledge, 1994.

Blazan, Sladja. "Haunting History: The Ghostliness of History in Susan Sontag's *In America* and Louise Erdrich's *Tracks*." *Cultural Memory and Multiple Identities*. Ed. Rüdiger Kunow and Wilfried Raussert. Berlin: LIT, 2008. 129–43.

Blinde, Patricia L. "The Icicle in the Desert: Perspective and Form in the Works of Two Chinese-American Women Writers." *MELUS* 6.3 (1979): 51–71. https://doi.org/10.2307/466953

Boehmer, Elleke. "Postcolonialism and Autobiography (review)." *Biography* 23.4 (2000): 756–58. https://doi.org/10.1353/bio.2000.0044

Boelhower, William. "The Making of Ethnic Autobiography in the United States." *American Autobiography: Retrospect and Prospect*. Ed. Paul J. Eakin. Madison, Wis.: The University of Wisconsin Press, 1991. 123–41.

Bowlby, John. *A Secure Base*. 1988. London and New York: Routledge Classics, 2005.

Brogan, Kathleen. *Cultural Haunting: Ghosts and Ethnicity in Recent American Literature*. 1st ed. Charlottesville: Univ. Press of Virginia, 1998.

Brooks, Peter. *The Melodramatic Imagination: Balzac, Henry James, Melodrama, and the Mode of Excess*. New Haven and London: Yale University Press, 1976.

Brouillette, Sarah. *Postcolonial Writers in the Global Literary Marketplace*. 2007. Houndmills, Basingstoke, Hampshire, New York: Palgrave Macmillan, 2011.

Bruhm, Steven. "The Contemporary Gothic: Why We Need It." *The Cambridge Companion to Gothic Fiction*. Ed. Jerrold E. Hogle. Cambridge, New York: Cambridge University Press, 2002. 259–76. https://doi.org/10.1017/CCOL0521791243.013

Buse, Peter, and Andrew Stott. "Introduction: A Future for Haunting." *Ghosts: Deconstruction, Psychoanalysis, History*. Ed. Peter Buse and Andrew Stott. Basingstoke: Macmillan Press [u.a.], 1999. 1–20. https://doi.org/10.1057/9780230374812_1 https://doi.org/10.1057/9780230374812

Capozzola, Christopher. "Transnationalizing Asian American Studies: Two Perspectives." *The Journal of Transnational American Studies* 4.1 (2012): 1–5.

Carballal, Ana I. "Postcolonial Theory and Autobiography by David Huddart." *Rocky Mountain Review of Language and Literature* 63.2 (2009): 285–87.

Carpenter, Lynette, and Wendy K. Kolmar. "Introduction." *Haunting the House of Fiction: Feminist Perspectives on Ghost Stories by American Women*. Ed. Lynette Carpenter and Wendy K. Kolmar. 1st ed. Knoxville: University of Tennessee Press, 1991. 1–25. https://doi.org/10.1007/978-1-349-12821-1_1

Cersowsky, Peter. "Allegory and the Fantastic in Literature: Poe's 'The Masque of the Red Death' and Alfred Rubin's 'The Other Side.'" *Sprachkunst: Beiträge zur Literaturwissenschaft* 13 (1982): 141–50.

Chambers, Claire. "Postcolonial Science Fiction: Amitav Ghosh's *The Calcutta Chromosome.*" *Journal of Commonwealth Literature* 3.1 (2003): 57–72. https://doi.org/10.1177/0021989404381006

Chang, Juliana. *Inhuman Citizenship: Traumatic Enjoyment and Asian American Literature*. Minneapolis, London: University of Minnesota Press, 2012. https://doi.org/10.5749/minnesota/9780816674435.001.0001

Chatman, Seymour. *Story and Discourse: Narrative Structure in Fiction and Film*. Ithaca and London: Cornell University Press, 1978.

Cheung, King-Kok. *Articulate Silences: Hisaye Yamamoto, Maxine Hong Kingston, Joy Kogawa*. Ithaca, New York: Cornell University Press, 1993.

Chiang, Mark. *The Cultural Capital of Asian American Studies: Autonomy and Representation in the University*. New York, London: New York University Press, 2009. https://doi.org/10.18574/nyu/9780814717004.001.0001

Chin, Frank, and Paul J. e. Chan. "Fifty Years of Our Whole Voice." *Aiiieeeee! An Anthology of Asian-American Writers*. Ed. Frank Chin and Paul J. e. Chan. Washington, D.C.: Howard University Press, 1974. xxi–xlviii.

---. "Preface." *Aiiieeeee! An Anthology of Asian-American Writers*. Ed. Frank Chin and Paul J. e. Chan. Washington, D.C.: Howard University Press, 1974. https://doi.org/10.1016/B978-0-12-170850-4.50004-3

Chin, Frank. "Come All Ye Asian American Writers of the Real and the Fake." *The Big Aiiieeeee! An Anthology of Chinese American and Japanese American Literature*. Ed. Paul J. e. Chan. New York: Meridan, 1991. 1–92.

Cho, Grace M. *Haunting the Korean Diaspora: Shame, Secrecy, and the Forgotten War*. Minneapolis, London: University of Minnesota Press, 2008.

Chuh, Kandice. *Imagine Otherwise: On Asian Americanist Critique*. Durham and London: Duke Univ. Press, 2003. https://doi.org/10.1215/9780822384427

Clifford, James. *Routes: Travel and Translation in the Late Twentieth Century*. Cambridge: Harvard University Press, 1997.

Csicsery-Ronay, Istvan, Jr. "What Do We Mean When We Say 'Global Science Fiction?': Reflections on a New Nexus." *Science Fiction Studies* 39.3 (2012): 478–93. https://doi.org/10.5621/sciefictstud.39.3.0478

Cumings, Bruce. *The Korean War: A History*. 2010. New York: A Modern Library Chronicles Book, 2011.

Damrosch, David. *What Is World Literature?* Princeton and Oxford: Princeton University Press, 2003.

Davis, Colin. *Haunted Subjects: Deconstruction, Psychoanalysis, and the Return of the Dead*. Basingstoke, New York: Palgrave Macmillan, 2007. https://doi.org/10.1057/9780230627413 https://doi.org/10.1057/9780230273948

Davis, Rocío G., and Sämi Ludwig. "Introduction: Asian American Literature in the International Context." *Asian American Literature in the International Context: Readings on Fiction, Poetry, and Performance*. Ed. Rocío G. Davis and Sämi Ludwig. Münster, Hamburg, London: LIT, 2002. 9–18. https://doi.org/10.1017/CBO9780511498763.002 https://doi.org/10.1515/9783110960198.23 https://doi.org/10.1201/9781420031454.fmatt https://doi.org/10.1385/1-59259-279-1:01 https://doi.org/10.1017/CBO9780511487651.002 https://doi.org/10.1002/0470858060.ch1 https://doi.org/10.1093/acprof:oso/9780199257249.003.0001 https://doi.org/10.1093/0199242402.003.0001 https://doi.org/10.1098/rsta.2002.1086

Davis, Rocío G. "The Self in the Text versus the Self as Text: Asian American Autobiographical Strategies." *Asian American Literary Studies*. Ed. Guiyou Huang. Edinburgh: Edinburgh University Press, 2005. 41–63.

---. "Mediating Historical Memory in Asian/American Family Memoirs: K. Connie Kang's *Home Was the Land of Morning Calm* and Duong Van Mai Elliot's *The Sacred Willow." Biography* 30.4 (2007): 491–511.

Derrida, Jacques. *Dissemination.* 1972. Chicago and London: The University of Chicago Press, 1981.

---. "The Law of Genre." 1980; 1986. *Acts of Literature.* Ed. Derek Attridge. New York and London: Routledge, 1992. 221–52.

---. *Specters of Marx: The State of the Debt, the Work of Mourning, and the New International.* New York, NY: Routledge, 1994.

---. "'This strange institution called literature:' an Interview with Jacques Derrida." *Deconstruction: Critical Concepts in Literary and Cultural Studies.* Ed. Jonathan Culler. 4 vols. London and New York: Routledge, 2003. 3–34. vol. 2.

Dimock, Wai C. "Introduction: Genres as Fields of Knowledge." *PMLA* 122.5 (2007): 1377–88. https://doi.org/10.1632/pmla.2007.122.5.1377

Dirlik, Arif. "Introduction: Pacific Contradictions." *What is in a Rim? Critical Pespectives on the Pacific Region Idea.* Ed. Arif Dirlik. 2nd ed. Lanham, MD: Rowman & Littlefield, 1998. 3–13.

Eakin, Paul J. "Introduction." *American Autobiography: Retrospect and Prospect.* Ed. Paul J. Eakin. Madison, Wis.: The University of Wisconsin Press, 1991. 3–22.

Entertainment Weekly, ed., 2015. Web. http://www.ew.com/article/2005/10/19/saving-fish-drowning.

Erll, Astrid. "Kollektives Gedächtnis und Erinnerungskultur." *Konzepte der Kulturwissenschaften: Theoretische Grundlagen – Ansätze – Perspektiven.* Ed. Ansgar Nünning and Vera Nünning. Stuttgart: Metzler, 2003. 156–85.

Fenkl, Heinz I. *A Few Notes on Memories of My Ghost Brother.* Web. http://heinzinsufenkl.net/haunting.html.

---. *Memories of My Ghost Brother.* 1996. no place: Bo-Leaf Books, 2005.

---. Interview by Piya Kochhar. *The Making of a Novel.*

Fishkin, Shelley F. "Crossroads of Cultures: The Transnational Turn in American Studies – Presidential Address to the American Studies Association." *American Quarterly* 57.1 (2005): 17–57. https://doi.org/10.1353/aq.2005.0004

Fluck, Winfried. *Das kulturelle Imaginäre: Eine Funktionsgeschichte des Amerikanischen Romans 1790–1900.* Frankfurt am Main: Suhrkamp, 1997.

Fludernik, Monika. *An Introduction to Narratology.* 2006. New York: Routledge, 2009.

Freud, Sigmund. "The Uncanny." *The Standard Edition of the Complete Psychological Works of Sigmund Freud*. Ed. James Strachey. London: Vintage, 2001. 218–52.

Gaines, Luan. *Review: Behold the Many*, 2006. Web. http://www.curledup.com/beholdtm.htm.

Garber, Marjorie. *Shakespeare's Ghost Writers: Literature as Uncanny Causality*. New York and London: Routledge, 1987.

Gelder, Ken. *Popular Fiction: The Logics and Practices of a Literary Field*. New York and London: Routledge, 2004.

Geok-lin Lim, Shirley, et al. "Introduction." *Transnational Asian American Literature: Sites and Transits*. Ed. Shirley Geok-lin Lim, et al. Philadelphia, Pa.: Temple Univ. Press, 2006. 1–26.

Gerould, Daniel C. "The Americanization of Melodrama." *American Melodrama*. Ed. Daniel C. Gerould. New York: Performing Arts Journal Publications, 1983. 7–29.

Ghosh, Amitav. *Author's Website*. Web. June 23, 20015. http://www.amitavghosh.com/bio.html.

---. *The Calcutta Chromosome*. 1995. London: John Murray, 2011.

Ghosh, Bishnupriya. "On Grafting the Vernacular: The Consequences of Postcolonial Spectrology." *boundary 2* 31.2 (2004): 197–218.

Gibson, Sharan. *Review: 'The Bonesetter's Daughter' by Amy Tan: Cheekiness of Tan – How Dare a Best-selling Novelist Continue to Write Good Books?*, 2001. Web. http://www.chron.com/life/article/The-Bonesetter-s-Daughter-by-Amy-Tan-2018953.php.

Goddu, Teresa A. *Gothic America: Narrative, History, and Nation*. New York: Columbia University Press, 1997.

Goellnicht, Donald C. "Blurring Boundaries: Asian American Literature as Theory." *An Interethnic Companion to Asian American Literature*. Ed. King-Kok Cheung. Cambridge: Cambridge University Press, 1997. 338–65.

Goh, Robbie B. H. "The Postclone-nial in Kazuo Ishiguro's *Never Let Me Go* and Amitav Ghosh's *The Calcutta Chromosome:* Science and the Body in the Asian Diaspora." *ARIEL: A Review of International English Literature* 41.3-4 (2011): 45–71.

Goodwin, Mary. "Stranger Fiction: The Asian Ghost Tales of Rudyard Kipling and Lafcadio Hearn." *Transnational Gothic: Literary and Social Exchanges in the Long Nineteenth Century*. 2013. Ed. Elbert, Monika and Bridget M. Marshall. Oxon and New York: Routledge, 2016. 237–55.

Gordon, Avery F. *Ghostly Matters: Haunting and the Sociological Imagination*. Minneapolis: Univ. of Minnesota Press, 2004.

---. *Ghostly Matters: Haunting and the Sociological Imagination*. 2nd ed. Minneapolis and London: University of Minnesota Press, 2008. Foreword by Janice Radway.

Green-Simms, Lindsey. “Occult Melodramas: Spectral Affect and West African Video-Film.” *Camera Obscura* 80.2 (2012): 24–59. https://doi.org/10.1215/02705346-1597204

Gu, Ming D. “Theory of Fiction: A Non-Western Narrative Tradition.” *Narrative* 14.3 (2006 October): 311–38. https://doi.org/10.1353/nar.2006.0013

Hall, Stuart. “The West and the Rest: Discourse and Power.” *Modernity*. Eds. Don Hubert and Kenneth Thompson, Cambridge: Blackwell Publishers, 1996. 184–227.

Hamilton, Patricia L. “Feng Shui, Astrology, and the Five Elements: Traditional Chinese Belief in Amy Tan’s *The Joy Luck Club.*” *MELUS* 24.2 (1999): 125–44. https://doi.org/10.2307/467703

Haselstein, Ulla. “Ghost Dance Literature: Spectrality in James Welch’s *The Heartsong of Charging Elk*.” *The Pathos of Authenticity: American Passions of the Real*. Ed. Ulla Haselstein, Andrew S. Gross, and MaryAnn Snyder-Körber. Heidelberg: Winter, 2010. 179–98.

Heinze, Ruediger. “Violations of Mimetic Epistemology in First-Person Narrative Fiction.” *Narrative* 16.3 (2008): 279–97. https://doi.org/10.1353/nar.0.0008

Hogle, Jerrold E. “The Gothic at our Turn of the Century: Our Culture of Simulation and the Return of the Body.” *The Gothic*. Ed. Fred Botting. Cambridge: D.S. Brewer, 2001. 153–79.

---. “Introduction: The Gothic in Western Culture.” *The Cambridge Companion to Gothic Fiction*. Ed. Jerrold E. Hogle. Cambridge, New York: Cambridge University Press, 2002. 1–20. https://doi.org/10.1017/CCOL0521791243 https://doi.org/10.1017/CCOL0521791243.001

Holland, Nancy J. “Genre Fiction and ‘The Origin of the Work of Art.’” *Philosophy and Literature* 26.1 (2002): 216–23. https://doi.org/10.1353/phl.2002.0014

Hollinger, David A. *Postethnic America: Beyond Multiculturalism*. 1995. New York: Basic Books, 2000. https://doi.org/10.1017/S0003161500030108

Holte, James C. “The Representative Voice: Autobiography and the Ethnic Experience.” *MELUS* 9.2 (1982): 25–46. https://doi.org/10.2307/466963

Hong, Grace K. “Ghosts of Camptown.” *MELUS* 39.3 (2014): 49–67. https://doi.org/10.1093/melus/mlu025

Hornung, Alfred. "Auto/Biography and Mediation: Introduction." *Auto/Biography and Mediation*. Ed. Alfred Hornung. Heidelberg: Universitäts verlag Winter, 2006. xi–xviii.

Huang, Betsy. *Contesting Genres in Contemporary Asian American Fiction*. New York: Palgrave Macmillan, 2010. https://doi.org/10.1057/9780230117327

Huddart, David. "Postcolonial Life Writing: Culture, Politics and Self-Representation (review)." *Biography* 33.3 (2010): 549–52. https://doi.org/10.1353/bio.2010.0990

Hutcheon, Linda. "The Politics of Postmodernism: Parody and History." *Cultural Critique* 5 (1985–1987): 179–207.

---. *A Poetics of Postmodernism: History, Theory, Fiction*. New York and London: Routledge, 1988.

Inouye, Charles S. "Japanese Gothic." *A New Companion to the Gothic*. Ed. David Punter. Chichester, UK: Blackwell Publishing Ltd, 2012. 442–54. https://doi.org/10.1002/9781444354959.ch30

Iser, Wolfgang. *The Fictive and the Imaginary: Charting Literary Anthropology*. Baltimore and London: The Johns Hopkins University Press, 1993.

Jackson, Peter, Philip Crang, and Claire Dwyer. "Introduction: The Spaces of Transnationality." *Transnational Spaces*. Ed. Peter Jackson, Philip Crang, and Claire Dwyer. 1. publ. London and New York: Routledge, 2004. 1–23. https://doi.org/10.2307/j.ctv16x58.7 https://doi.org/10.4324/9780203465165_Introduction https://doi.org/10.1093/0195166418.003.0001 https://doi.org/10.1002/3527603891.ch1 https://doi.org/10.1080/713659798

Jackson, Rosemary. *Fantasy: The Literature of Subversion*. London and New York: Methuen & Co. Lt, 1981. https://doi.org/10.4324/9780203328446

James, Jamie. *This Hawaii Is Not For Tourists*, 1999. Web. http://www.theatlantic.com/magazine/archive/1999/02/this-hawaii-is-not-for-tourists/377458/.

Jenkins, Ruth Y. "Authorizing Female Voice and Experience: Ghosts and Spirits in Kingston's *The Woman Warrior* and Allende's *The House of Spirits*." *MELUS* 19.3 (1994): 61–73. https://doi.org/10.2307/467872

Jentsch, Ernst. "Zur Psychologie des Unheimlichen." *Psychiatrisch-Neurologische Wochenschrift* 22 (1906): 195–205.

Kelleter, Frank, and Ruth Mayer. "The Melodramatic Mode Revisited: An Introduction." *Melodrama! The Mode of Excess from Early America to Hollywood*. Ed. Frank Kelleter, Barbara Krah, and Ruth Mayer. Heidelberg: Universitätsverlag Winter, 2007. 7–17.

Kendall, Laurel. “Wives, Lesser Wives, and Ghosts: Supernatural Conflict in a Korean Village.” *Asian Folklore Studies* 43 (1984): 215–25. https://doi.org/10.2307/1178010

---. *Shamans, Nostalgias and the IMF: South Korean Popular Religion in Motion*. Honolulu: University of Hawai’i Press, 2009.

Khan, Nyla A. “Transporting the Subject: The Fiction of Nationality in an Era of Transnationality.” UMI Microform 3119185. *University of Oklahoma*.

Kim, Elaine H. *Asian American Literature: An Introduction to the Writings and their Social Context*. Philadelphia: Temple University Press, 1982.

Kim, Jodi. *Ends of Empire: Asian American Critique and the Cold War*. Minneapolis and London: University of Minnesota Press, 2010. https://doi.org/10.5749/minnesota/9780816655915.001.0001

Kingston, Maxine H. *The Woman Warrior: Memoirs of a Girlhood Among Ghosts*. 1977. London: Picador, 1981.

---. “Cultural Mis-Readings by American Reviewers.” *Critical Essays on Maxine Hong Kingston*. Ed. Laura E. Skandera-Trombley. New York: G.K. Hall & Co, 1998. 95–106.

Kirkus Review, ed. *Review: Behold the Many*, February 7th, 2006. Web. https://www.kirkusreviews.com/book-reviews/lois-ann-yamanaka/behold-the-many/#review.

---. *Review of Ghost Month*, June 19th 2014. Web. https://www.kirkusreviews.com/book-reviews/ed-lin/ghost-month/.

Kong, Belinda. “The Asian-American Hyphen Goes Gothic: Ghosts and Doubles in Maxine Hong Kingston and lê thi diem thúy.” *Asian Gothic: Essays on Literature, Film and Anime*. Ed. Andrew H. S. Ng. Jefferson, North Carolina and London: McFarland & Company, Inc., Publishers, 2008. 123–39.

Krumholz, Linda. “The Ghosts of Slavery: Historical Recovery in Toni Morrison’s *Beloved.*” *African American Review* 26.3 (1992): 395–408. https://doi.org/10.2307/3041912

Künnemann, Vanessa, and Ruth Mayer. “Transnational Nationalisms – China and the United States in a Pacific World: An Introduction.” *Trans-Pacific Interactions: The United States and China, 1880–1950*. Ed. Vanessa Künnemann and Ruth Mayer. New York: Palgrave Macmillan, 2009. 1–17. https://doi.org/10.1057/9780230101302 https://doi.org/10.1057/9780230101302_1

Lawn, Jennifer. “From the Spectral to the Ghostly: Postcolonial Gothic and New Zealand Literature.” *Australasian Canadian Studies.* 24.2 (2006): 143–69.

Lee, Jin-Kyung. *Service Economies: Militarism, Sex Work, and Migrant Labor in South Korea*. Minneapolis and London: Univ. of Minnesota Press, 2010.

Lee, Ken-fang. "Cultural Translation and the Exorcist: A Reading of Kingston's and Tan's 'Ghost Stories.'" *MELUS* 29.2 (2004): 105–27. https://doi.org/10.2307/4141821

Lee, Kun J. "Heinz Insu Fenkl's *Memories of My Ghost Brother:* An Amerasian Rewriting of Rudyard Kipling's *Kim." Journal of American Studies* 42.2 (2008): 317–40. https://doi.org/10.1017/S0021875808004702

Lee, Rachel C. *The Americas of Asian American Literature: Gendered Fictions of Nation and Transnation*. Princeton, New Jersey: Princeton University Press, 1999. https://doi.org/10.2307/j.ctt7t0vn.1 https://doi.org/10.2307/j.ctt7t0vn.4 https://doi.org/10.1353/chapter.1227821 https://doi.org/10.2307/j.ctt7t0vn.8 https://doi.org/10.2307/j.ctt7t0vn.5 https://doi.org/10.1353/book.29795 https://doi.org/10.2307/j.ctt7t0vn.2 https://doi.org/10.2307/j.ctt7t0vn https://doi.org/10.2307/j.ctt7t0vn.12 https://doi.org/10.2307/j.ctt7t0vn.7 https://doi.org/10.2307/j.ctt7t0vn.10 https://doi.org/10.2307/j.ctt7t0vn.14 https://doi.org/10.1515/9781400823208 https://doi.org/10.2307/j.ctt7t0vn.9 https://doi.org/10.2307/j.ctt7t0vn.11 https://doi.org/10.2307/j.ctt7t0vn.13 https://doi.org/10.2307/j.ctt7t0vn.6

Lee, Robert G. *Orientals: Asian Americans in Popular Culture*. Philadelphia: Temple Univ. Press, 1999.

Lee, Sue-Im. "Introduction: The Aesthetic in Asian American Literary Discourse." *Literary Gestures: The Aesthetic in Asian American Writing*. Ed. Rocío G. Davis and Sue-Im Lee. Philadelphia: Temple Univ. Press, 2006. 1–14. https://doi.org/10.1017/CBO9780511584541.001 https://doi.org/10.1017/CBO9780511617508.002 https://doi.org/10.4135/9781412983341.n1 https://doi.org/10.1142/9789812707130_0001 https://doi.org/10.1142/9789812773494_0001 https://doi.org/10.1201/9781420011340.fmatt https://doi.org/10.1111/j.0083-2919.2006.00458.x https://doi.org/10.1053/j.sembd.2006.10.006

Lehmann, Florian. "Einführung: Das Unheimliche als Phänomen und Konzept." *Ordnungen des Unheimlichen: Kultur – Literatur – Medien*. Ed. Florian Lehmann. Würzburg: Königshausen & Neumann, 2016. 9–28.

Lejeune, Philippe. "The Autobiographical Contract." *French Literary Theory Today*. Ed. Tzvetan Todorov. Cambridge: Cambridge University Press, 1982. 193–222.

Lelia T. *Book Reviews: Ghost Month by Ed Lin and A Dark and Twisted Tide by Sharon Bolton*, May 18th, 2015. Web. https://cncbooksblog.wordpress.com/2015/05/18/book-reviews-ghost-month-by-ed-lin-and-a-dark-and-twisted-tide-by-sharon-bolton/.

Leong, Russell C. "Discovering a Rich Resource: Literature by and about Asian Americans." *Change* 21.6 (1989): 64–68. https://doi.org/10.1080/00091383.1989.9937608

Li, David L. *Imagining The Nation: Asian American Literature and Cultural Consent*. [Nachdr.]. Stanford, Calif: Stanford Univ. Press, 1998.

Liem, Ramsay. "History, Trauma, and Identity: The Legacy of the Korean War for Korean Americans." *Amerasia Journal* 29.3 (2003–2004): 111–29. https://doi.org/10.17953/amer.29.3.k2t76468016pg455

Lim, Bliss C. *Translating Time: Cinema, the Fantastic, and Temporal Critique*. Durham and London: Duke University Press, 2009. https://doi.org/10.1215/9780822390992

Lin, Ed. *Ed Lin For President: The Official Website of Author Ed Lin*. Web. http://www.edlinforpresident.com/about-ed-lin/who-is-ed-lin/.

---. *Ghost Month*. New York: Soho Press, 2014.

Ling, Amy. *Between Worlds: Women Writers of Chinese Ancestry*. New York, Oxford, Beijing et.al.: Pergamon Press, 1990.

Ling, Jinqi. *Narrating Nationalisms: Ideology and Form in Asian American Literature*. New York, Oxford: Oxford University Press, 1998.

Lloyd-Smith, Allan. *American Gothic Fiction: An Introduction*. New York, London: Continuum, 2004.

Lowe, Lisa. *Immigrant Acts: On Asian American Cultural Politics*. Durham: Duke University Press, 1996.

---. "The Intimacies of Four Continents." *Haunted By Empire: Geographies of Intimacy in North American History*. Ed. Laura A. Stoler. Durham: Duke University Press, 2006. 192–212. https://doi.org/10.1215/9780822387992

Luckhurst, Roger. "The Contemporary London Gothic and the Limits of the 'Spectral Turn.'" *Textual Practice* 16.3 (2002): 527–46. https://doi.org/10.1080/09502360210163336

Madsen, Deborah L. "Introduction." *Asian American Writers*. Ed. Deborah L. Madsen. Detroit, New York, San Francisco et.al., 2005. xvii–xxiv.

---. "Chinese American Writers of the Real and the Fake: Authenticity and the Twin Traditions of Life Writing." *Canadian Review of American Studies* 36.3 (2006): 257–71. https://doi.org/10.3138/CRAS-s036-03-02 https://doi.org/10.1353/crv.2007.0005

Mailloux, Steven. "Hermeneutics, Deconstruction, Allegory." *The Cambridge Companion to Allegory*. Ed. Copeland, Rita and Peter Struck. Cambridge, New York: Cambridge University Press, 2010. 254–65. https://doi.org/10.1017/CCOL9780521862295.019

Majithia, Sheetal. “Rethinking Postcolonial Melodrama and Affect.” *Modern Drama* 58.1 (2015): 1–23. https://doi.org/10.3138/MD.S84R.1

Man, Paul de. *Blindness and Insight: Essays in the Rhetoric of Contemporary Criticism*. Minneapolis: University of Minnesota Press, 1983.

Mannur, Anita. “Food.” *Keywords for Asian American Studies*. Ed. Schlund-Vials, Cathy, Linda Trinh Vo, and K. Scott Wong. New York and London: New York University Press, 2015. 95–97.

Maron, Jeremy. “Affective Historiography: Schilder’s List, Melodrama and Historical Representation.” *Shofar – An Interdisciplinary Journal of Jewish Studies* 27.4 (2009): 66–94. https://doi.org/10.1353/sho.0.0422

Mason, Jeffrey D. *Melodrama and the Myth of America*. Bloomington and Indianapolis: Indiana University Press, 1993.

Masschelein, Anneleen. *The Unconcept: The Freudian Uncanny in Late-Twentieth-Century Theory*. New York: Suny Press, 2011.

Mayer, Ruth. *Diaspora: Eine kritische Begriffsbestimmung*. Bielefeld: transcript-Verl., 2005.

---. “Paper Citizens and Biometrical Identification: Immigration, Nationality, and Belonging in Chinese America During the Exclusion Era.” *Trans-Pacific Interactions: The United States and China, 1880–1950*. Ed. Vanessa Künnemann and Ruth Mayer. New York: Palgrave Macmillan, 2009. 85–104. https://doi.org/10.1057/9780230101302

---. “Postcolonial/Transcultural/Transnational: American Studies, American Literature, and the World.” *American Studies Today: New Research Agendas*. Ed. Winfried Fluck, Erik Redling, Sabine Sielke, and Hubert Zapf. Heideberg: Universitäts-Verlag Winter, 2014. 139–156.

McKay, Nellie Y. “Introduction.” *Toni Morrison’s Beloved: A Casebook*. Ed. William L. Andrews and Nellie Y. McKay. New York and Oxford: Oxford University Press, 1999. 3–19. https://doi.org/10.1017/CBO9780511549397.001

McMillin, Calvin. “The Hardboiled and the Haunted: Race, Masculinity, and the Asian American Detective.” Dissertation. *UC Santa Cruz*, 2012. Web. https://escholarship.org/uc/item/2jr6h026#page-49.

Mejia-LaPerle, Carol. “The Ghostly Rhetoric of Autobiography: Maxine Hong Kingston’s *The Woman Warrior* as American Gothic Narrative.” *Asian Gothic: Essays on Literature, Film and Anime*. Ed. Andrew H. S. Ng. Jefferson, North Carolina and London: McFarland & Company, Inc., Publishers, 2008. 108–22.

Moraga, Cherríe, and Gloria Anzaldúa. "Introduction." *This Bridge Called My Back: Writings By Radical Women of Color*. Ed. Cherríe Moraga and Gloria Anzaldúa. Watertown, Massachusetts: Persiphone Press, 1981. xxiii–xxvi.

Morrison, Toni. *Unspeakable Things Unspoken: The Afro-American Presence in American Literature*, 1988. Web. http://tannerlectures.utah.edu/_documents/a-to-z/m/morrison90.pdf.

---. *Playing in the Dark: Whiteness and the Literary Imagination*. Cambridge: Harvard University Press, 1992.

Napier, Susan J. *The Fantastic in Modern Japanese Literature: The Subversion of Modernity*. London and New York: Routledge, 1996.

Nasta, Susheila. "Editorial." *Wasafiri* 21.2 (2006): 1–2. https://doi.org/10.1080/02690050600694547

Nayar, Pramod K. "The Postcolonial Uncanny: The Politics of Dispossession in Amitav Ghosh's *The Hungry Tide.*" *College Literature* 37.4 (2010): 88–119. https://doi.org/10.1353/lit.2010.0011

Nelson, Diane M. "A Social Science of Fevers, Delirium and Discovery: 'The Calcutta Chromosome,' the Colonial Laboratory, and the Postcolonial New Human." *Science Fiction Studies* 30.2 (2003): 246–66.

Newman, Judie. "Postcolonial Gothic: Ruth Prawer Jhabvala and the Sobhraj Case." *MFS – Modern Fiction Studies* 40.1 (1994): 85–100. https://doi.org/10.1353/mfs.0.0304

Ng, Andrew H. S. *Interrogating Interstices: Gothic Aesthetics in Postcolonial Asian and Asian American Literature*. Bern: Peter Lang, 2007.

---. "Introduction: The Gothic Visage of Asian Narratives." *Asian Gothic: Essays on Literature, Film and Anime*. Ed. Andrew H. S. Ng. Jefferson, North Carolina and London: McFarland & Company, Inc., Publishers, 2008. 1–15.

Nguyen, Viet T. *Race and Resistance: Literature and Politics in Asian America*. Oxford, New York et. al.: Oxford University Press, 2002. https://doi.org/10.1093/acprof:oso/9780195146998.001.0001

NPR News Weekend Edition, ed. *Transcript: Interview with Lynn Neary and Amy Tan*, 2005. Web. http://www.npr.org/templates/story/story.php?storyId=5020636.

O'Briant, Don. *Review: Behold the Many*, 2006. Web. http://www.pastemagazine.com/articles/2006/03/loisann-yamanaka.html.

O'Connell, Hugh C. "Mutating Toward the Future: The Convergence of Utopianism, Postcolonial SF, and the Postcontemporary Longing for Form in Amitav Ghosh's *The Calcutta Chromosome.*" *MFS - Modern Fiction Studies* 58.4 (2011): 773–95. https://doi.org/10.1353/mfs.2012.0061

Odabas, Janna. "Do Ghosts Grow Up? Ghostliness in Maxine Hong Kingston's *The Woman Warrior* and *China Men." On the Legacy of Maxine Hong Kingston: The Mulhouse Book*. Ed. Sämi Ludwig and Nicoleta Alexoae-Zagni. Wien, Berlin: LIT, 2014. 147–60.

---. "Gespenstisches Amerika: Geister als Figuren der Selbstdarstellung und die Heimsuchung des ‚Weißen Amerikas' in Louis Erdrichs *Tracks." Ordnungen des Unheimlichen: Kultur – Literatur – Medien*. Ed. Florian Lehmann. Würzburg: Königshausen & Neumann, 2016. 219–28.

Okamura, Jonathan. *Ethnicity and Inequality in Hawai'i*. Philadelphia: Temple Univ. Press, 2008.

Oppolzer, Markus. "Todorov's Hesitation; or, In the Reader We Trust." *What Constitutes the Fantastic?* Ed. Sabine Coelsch-Foisner, et al. Szeged: JatePress, 2009. 45–55.

Parikh, Crystal. "Blue Hawaii: Asian Hawaiian Cultural Production and Racial Melancholia." *Journal of Asian American Studies* 5.3 (2002): 199–216. https://doi.org/10.1353/jaas.2003.0020

Parks, Tim. "The Dull New Global Novel." *The New York Times Review of Books* February 9th, 2010: http://www.nybooks.com/blogs/nyrblog/2010/feb/09/the-dull-new-global-novel/.

Pearl Buck. "Pearl Buck – Noble Lecture." Nobel Lectures. 12 Dec. 1938.

Penguiun Randomhouse, ed. *Author Q & A: A Conversation with Amy Tan*. Web. http://www.penguinrandomhouse.com/books/176370/saving-fish-from-drowning-by-amy-tan/.

Plasa, Carl. "Introduction." *Toni Morrison: Beloved*. Ed. Carl Plasa. New York: Columbia University Press, 1998. 5–13.

Punter, David. *The Literature of Terror: A History of Gothic Fictions from 1765 to the Present Day*. London and New York: Longman, 1980.

Rand, Nicholas T. "Introduction: Renewals of Psychoanalysis." *The Shell and the Kernel: Renewals of Psychoanalysis*. Ed. Nicolas Abraham, Maria Torok, and Nicholas T. Rand. Chicago and London: Univ. of Chicago Press, 1994. 1–22. https://doi.org/10.1515/9781400863945.91

---. "New Perspectives in Metapsychology: Cryptic Mourning and Secret Love." *The Shell and the Kernel: Renewals of Psychoanalysis*. Ed. Nicolas Abraham, Maria Torok, and Nicholas T. Rand. Chicago and London: Univ. of Chicago Press, 1994. 99–106.

---. "Secrets and Posterity: The Theory of the Transgenerational Phantom." *The Shell and the Kernel: Renewals of Psychoanalysis*. Ed. Nicolas Abraham, Maria Torok, and Nicholas T. Rand. Chicago and London: Univ. of Chicago Press, 1994. 165–69.

Royle, Nicholas. *The Uncanny*. New York: Routledge, 2003.

Rudd, Alison. *Postcolonial Gothic Fictions: from the Caribbean, Canada, Australia and New Zealand*. Cardiff: University of Wales Press, 2010.

Russel, Keith A. "Dislocated: Trauma and Narrative Distance in Korean American Literature." Dissertation Manuscript. *Southern Illinois University*, 2007.

Safran, William. "Diasporas in Modern Societies: Myths of Homeland and Return." *Diaspora* 1.1 (1991): 83–89. https://doi.org/10.1353/dsp.1991.0004

Saldivar, Ramon. "The Second Elevation of the Novel: Race, Form, and the Postrace Aesthetic in Contemporary Narrative." *Narrative* 21.1 (2013): 1–18. https://doi.org/10.1353/nar.2013.0000

---. "Historical Fantasy, Speculative Realism, and Postrace Aesthetics in Contemporary American Culture." Presentation. Berlin. 28 Jun. 2013.

Sato, Gayle K. F. "Ghosts as Chinese-American Constructs in Maxine Hong Kingston's *The Woman Warrior*." *Haunting the House of Fiction: Feminist Perspectives on Ghost Stories by American Women*. Ed. Lynette Carpenter and Wendy K. Kolmar. 1st ed. Knoxville: University of Tennessee Press, 1991. 193–214.

Schwab, Gabriele. *Haunting Legacies: Violent Histories and Transgenerational Trauma*. New York: Columbia University Press, 2010.

Sedlmeier, Florian. "Rereading Literary Form: Paratexts, Transpositions, and Postethnic Literature around 2000." *JLT* 6.1 (2012): 213–33. https://doi.org/10.1515/jlt-2011-0006

Shakespeare, William. *Hamlet*. approximately 1604. London, New York, et. al.: Penguin Books, 1994.

Shinn, Christopher A. "On Machines and Mosquitoes: Neuroscience, Bodies, and Cyborgs in Amitav Ghosh's 'The Calcutta Chromosome.'" *MELUS* 33.4 (2007): 145–66. https://doi.org/10.1093/melus/33.4.145

Silva, Noenoe K. *Aloha Betrayed: Native Hawaiian Resistance to American Colonialism*. Durham and London: Duke University Press, 2004. https://doi.org/10.1215/9780822386223

Slowik, Mary. "When the Ghosts Speak: Oral and Written Narrative Forms in Maxine Hong Kingston's *China Men*." *MELUS* 19.1 (1994): 73–88. https://doi.org/10.2307/467789

Smith, Sidonie. "Presidential Address 2011: Narrating Lives and Contemporary Imaginaries." *PMLA* 126.3 (2011): 564–74. https://doi.org/10.1632/pmla.2011.126.3.564

Smith, Andrew and William Hughes. "Introduction: Enlightenment Gothic and Postcolonialism." *Empire and the Gothic: The Politics of Genre*. Ed. Smith,

Andrew and William Hughes. Houndmills, New York: Palgrave Macmillan, 2003. 1–12. https://doi.org/10.1057/9781403919342 https://doi.org/10.1057/9781403919342_1

Solomon, Andrew. *Review:* Saving Fish From Drowning: *Bus of Fools*, 2005. Web. http://www.nytimes.com/2005/10/16/books/review/16solomon.html?pagewanted=all&_r=0.

Solomon, Barbara H. "Introduction." *Critical Essays on Toni Morrion's Beloved.* Ed. Barbara H. Solomon. New York: G.K. Hall & Co, 1998. 1–35. https://doi.org/10.1093/0195108647.003.0001

"Success of One Minority Group In U.S." 1966. *Asian American Studies: A Reader.* Ed. Jean Y.-w. S. Wu and Min Song. New Brunswick, New Jersey, and London: Rutgers University Press, 2000. 158–63.

Takaki, Ronald. *Strangers From a Different Shore: A History of Asian Americans.* 1989. New York, Boston: Little, Brown and Co., 1998.

Tan, Amy. "A Conversation With Amy Tan." *Saving Fish From Drowning.* 2–15.

---. *Amy Tan Website: Biography Section.* Web. https://www.amytan.net/bio-1.html.

---. *Saving Fish From Drowning.* 2005. London, New York, Toronto and Sydney: Harper Perennial, 2006.

te Velde, Herman. *Seth, God of Confusion: A Study of His Role in Egyptian Mythology and Religion.* Leiden: Brill, 1967.

The Creative Writing Program at SUNY New Paltz. Heinz Insu Fenkl. Web. 16 Sep. 2015. https://newpaltzcwprogram.wordpress.com/heinz-insu-fenkl/.

Thrall, James H. "Postcolonial Science Fiction? Science, Religion and the Transformation of Genre in Amitav Ghosh's *The Calcutta Chromosome.*" *Literature & Theology* 23.3 (2009): 289–302. https://doi.org/10.1093/litthe/frp041

Todorov, Tzvetan. *The Fantastic: A Structural Approach to a Literary Genre.* 1970. Ithaca, New York: Cornell University Press, 1973.

Torok, Maria. "Story of Fear: The Symptoms of Phobia – the Return of the Repressed or the Return of the Phantom?" *The Shell and the Kernel: Renewals of Psychoanalysis.* Ed. Nicolas Abraham, Maria Torok, and Nicholas T. Rand. Chicago and London: Univ. of Chicago Press, 1994. 177–86.

Ty, Eleanor. "Rethinking the Hyphen: Asian North American and European Ethnic Texts as Global Narratives." *Canadian Review of American Studies* 32.3 (2002): 239–52. https://doi.org/10.3138/CRAS-s032-03-01

---. "Representing 'Other' Diasporas in Recent Global Canadian Fiction." *College Literature* 38.4 (2011): 98–114. https://doi.org/10.1353/lit.2011.0047

Uchmanowicz, Pauline. *Heinz Insu Fenkl Traces His Korean-American Experience*, 2000–2015. Web. http://www.catskillmtn.org/guide-magazine/articles/2001-11-heinz-insu-fenkl-traces-his-korean-american-experience.html.

Varvogli, Aliki. *Travel and Dislocation in Contemporary American Fiction*. New York and London: Routledge, 2012.

Wagner-Egelhaaf, Martina. *Autobiographie*. 2nd ed. Stuttgart and Weimar: J.B. Metzler, 2005. https://doi.org/10.1007/978-3-476-05087-8

Wakatsuki Houston, Jeanne. *Review: Behold the Many*. Web. http://www.waterbridgereview.org/032007/rvw_behold.php.

Wald, Priscilla. *Contagious: Cultures, Carriers, and the Outbreak Narrative*. Durham and London: Duke University Press, 2008.

Waller, Nicole. "Transpazifische und transatlantische Gespenster in Maxine Hong Kingstons *The Woman Warrior* und Toni Morrisons *Beloved.*" *Gespenster: Erscheinungen – Medien – Theorien*. Ed. Moritz Baßler, Bettina Gruber, and Martina Wagner-Egelhaaf. Würzburg: Königshausen & Neumann, 2005. 267–78.

Warren W., Kenneth. *What Was African American Literature*. Cambridge, Massachusetts, and London: Harvard University Press, 2011.

Wassef, Hind. "Beyond the Divide: History and National Boundaries in the Work of Amitav Ghosh." *Alif: Journal of Comparative Poetics* 18 (1998): 75–95. https://doi.org/10.2307/521882

Weinstock, Jeffrey A. "Introduction: The Spectral Turn." *Spectral America: Phantoms and the National Imagination*. Ed. Jeffrey A. Weinstock. Madison, Wis.: Univ. of Wisconsin Press/Popular Press, 2004. 3–17.

Williams, Linda. *Playing the Race Card: Melodramas of Black and White From Uncle Tom to O.J. Simpson*. Princeton and Oxford: Princeton University Press, 2001.

Winsbro, Bonnie. *Supernatural Forces: Belief, Difference, and Power in Contemporary Works by Ethnic Women*. Amherst: The University of Massachusetts Press, 1993.

Wong, Sau-ling C. "Immigrant Autobiography: Some Questions of Definition and Approach." *American Autobiography: Retrospect and Prospect*. Ed. Paul J. Eakin. Madison, Wis.: The University of Wisconsin Press, 1991. 142–70.

---. "Autobiography as Guided Chinatown Tour? Maxine Hong Kingston's *The Woman Warrior* and the Chinese-American Autobiographical Controversy."

Multicultural Autobiography: American Lives. Ed. James R. Payne. Knoxville: University of Tennessee Press, 1992. 248–79.

---. *Reading Asian American Literature: From Necessity to Extravagance*. Princeton, New Jersey: Princeton University Press, 1993.

---. "'Sugar Sisterhood:' Situating the Amy Tan Phenomenon." *The Ethnic Canon: Histories, Institutions, and Interventions*. Ed. David Palumbo-Liu. Minneapolis: University of Minnesota Press, 1995.

Xiaojing, Zhou. "Introduction: Critical Theories and Methodologies in Asian American Literary Studies." *Form and Transformation in Asian American Literature*. Ed. Xiaojing Zhou and Samina Najmi. Seattle, London: University of Washington Press, 2005. 3–29.

Yamanaka, Lois-Ann. *Behold the Many*. New York: Picador, 2006.

Yep, Laurence. "Fantasy and Reality." *The Horn Book Magazine* (1978): np. Web. http://archive.hbook.com/magazine/articles/1970s/apr78_yep.asp.

Yin, Xiao-huang. *Chinese American Literature since the 1850s*. Urbana and Chicago: University of Illinois Press, 2000.

Yuh, Ji-Yeon. *Beyond the Shadow of Camptown: Korean Military Brides in America*. New York and London: New York University Press, 2002.

Yurkovsky, Alexandra. *Review of Hotel World by Ali Smith: Maid's Nostalgic Ghost Makes a Haunting Narrator: Novel's Life-and-Death Ambiguities Add to Its Complexity*, 2004. Web. http://www.sfgate.com/books/article/Maid-s-nostalgic-ghost-makes-a-haunting-narrator-2878287.php

Cultural Studies

Gundolf S. Freyermuth
Games | Game Design | Game Studies
An Introduction
(With Contributions by André Czauderna, Nathalie Pozzi and Eric Zimmerman)

2015, 296 p., pb.
19,99 € (DE), 978-3-8376-2983-5
E-Book: 17,99 € (DE), ISBN 978-3-8394-2983-9

Andréa Belliger, David J. Krieger
Network Publicy Governance
On Privacy and the Informational Self

February 2018, 170 p., pb.
29,99 € (DE), 978-3-8376-4213-1
E-Book: 26,99 € (DE), ISBN 978-3-8394-4213-5

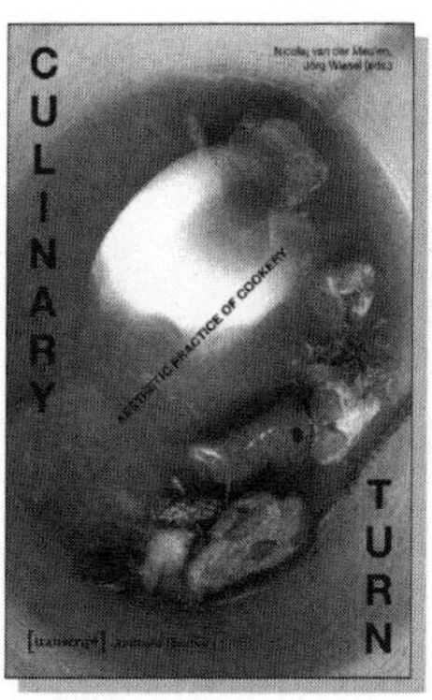

Nicolaj van der Meulen, Jörg Wiesel (eds.)
Culinary Turn
Aesthetic Practice of Cookery
(In collaboration with Anneli Käsmayr and in editorial cooperation with Raphaela Reinmann)

2017, 328 p., pb., col. ill.
29,99 € (DE), 978-3-8376-3031-2
E-Book available as free open access publication
ISBN 978-3-8394-3031-6

All print, e-book and open access versions of the titles in our list are available in our online shop www.transcript-verlag.de/en!